YOUNG PEOPLE'S

SCIENCE

ENCYCLOPEDIA

VOLUME 13
OI - PI

ALFRED B. NOBEL
1833–1896 •
Invented dynamite,
started Nobel Prizes

HIPPOCRATES
460–370? B.C •
"Father of Medicine"

MARIE CURIE
• 1867–1934
Discovered radium
and polonium

ENRICO FERMI
• 1901–1954
Produced first atomic pile and first
controlled nuclear chain reaction

THOMAS ALVA EDISON
1847–1931 •
Invented light bulb,
phonograph and mimeograph

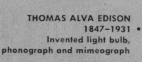

NICOLAUS COPERNICUS
• 1473–1543
First astronomer to say that Earth
goes around the sun

LUTHER BURBANK
• 1849–1926
Invented new
varieties of plants

EDWARD JENNER
1749–1823 •
Discovered smallpox vaccine

CHARLES DARWIN
1809-1882 •
Conceived the Theory of Evolution
through Natural Selection

WILLIAM HARVEY
• 1578–1657
Discovered the circulation
of the blood

GEORGE WASHINGTON CARVER
1864–1943 •
Experimented with
practical botany

SAMUEL F. B. MORSE
• 1791–1872
Invented telegraph and Morse code

LOUIS PASTEUR
• 1822–1895
Invented pasteurization

BENJAMIN FRANKLIN
• 1706–1790
Invented lightning rod

GALILEO GALILEI
1564–1642 •
Discovered law of pendulum motion

CAROLUS LINNAEUS
• 1707–1778
Classified the plant
and animal kingdoms

SIGMUND FREUD
• 1856–1939
Started psychoanalysis

GREGOR JOHANN MENDEL
1822–1884 •
Discovered principles of heredity

BARON ERNEST RUTHERFORD
1871–1937 •
Contributed to knowledge of
radioactivity and atomic structure

GUGLIELMO MARCONI
• 1874–1937
Invented the wireless telegraph

LOUIS AGASSIZ
• 1807–1873
Investigated glacial motion
and marine life

MICHAEL FARADAY
1791–1867 •
Discovered electromagnetic induction

SIR ISAAC NEWTON
• 1642–1727
Discovered laws of light,
gravity, motion and color

ALBERT EINSTEIN
1879–1955 •
Conceived the Theory of Relativity

WILHELM KONRAD ROENTGEN
• 1845–1923
Discovered X-rays

ALEXANDER GRAHAM BELL
1847–1922 •
Invented
the telephone

JOSEPH LISTER
• 1827–1912
Started antiseptic surgery

YOUNG PEOPLE'S
SCIENCE
ENCYCLOPEDIA

Edited by the Staff of

NATIONAL COLLEGE OF EDUCATION, Evanston, Ill.

ASSOCIATE EDITORS

HELEN J. CHALLAND, B.E., M.A., PH.D.
Chairman, Science Department, National
College of Education

DONALD A. BOYER, B.S., M.S., PH.D.
Science Education Consultant, Winnetka
Public Schools, Winnetka, Ill., Science,
National College of Education

W. RAY RUCKER, B.A., M.A., ED.D.
Former Dean of the College, National College of Education

EDITORIAL CONSULTANTS
ON THE STAFF OF NATIONAL COLLEGE OF EDUCATION

Elizabeth R. Brandt, B.A., M.Ed.

Eugene B. Cantelupe, B.A., M.F.A., Ph.D.

John H. Daugherty, B.S., M.A.

Irwin K. Feinstein, B.S., M.A., Ph.D.

Mary Gallagher, A.B., M.A., Ph.D.

Beatrice B. Garber, A.B., M.S., Ph.D.

Robert R. Kidder, A.B., M.A., Ph.D.

Jean C. Kraft, B.S., M.A., Ph.D.

Elise P. Lerman, B.A., B.F.A., M.F.A.

Mary-Louise Neumann, A.B., B.S. in L.S.

Lavon Rasco, B.A., M.A., Ph.D.

SPECIAL SUBJECT AREA CONSULTANTS

Krafft A. Ehricke, B.A.E., H.L.D.

Charles B. Johnson, B.S., M.A., M.S.

Raymond J. Johnson, B.B.A., Senior
Certificate in Industrial Engineering

Norma R. Rucker, B.S.

H. Kenneth Scatliff, M.D.

Ray C. Soliday, B.A., B.S., M.A.
(Deceased)

Fred R. Wilkin, Jr., B.S., M.Ed.

THE STAFF

PROJECT DIRECTOR · WALLACE B. BLACK

COORDINATING EDITOR · JEAN F. BLASHFIELD

ART DIRECTOR · BEN ROSEN

PHOTO AND ART EDITOR · MARTHA O'ROURKE

PRODUCTION EDITOR · ORLANDO T. CURCIO

YOUNG PEOPLE'S
SCIENCE
ENCYCLOPEDIA

Edited by the Staff of

NATIONAL COLLEGE OF EDUCATION
Evanston, Illinois

VOLUME 13
OI - PI

CHILDRENS PRESS, INC.
Chicago

Revised Edition 1966
©Copyright 1964, U. S. A.
by CHILDRENS PRESS, INC.

All rights reserved
Printed in the United States of America
Library of Congress Catalogue Card Number 61-17925

9 10 11 12 13 14 15 16 17 18 19 20 21 22 23 24 25 R 75 74 73 72 71 70 69 68 67

A working oil field with wells and derricks

Oil well If one visited an oil field, he might see men smelling handfuls of mud from a pit. These oil workers, called *drillers,* are testing this mud for traces of oil. They can identify it by its smell.

Oil is one of the most valuable deposits in the earth's crust. Because of its many uses, it is poetically called "black gold." Chemically, it is a natural mixture of HYDROCARBONS because it contains a compound of hydrogen and carbon.

Oil is always found in such sedimentary rock layers as sandstone. Oil geologists look for layers that are shaped like a dome. The oil deposits found in the dome are called *anticlinal accumulations.* In most cases, oil is found near rock layers containing fossils. These are the remains of sea animals, such as clams or corals. Some oil is found in limestone or shale layers.

In addition to the dome deposits, the porous sandstone also acts as a reservoir to hold some of the liquids and gases. Oil men often speak of an *oil pool.* This does not, however, really mean a pool of oil. Oil is lighter than water and therefore is above water. When oil is trapped in a porous rock, some of the oil evaporates and exerts pressure on the surface. When a well is drilled down to the oil, the gas on top escapes or is tapped off. The rest of the gas may push out the oil with so much force that it causes a gusher. When this gusher occurs, the drillers cap the well, then put in pipes to storage tanks nearby.

The crude oil is allowed to flow into the tanks until the pressure of the gas lessens. Then the oil must be pumped. These wells are pumped until they cease to produce economically. Some wells can be pumped for years, while others are short-lived. Many wells can be drilled into the same pool to draw off the oil more rapidly. In big oil fields the derricks are almost as thick as trees in a forest.

The first successful oil well in the United States was drilled in Titusville, Pennsylvania, in 1859. It required drilling to only 69 feet to reach this first well. Today drillers probe to much greater depths for oil. There are wells in Texas that reach down as far as 26,000 feet.

Oil is too valuable and drilling too costly merely to guess where it is located. Wells are drilled where the best scientific evidence indicates likely success. A dry hole or a *duster,* as drillers call a well that does not produce, is a costly mistake to investors.

Oil geologists use the magnetometer, seismograph, and gravimeter in finding oil. These instruments help them locate the proper rock formations where oil may be found. The geologists also study the walls of canyons to look for outcroppings of particular rock formations. Aerial photographs are also studied. Even changes in the number and kinds of plants in an area may offer a clue. The geologists take particular notice of folding or faulting of terrain.   V. V. N.

SEE ALSO: NATURAL RESOURCES, PETROLEUM

Ointment An ointment is a semisolid fatty or oily substance used simply for its protective effect or to hold medicine which must be administered locally.

SEE: DRUGS, SALVE

Okapi see Giraffe

Okra (OH-kruh) *Gumbo* is the Spanish word for okra. The fruit from this green plant is a long pod. It is used as a vegetable and in soups and stews. The unripe seeds are cooked and eaten as one would eat lima beans.

Okra is an annual herb belonging to the MALLOW family. It is native to Africa and has been cultivated in the Old World for less than 2000 years. It is grown in the warm areas of the United States. Okra is propagated from seed.

Okra grows up to seven feet high. The large leaves have prominent veins. The flower is yellow with a red center. The fibers in the stem are extracted and used in making textiles and paper.   H. J. C.

Oleander see Wild flowers

Olfactory see Nose

Oligocene see Cenozoic Era, Geologic time table

Olive The olive is an evergreen tree which grows up to forty feet tall. It has green fruit which turns to a purple color when ripe. It grows in a warm dry climate as in California, Florida and Arizona. It cannot survive below 15° Fahrenheit. Olives are native to the Mediterranean area.

Olive trees can live for over a century. The leaves are opposite, leathery and have a smooth margin. The white flower has parts in fours or divisible by fours. The fruit is classified botanically as a DRUPE. The exocarp and mesocarp is oily, fleshy and edible. The stony endocarp or pit contains one seed. Olive trees are propagated by stem cuttings, seeds or by *knaurs,* woody knots on the old trunk.

The olive has a *glucoside* which gives the raw fruit a very bitter taste. A solution of lye and sodium hydroxide removes it.

Olive is also the name of a plant family (*Oleaceae*) which includes syringa, privet, and forsythia.   H. J. C.

Okra plant and cut fruit section

Olive tree and branch

Olivine Olivine is a mineral that is also called *chrysolite* or *peridot*. It is the most common member of a group of silicates. It is colored various shades of green with rare brown tints. Olivine is a MAGNESIUM iron silicate.
SEE: MINERALS

Omnivore (OHM-nih-vohr) An omnivore is one of a group of animals that eats both animals and plants for its food.
SEE: BALANCE OF NATURE

Omnivorous see Animals, classification of; Balance of nature

Red and green onions

Onion (UN-yuhn) An onion is a BIEN-NIEL herb related to the LILY. The bulbs are used as vegetables and for flavoring other foods. A chemical, *allyl sulfide,* escapes when the onion is cut and affects nerve endings in the nose. The nerve endings stimulate tears to flow from the eyes.

The onion grows to be two or three feet tall. The stem is flat, disk-like and underground. The fleshy underground leaves surrounding the stem are white. As they grow and receive sunlight, chlorophyll is produced. In the second year of growth, a flower stalk produces a flower cluster.

Onions are propagated by *seed sets* (small bulbs) and by bulblets that grow at the top of the stem instead of flowers.   H. J. C.

J. Daniel Willems
Black onyx

Onyx (AHN-icks) Onyx is a semiprecious stone. Greek myths spoke of onyx as the fingernails of a goddess which were turned into stone as they touched water. The name *onyx* comes from the Latin word, *oniscus,* which means "lined" or "partly transparent," as a fingernail. The lines in this stone are parallel. They are white with brown, red, or green variations.

True onyx is a variety of AGATE, which is a form of quartz. It is formed from the dissolved mineral *silica,* which has been deposited in areas of ancient lava beds or petrified wood. The colors are caused by the deposition of other minerals. Mexican onyx is actually miscalled because it is a limestone variety, frequently found as cave or hot springs deposits. This is sometimes called *onyx marble.* It is more translucent than the true onyx.

Onyx is easily carved and takes a high polish. It is used as jewelry, ornamental stonework, mantles, and pillars.   J. A. D.
SEE ALSO: GEM, QUARTZ

Opal (OH-puhl) The opal is one of the main precious stones. It has been mined for thousands of years for use as a jewel. Long ago, people thought the opal had magic powers. Some thought it brought bad luck, but the Romans wore opals as good luck charms. At the present time, Hungary and Australia produce the best opals, but the stone can also be found in many other parts of the world.

J. Daniel Willems

Black and white Australian opals

The common opal has a body color of milky white, pale yellow, or black. The better opals are iridescent, which means they show shifting lights of reds, yellows, blues, and greens. Opals are a variety of QUARTZ. Their origins date back to prehistoric times when water, seeping through volcanic ash, dissolved the mineral silica and was then deposited in petrifying wood or rock cavities. The "opalescence" or iridescence of this gem, which is its source of beauty, is also its weakness. The lines of varying colors are actually fractures or lines of strain formed in its development. While these lines reflect light, they can also cause breakage in the stone. An opal cannot be cut into facets but must be polished into a rounded surface and carefully mounted.

J. A. D.

SEE ALSO: GEM

Opaque (oh-PAYK) Opaque means not TRANSPARENT to human eyes; able to stop light rays and other forms of radiant energy such as infrared rays by absorption and reflection.

SEE: LIGHT, TRANSLUCENT

Window is translucent; wall is opaque

Open hearth process As the use of steel grew rapidly in Europe years ago, large quantities of rusty scrap iron were created. However, there was no readily available market for this type of metal. Sir William Siemens of England, therefore, felt compelled to invent a furnace which would re-melt the scrap and turn it into new steel. He accomplished this in 1856 with the discovery of the open hearth furnace. In 1864, Emile and Pierre Martin of France improved the process. Today it is alternately known as the *Siemens-Martin process.*

The open hearth process is the one generally used in the United States for making a good-quality steel. In 1942, over 90 per cent of the steel produced in this country was made by this method. The quality steel is used for the better class of rails; for structural steel such as girders for bridges, buildings, and tunnels; for shafts, armor-plate, and heavy guns; and wherever steel is to be subjected to much vibration. In addition to the very high-grade steel produced in this process, open hearth steel has three additional advantages. First, almost any kind of iron can be used as the charge. The *charge* consists of the impure materials which are refined in the process. Second, large quantities of steel can be made at one time. Third, the carbon content of the steel can be easily controlled.

In this process, the open hearth furnace, or *converter,* consists of a shallow, wide, saucer-shaped hearth and a low roof. It may be as long as fifty feet and as wide as twenty feet, with a basin about two feet deep. It is lined with either silica brick in the acid process, or with magnesia dolomite brick in the basic process (which is the process used in this country). The hearth holds the charge of scrap iron, solid pig iron, and molten pig iron direct from the blast furnace. Limestone is also added as a flux. A *flux* is a material purposely added to unite with the impurities. The waste product then formed is called the *slag.*

Natural gas or producer gas is the fuel burned to melt the charge. Pre-heated air and fuel gas (at temperatures of 2800° to

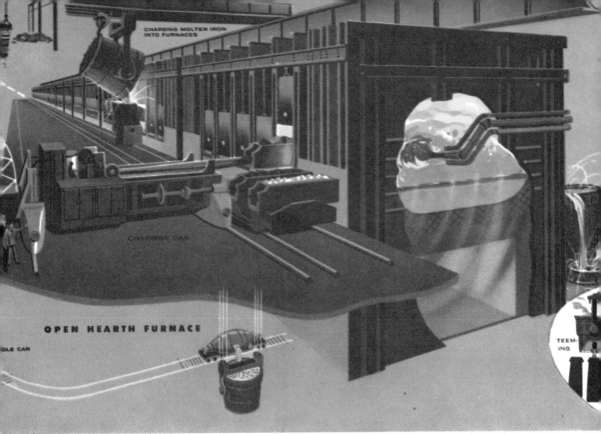

CHARGING MOLTEN IRON
INTO FURNACES

CHARGING CAR

OPEN HEARTH FURNACE

DLE CAR

TEEM-
ING

Inland Steel, United States Steel

(Above) Diagram of a large open hearth furnace as used in modern steel factories. (Right) Near the end of the process, the slag is drained from the top of a ladle of freshly-poured steel

3100° F) enter from one compartment and burn above the charge, which is heated by reflection from the roof of the furnace. The hot waste gases heat a similar compartment as they pass out from above the hearth. The compartments form a system of fire brick checkerwork. After about twenty minutes, the compartments are interchanged so that the direction of the incoming gases is reversed, offering great economy of heating. This change is called the *Siemens regenerative process*.

While the charge is melting, some iron oxide is added as a flux—to oxidize the impurities to oxides of carbon, sulfur, phosphorous, silicon, and manganese. The oxygen of the iron oxide combines with the carbon to form carbon dioxide, which passes off with the flue gases. Other oxidized elements combine with the basic lining and form a slag which floats to the surface of the molten mass. This also prevents further oxidation of the iron. Since no air is blown

Inland Steel

"Tapping" the furnace, letting the molten steel run into the ladle

Inland Steel

Pouring molten steel from the open hearth ladle into ingot molds

through the molten mass, as in the Bessemer process, there is less iron oxide and dissolved gas in the finished product. By using as much as fifty per cent scrap iron or scrap steel, the oxidation of the impurities is speeded up considerably.

During the process, samples of molten steel are taken out at frequent intervals and allowed to cool and solidify. An analysis is made of the quality. Such treatment would be impossible in the Bessemer converter.

After eight or ten hours, the run is completed and the steel is tapped from the furnace. The slag is skimmed off from the top. Some *spiegeleisen*—a carbon-iron-manganese alloy—is then added to give the steel the desired composition of carbon and manganese.

Molten steel dissolves considerable quantities of carbon monoxide and other gases such as oxygen and nitrogen, which are liberated as the steel cools. This causes blowholes in the steel. To prevent this from happening, small portions of reducing agents such as metallic aluminum, silicon, or alloys of iron (ferro-titanium, ferro-vanadium) are added to the molten metal just before it is poured. The small, desired additions are called *scavengers*. The oxides they form are removed in the slag.

Fifty tons of steel or more are produced in the open hearth furnace every eight hours. In recent years, new steel processes using pure oxygen are being developed. They may replace some of the open hearth and Bessemer methods for making steel efficiently.   D. L. D.

SEE ALSO: BESSEMER PROCESS, STEEL

Operation see Surgery

Opiate see Narcotics, Opium

Opium (OH-pee-um) Opium has been used since ancient times. It is a narcotic drug made from the dried milk or juice from the pod of the unripe poppy *(Papaver somniferum)*. However, various useful drugs, such as codein, morphine, laudanum and paregoric, are obtained from opium. It has been said that opium has brought more relief to the world through its legal uses and more unhappiness through its illegal uses than anything else known to man.

Doctors use the useful opium drugs mainly for the relief of pain. Every American soldier in World War II carried morphine (from opium) in case he was wounded.

Improper use of opium derivatives (*opiates*) can lead to drug addiction—physical dependence on the drugs. Heroin, obtained from morphine, is the most widely used drug in illegal trade. Continued use of these drugs may lead to inability to follow a normal useful life and eventually leads to complete physical ruin and death. There is no known drug that will counteract the use of opium and its related NARCOTICS.

H. J. C.

Opium is obtained from the pod of an opium poppy

After the baby opossums are old enough to come out of the marsupial pouch, they ride on the mother's back

Opossum

Opossum (oh-PAHS-um) The opossum is a *marsupial,* an animal with a pouch. Opossums are the only pouched animals in North America. This *common* or *Virginia opossum* is about the size of a cat and has grayish fur. It has a long, light-gray snout. With its long, hairless tail, the opossum can carry things or even hang upside down from a tree branch.

The opossum does not seem to be a very intelligent animal. Its only interests seem to be in keeping safe, comfortable, and free from hunger. It will eat anything—insects, fruits, other animals, eggs, or roots. The meat of the opossum is edible. When surprised by a hunter, an opossum falls into a state of shock and paralysis and appears to be dead. It is fear, not intelligence, that gives it this trick of "playing 'possum."

Opossums belong to a group of marsupials called *didelphids,* meaning that the female has two wombs. There is no placenta, however, which would be the source of food for the unborn offspring. As a result, newborn opossums are very small, undeveloped creatures. A litter often contains more infants than the mother can feed. First arrivals attach themselves to a nipple and the late ones starve. The survivors grow rapidly and crawl out of the pouch and attach themselves to the mother's back, where they ride until they can take care of themselves.

There are numerous other varieties of opossum in South and Central America. Like the North American opossum, they are generally neither friendly, beautiful, nor intelligent. The opossum has survived unchanged and untamed for thousands of years.   C. L. K.

SEE ALSO: MAMMALIA, MARSUPIAL

Oppenheimer, J. Robert

Oppenheimer, J. Robert (1904-   )
J. Robert Oppenheimer is the brilliant American physicist who is largely credited with building the first atomic bomb. He did not, of course, build the bomb by himself. He was the chief of scientists at the Los Alamos, New Mexico, laboratory where the work was done.

J. Robert Oppenheimer was born on April 22, 1904. His parents were gentle, cultured, and wealthy, having earned their fortune from importing textiles. Young Robert had every opportunity to succeed, and he made superb use of his good fortune. He was a brilliant boy, and was interested in everything except sports.

When he was five, the young Oppenheimer's grandfather gave him a small collection of rocks which led the boy to study geology. His mother taught him painting and music. When he was seven he began to write poetry, and his favorite toy was his microscope.

He returned to his interest in geology and began to correspond with professors of geology throughout America. By typing his letters so they would not betray his youthful age, he was nominated by one of the professors to the New York Mineralogical Club. Oppenheimer was eleven at the time. A year later he accepted an invitation to present a lecture to the members of the club on the minerals that form the bedrock of Manhattan Island. The members of the club were so astonished at his age that he had to allow them to recover their composure before delivering the lecture.

At nineteen, Oppenheimer enrolled at Harvard University, taking the required work and as many additional courses as possible. In three years he graduated with the highest scholastic record ever achieved at that university. He knew by then that

J. Robert Oppenheimer

he wanted to be a physicist, and he went to the famous Cavendish Laboratory in England to study with the great Ernest Rutherford and Niels Bohr. There he studied intently the structure of the atom. After leaving the laboratory he traveled to Göttingen, Germany, where he learned German and earned a Ph.D. degree by writing a paper in German on quantum mathematics.

Leaving Germany, he went to Zurich, Switzerland, and then on to Leyden, Netherlands, where after six weeks he was able to lecture in Dutch. He finally returned to the United States where he accepted positions simultaneously at the California Institute of Technology and the University of California.

Meanwhile, ALBERT EINSTEIN was gravely concerned by the success of the German program of atomic research, and strongly urged President Franklin D. Roosevelt to establish a research laboratory to help safeguard the future of the free world. After two letters of warning from the eminent Einstein, the government established the Los Alamos laboratory.

As one of the leading theoretical physicists in the world, J. Robert Oppenheimer was the logical man to take charge of the project. In 1943, at the age of thirty-nine, he accepted the post and was placed over a staff of 4,500 workers. Two months after the first successful atomic bomb explosion, Oppenheimer resigned. He aided Congress in drafting the first laws to be concerned with the control and use of atomic energy, and he strongly urged the formation of an international organization to develop this energy.

In 1947 he was made director of the Institute for Advanced Study at Princeton, New Jersey, and continued to serve as a consultant to the Atomic Energy Commission. However, soon after the explosion of the first hydrogen bomb, he was suspended while being investigated by the government. In a dramatic summary, the board of examiners confirmed his loyalty, but advised that the nation's atomic secrets be withheld from him. At the present time all the facts surrounding the final decision are still not known.   D. H. J.

Optic nerve see Eye, Nervous system

Optical illusions see Camouflage

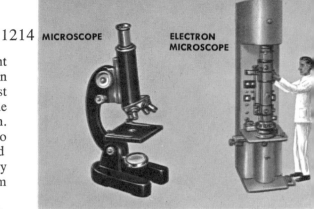

MICROSCOPE   ELECTRON MICROSCOPE

Optical instruments Optical instruments are devices in which light is passed through lenses or prisms. Among the common optical instruments are the microscope, binoculars, camera, spectroscope, periscope, and telescope.

In the 1500's and 1600's, the first optical instruments were developed, following the discovery of the glass lens. The earliest telescopes and microscopes evolved because of the lens.

One of the original optical instruments to undergo numerous improvements was the spectroscope. In 1666 Isaac Newton sent a beam of light through a prism. The beam broke into a band of colored light, similar to a rainbow.

One kind of SPECTROSCOPE is basically a glass PRISM. All materials, when heated hot enough, radiate light. When this light from a particular substance is beamed through a prism, it divides into colored areas that are distinct for the elements in that substance. A trained spectroscopist can use this instrument to determine the chemical composition of laboratory "unknowns" and the elements in the stars and the sun.

Intensity of light is measured by one or another type of light meter. Photoelectric-cell meters convert light to electricity, and then the light strength is read on a dial. A laboratory PHOTOMETER compares a standard light source at a given distance with an unknown light at a measured distance; then by use of the *inverse square law,* the strength of the unknown light can be figured. Measurement units of intensity for light instruments are either in FOOT CANDLES or in the new units, *candelas.*

The speed of light can be measured by an optical instrument developed by Albert A. Michelson of the University of Chicago. He

TELESCOPE

BINOCULARS

CAMERA LENS

POLARIZED LENS,

WHEN CROSSED WILL STOP THE LIGHT

determined that light in a vacuum travels at the speed of 186,284 miles per second.

Some instruments use *polarized light*. This is ordinary light that has been passed through a device that makes all its waves vibrate in one direction only instead of moving in several planes. This is done by directing the light either through crystals having a slit-like molecular arrangement, or else through plastic sheets coated with certain chemicals. Polarized light devices include camera filters, glare-reducing sunglasses, and car headlights. Biochemists use it in an instrument that measures strength of sugar solutions. Engineers who work with construction and manufacturing materials use polarized beams to reveal strains in glass and plastics.

From the time of Columbus to the present, optical instruments have become increasingly important to the scientist. He relies upon the microscope to see the micro, or small world, and upon the telescope to see the universe. Many discoveries in atomic physics, and in chemistry are due to the spectroscope. An even smaller world is now visible with the electron microscope.

Eye glasses, cameras, and binoculars are examples of the modern uses and improvements in optical instruments.   P. F. D.

SEE ALSO: BINOCULAR; CAMERA; GLASS; LENS, MAN-MADE; LIGHT; MICROSCOPE; MICRO-SCOPE, ELECTRON; MIRROR; PERISCOPE; PRISM; TELESCOPE

Optics Optics is that branch of science dealing with the generation, transmission and detection of electromagnetic waves with wave lengths greater than X-RAYS and shorter than microwaves. It includes the laws of LIGHT and its relation to vision, and also deals with the construction of lenses.

SEE: ELECTROMAGNETIC SPECTRUM; LENS, MAN-MADE

Optometry (ahp-TAHM-uh-tree) Optometry is a profession specializing in the protection and improvement of vision. The optometrist is one who practices the art and science of vision care. He is trained and licensed to make tests to determine the person's visual skills, especially in relation to his specific needs. When visual errors are found, he prescribes and provides any corrective lenses or visual training needed for adequate and comfortable sight.

The roots of the profession of optometry lie in the development of research in physics, mathematics, and optics, as well as in physiology and psychology. Modern optometry, however, really dates from the 19th century, when such men as Thomas Young, Herman von Helmholtz, Eduard Jaeger, and others, were busily engaged in Europe in measuring the eye and inventing instruments for testing sight. The results of their research are found in the applications used today. Development in the field of refraction led to the refractive testing of the eye, or optometry, as it is now known.

The word "optometry," in the sense of "diagnosis of refractive error" first appeared in 1870, and in the next thirty years optometry slowly evolved as a specialized vocation. Two outstanding leaders in the United States responsible for developing the profession were Charles F. Prentiss, who campaigned for legal recognition of the group, and Andrew J. Cross, who devoted himself to the establishment and improvement of the optometric educational facilities. By 1901, the first state law regulating the practice of optometry was passed in Minnesota. At the present time, the practice of optometry is recognized and regulated by state

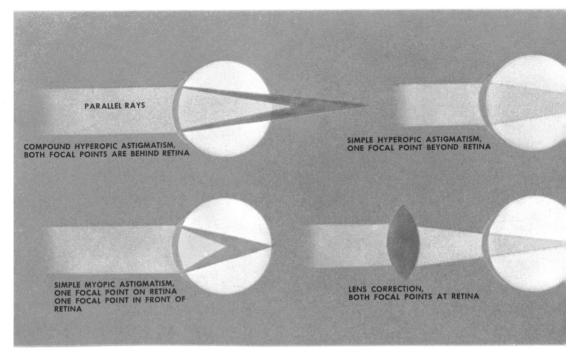

PARALLEL RAYS

COMPOUND HYPEROPIC ASTIGMATISM,
BOTH FOCAL POINTS ARE BEHIND RETINA

SIMPLE HYPEROPIC ASTIGMATISM,
ONE FOCAL POINT BEYOND RETINA

SIMPLE MYOPIC ASTIGMATISM,
ONE FOCAL POINT ON RETINA
ONE FOCAL POINT IN FRONT OF
RETINA

LENS CORRECTION,
BOTH FOCAL POINTS AT RETINA

laws in every state in the Union and by Federal law in the District of Columbia.

Optometry has encompassed new responsibilities in helping people's eyes to function properly under the increasing strain of modern living.

Contact lenses are optometry's contribution to many whose careers in athletics, aviation, on the stage, screen and television, depend on being able to see safely or to present the most aesthetic appearance.

Telescopic spectacles have been instrumental in returning the near blind to usefulness by helping them to see more than was previously thought possible.

The use of visual training and orthoptics (eye exercise) in the correction of squint (crossed eyes) and in the development or re-education of the visual skills for the improvement of visual performances was also due to the influence of optometry.

Vision is only one of the senses, but people rely on it more than on all the others put together. Most vision problems are due to *refractive errors* or inability of the eyes to focus light rays in the proper way. Glasses are the most common remedy for these errors. By relieving strain and permitting the eyes to function normally, glasses enable the individual not only to see clearly, but also to see efficiently and comfortably.

Faults of vision may be grouped into five classes: hyperopia (farsightedness), myopia (nearsightedness), astigmatism, presbyopia (aging eyes), and strabismus (cross-eye).

The condition describing a normal eye is known as *emmetropia*. A properly functioning eye refracts rays of light coming from a distant object (20 or more feet away) so that the image is brought to a focus at the retina when that eye is at rest.

Hyperopia is a state or condition of an eye which refracts parallel rays of light to a focus at a point behind the retina when the eye is at rest. In this case, the retina intercepts the converging rays of light before they reach their focal point. Farsightedness is corrected by placing a convex, or plus, lens before the eye. The power of the lens is such that it will converge the rays before they reach the eye enabling them to focus on the retina.

Myopia is a state or condition of an eye which refracts parallel rays of light to a focus at a point in front of the retina when the eye is at rest. In such a case, the retina intercepts the rays of light after they have converged to a focal point. Nearsightedness is corrected by placing a concave, or minus, lens before the eye. The power of the lens is such that it will diverge the rays before they reach the eye enabling them to focus on the retina.

Astigmatism is the most common refrac-

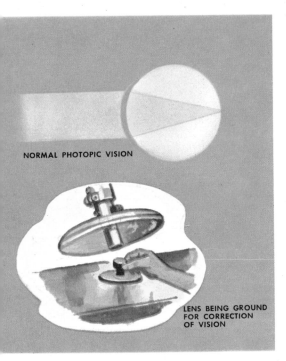

NORMAL PHOTOPIC VISION

LENS BEING GROUND
FOR CORRECTION
OF VISION

Courtesy Society For Visual Education, Inc.

A young orangutan

tive error. It is a condition of an eye which refracts parallel rays of light so that they do not focus at one point. In most cases, astigmatism is the result of the cornea not being truly spherical. There are many forms of astigmatism. The correction of an astigmatic eye is obtained by placing a cylindrical or sphero-cylindrical lens before the eye.

Presbyopia means literally "old sight." It is a state or condition in which the near point of any eye gradually recedes. Presbyopia is the result of a gradual hardening of the lens in the eye, and is universally present in persons 40 years or older. The addition of a convex, or plus lens makes up for the loss in power and thus, allows clear vision at near distances.

Strabismus is a Greek word meaning "squint" and describes what is commonly recognized as cross-eye. This is usually caused by imbalance in the eyes. The two eyes do not function together and the ability to see three-dimensionally suffers. This condition is correctable by lenses, and/or visual training, and/or surgery.　J. H. D.

Oral Oral means spoken and pertains to the mouth. In ZOOLOGY it refers to the same side of the animal as the mouth or mouth region.

SEE: ANIMAL

Orange see Citrus fruits

Orangutan (oh-RANG-oo-tann) *Orang* means "man" and *utan* means "jungle." Thus the orangutan is called "man-of-the-woods." It belongs to the APE family, and spends most of its life in tree tops, coming down to the ground only for water. An orangutan, if captured young, can be easily trained. Within weeks, it can be taught to eat, dress, and act well-behaved.

Some orangutans have reached the height of four and one-half feet. The males may weigh 200 pounds, the females are usually smaller. In spite of their great weight, they travel very rapidly; for though their legs are little and weak, their arms are strong and muscular, enabling them to swing rapidly from tree to tree rather than leap as many other PRIMATES do. Their long, loose hair ranges from brick-red to brownish-orange, and their cheeks are wide and flat.

Orangutans are chiefly vegetarians, feasting on wild fruit, especially on the fruit of durain, shoots of screw pine, and fleshy leaves of various kinds.　H. J. C.

Orbit The word *orbit* can be used to describe the path of any body revolving around another body. The path may be as simple as a circle, or as complicated as an ellipse.

Probably one of the oldest significant uses of the word orbit refers to the paths of celestial bodies as they revolve around the sun. Earth and other planets move in specific orbits as they travel around the sun, under the force of the sun's gravitational pull. Planets with natural satellites are the centers of the satellites' orbits.

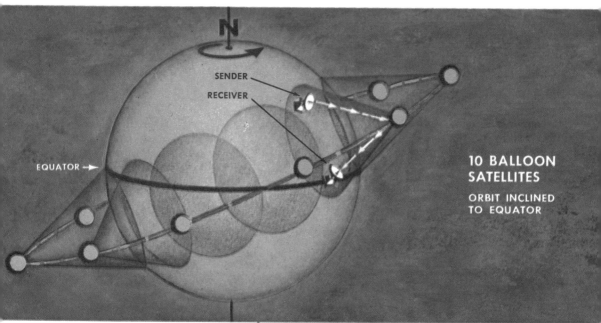

SENDER
RECEIVER

EQUATOR →

**10 BALLOON
SATELLITES**

**ORBIT INCLINED
TO EQUATOR**

Figure 1—Example of a 10 satellite orbital system; circles indicate the approximate area in which ground stations can use the respective satellite for communications purposes

The revolving body always has some sort of massive center or nucleus around which it makes its orbit. For the planets, the sun is the center. Atoms also have particles which can be referred to as traveling in an orbit. These particles are the electrons which revolve about a nucleus composed of protons, neutrons, and other subatomic particles. At one time it was thought that these orbits were as simple as a circle. Now the paths of the electrons are recognized as three-dimensional orbits. If the path of the electron were to be traced, in time it would form a sort of "shell" around the nucleus. These paths are called *orbitals*.

The most recent application of the word describes the paths taken by the various man-made satellites as they revolve around the earth. Generally, these satellites have elliptical orbits with the ellipse oriented in various positions relative to the earth.

Regardless of how large or small the revolving body may be, there must always be a mass or nucleus around which the body can describe an orbit. The mass or nucleus plays a very important role in maintaining the balance of forces on the revolving body. If there were no nucleus, the body would no longer experience a force of attraction and it would float off into space. A. E. L.

SEE ALSO: APOGEE, ORBITAL SYSTEMS, PERIGEE, SPACE TRAVEL

Orbital systems Once a rocket or spaceship escapes the pull of the earth's gravity, it can be made to travel in an orbit or path around the earth. *Orbital system* is a term used in astronautics to refer to a group of such objects or satellites traveling in the same orbit, or in a certain set of orbits about the earth.

Typical examples of such systems are (1) a group of balloon satellites serving as passive repeater communication satellites, more or less equally spaced in an orbit a few hundred miles high so that at least one satellite is always in the line of sight of a given ground station; (2) two groups of satellites, each group spaced in a different orbit with the two orbits, for example, perpendicular to each other; and (3) a cluster of orbital installations made up of a space station and vehicles which ascend from the earth to meet the satellite cluster in orbit.

Figure 1 above shows the earth, its north pole slightly tipped and a satellite orbit which is inclined with respect to the equator. Suppose that passive repeater satellites are to be placed into this orbit in such a manner that before a satellite leaves the field of view of a given ground station, the next satellite enters it. In this manner one can make sure that the particular radio or television station always has at least one satellite available from which to bounce messages to other parts of the earth. The field of view of the satellite looking down on the earth is roughly circular, as is shown. The lower the orbital altitude, the smaller will be the diameter of this circle. In order to assure continuous coverages (that is, visibility of at least one satellite from a ground station at all times), the fields of view of the individual satellites must overlap. In other words, the coverage circles must be "linked" together. Each "link" involves two intersections for each of the two adjacent circles. Only the area between the intersections (cross-hatched) is covered all the time. The region above the northern intersection and below the southern intersection is covered only at times. It is easily seen that the lower the satellite orbit, the more satellites are required to provide continuous coverage, and the smaller will be the band which has coverage all the time. But as the number of satellites is increased, it becomes more difficult to keep them evenly spaced in the orbit. Slight differences in speed or direction of flight, as well as a twisting effect caused by the earth's equatorial bulge and, to a lesser extent, by the gravitational pull of sun and moon, will cause the satellites to drift slowly off course. As a result, the coverage circles will overlap more in one region, causing temporary "holes" in other regions. Keeping all these satellites in reasonable nearness to their intended places in the orbit is, therefore, like a very complicated juggling act.

Things become somewhat easier when the satellites are placed in orbits of greater altitude. The coverage circles are much larger so that fewer satellites are needed for continuous coverage of a particular zone of the earth. In addition, coverage can be increased greatly by spreading the orbital system over two or more orbits. Fig. 2 shows an example for two high-altitude orbits which are perpendicular to each other; in this case, one group of satellites travels in the plane of the equator, the other in a polar orbit. Because of the greater altitude than in Fig. 1, only four satellites are needed in the equatorial orbit and four in the polar orbit for continuous coverage of almost the entire globe. Thus, much greater coverage for communication or observation purposes can be

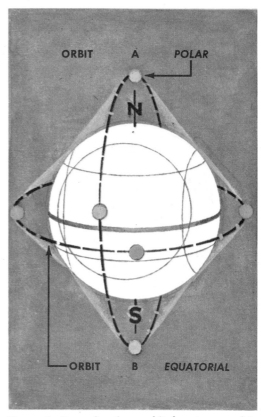

Figure 2—Example of an orbital system consisting of two orbits perpendicular to each other with four satellites in each orbit

achieved than with the larger number of satellites in the example in Fig. 1.

Fig. 3 shows an orbital system which consists of a cluster of objects in a given orbit, and of vehicles which ascend from the earth's surface at more or less regular periods of time to join the cluster for a limited period before returning to the earth. Fig. 3 shows the example of a rather highly inclined orbit. It is more difficult to get into such an orbit from a launch site at a given altitude than if both launch site and orbit were located in the plane of the equator. As shown in Fig. 3, the launch site crosses the plane of the satellite *twice* during one rotation of Earth. One of these crossings lies on the other side of the globe in Fig. 3. A launch is practical only when the launch site is near one of the two crossings.

Fig. 3 shows the ascent of a vehicle into the plane of the orbit. After the vehicle has completed this phase of its flight, it could theoretically continue to ascend directly into the satellite orbit. It is likely, however, that the satellite did not have the

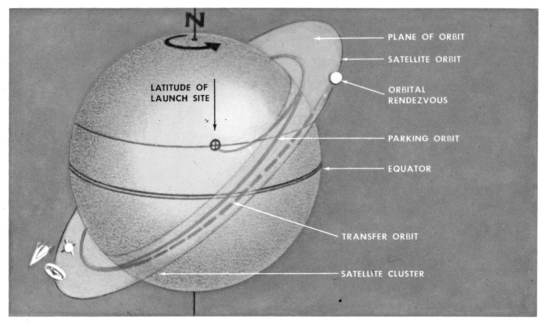

Figure 3—Example of an orbital system consisting of a satellite cluster and rendezvous vehicles for contact with the earth's surface

right position when the vehicle arrived in the orbit plane. The vehicle, therefore, would not meet the satellite when arriving in the orbit, just as bullets of the duck hunter's gun might cross the path of the duck's flight, but travel before or behind the ducks, missing them. It might, therefore, be necessary for the ascending vehicle to "wait" after arrival in the plane of the orbit until the right positions (*constellation*) of vehicle and satellite are formed. During the waiting period, the vehicle is "parked" in an orbit of lower altitude than the satellite orbit, but in the same plane. While in this parking orbit, the vehicle moves somewhat faster than the satellite. The right transfer constellation is, therefore, bound to occur sooner or later. For a vehicle in a parking orbit of, say 120 miles altitude with the satellite in an orbit of an altitude of several hundred miles, the waiting period in the parking orbit will be no greater than 1.5 days; in many cases, it is only a few hours. Once the correct transfer constellation is attained, the vehicle's rocket engines are ignited again and propel the spacecraft into a transfer orbit which enables it to climb to the height and position of the satellite cluster. This is shown in Fig. 3. Once the vehicle enters the transfer orbit, it will arrive, about 40 minutes later, at the orbital rendezvous point. *Rendezvous* is French, and

means "appointment" or "meeting." This encounter is, therefore, frequently referred to as "rendezvous maneuver." It will play a very important role in manned space flight.

K. A. E.

SEE ALSO: SPACE TRAVEL, SPACE VEHICLES

Orchard An orchard is a collection of fruit-bearing trees, especially APPLE, PEAR, PEACH, PLUM, CHERRY, APRICOT and QUINCE. Factors such as wind, light, nourishment, cold and heat influence the selection of a site for an orchard.

A two-year-old lemon orchard planted on the contour

U.S. Department of Agriculture photo

Helen J. Challand
Yellow orchids

F. A. Blashfield
Purple orchids, most popular for corsages

Orchid (OHR-kid) The orchid is one of the most interesting and beautiful of all flowers. It has many different shapes and colors. All of the 12,000 known species resemble one another, but some are shaped more like a butterfly, some like a dove, and some like a lady's slipper. These exciting blooms, which come from the tropics and subtropics, may be colored white, yellow, purple, green, or brown.

There are two classes of orchids: those that take their food from the ground (*terrestrial*) and those that take their food from the air (*epiphytal*). The terrestrial orchids are found in moist, marshy places and in greenhouses. They are known as hardy, native varieties and have their resting period in the winter months. The epiphytal orchids attach themselves to the bark of trees and depend upon the moist, humid atmosphere for water. Sometimes these orchids are incorrectly called *parasites*. They merely cling to the trunks and limbs of trees and take nothing from the tree itself. In this group of orchids are the most beautiful and most valuable species.

The orchid flower is irregular. Two of the three petals are alike. The third one takes on many shapes, forming a *lip,* or *labellum.* This structural arrangement facilitates insect pollination. One pistil and one or two stamens are joined together. The roots are fibrous, tuberous or bulbous.

Orchids are propagated by division of the rhizome, stem cuttings and by seeds. The latter are very small and require very sterile germinating materials. One variety of climbing orchid produces a long pod that is dark brown when ripe. VANILLA is extracted from this plant. J. K. K.

Order see Animals, classification of; Plants, classification of

Ordovician see Geologic time table, Paleozoic Era

Ore The ground that man walks on is made of soil and loosened rocks. Under this surface lies the earth's crust of solid rock, often containing valuable metals and other chemicals. Such matter is called *ore* and is taken from the earth (mined) and refined into materials useful to man. A number of refining processes are used to separate the valuable substances from the surrounding rocks.

Roasting, smelting, and electrolysis are commonly used in refining such metals as IRON, silver, gold, copper, aluminum, lead, and nickel. The presence of rich ore deposits adds greatly to a nation's wealth. Ore gives rise to industries that affect the lives of all people.

Ores are classified as two main kinds: *native elements* and *chemical compounds.* Native ore is found in nearly pure masses or bands interlayered but not chemically mixed with the enclosing rock. About 15 elements occur in nature, but only copper, silver, gold, platinum, carbon (graphite) and sulfur are found in dependable quantities. Thousands of other ores occur as compounds of the desired elements, commonly with oxygen, silicon, and sulfur. For example, iron ore is plentifully found as the oxide, HEMATITE, and zinc as the dark sulfide, *sphalerite.*

The chief factors in the formation of ore seem to be time—millions and billions of years—and extremes of heating, cooling, and pressure. In the case of some iron ores, it is believed that formation began long before there was any life on earth. E. M. N.
SEE ALSO: MINERALS, STEEL

Unloading Chilean lump iron ore
Courtesy Inland Steel

Oregano

Oregano (oh-RAY-gah-no) Oregano is an HERB that belongs to the mint family. Although some people call wild marjoram *origanum,* botanists say that origanum is a separate genus.

Oregano is a beautiful leafy perennial grown widely in the United States, Mexico, Italy, and Spain. It is used in powdered or dried-leaf form to season Mexican and Italian dishes, hot sauces, and bean dishes.

The herb plant may grow three feet high in warmer climates, has large clusters of pale, purplish-pink flowers, and oval, gray-green leaves. The flavor of oregano is much more pungent than the flavor of MARJORAM.

J. K. K.

SEE ALSO: MINT

Organ An organ is a many-celled part of an animal or plant made up of various tissues which work together to carry out some definite function. Examples are PLANT leaves and roots, and ANIMAL hearts and lungs.

SEE: ANATOMY, HISTOLOGY

Organic compounds Chemical compounds containing CARBON are defined as organic compounds. Most of the organic compounds also contain hydrogen, and a large number contain oxygen. Many contain nitrogen, sulfur, phosphorus, and other elements. The branch of chemistry now known as *organic chemistry* grew out of earlier studies of substances obtained from living organisms.

Natural organic compounds are found in plant and animal tissues. Familiar organic substances include sugar, fat, and petroleum.

Prehistoric peoples were familiar with organic compounds only in a practical way. In the production of wine, they fermented grape juice and produced alcohol. Soap was made from animal fats and olive oil. Dyes, such as indigo (a vegetable dye), alizarin (from a plant root), and Tyrian purple (from a Mediterranean species of mollusk) were used by the Romans and Greeks.

For many years people believed that organic compounds were obtainable only from living organisms. Compounds derived from plant or animal sources were designated organic material. In recent years, many of the natural organic compounds have been made, or *synthesized,* by artificial processes. A familiar example is synthetic rubber. Moreover, thousands of carbon compounds, unknown to man in nature, have been synthesized.

While organic compounds are those containing carbon, inorganic compounds are those which do not contain carbon. Organic compounds outnumber inorganic compounds. Carbon atoms form *covalent bonds* with other atoms, linking them together in chains and rings of many different sizes and compositions and producing the practically unlimited number of organic compounds.

Organic compounds, with very few exceptions, are combustible. Inorganic salts, as a rule, do not burn. Organic compounds usually exist as gases, liquids, or low-boiling-point solids. Inorganic salts have very high melting points. Although alcohol, sugar, and similar compounds are readily soluble in water, water solubility for organic compounds is the exception rather than the rule. Many inorganic salts, on the other hand, are soluble in water. The difference in solubility may be attributed to the electronic structure and type of bonding of the compounds.

Familiar organic compounds are the hydrocarbons. Hydrocarbons occur plentifully in nature, particularly in PETROLEUM. NATURAL GAS, the gas used for cooking and heating in homes, is composed mostly of methane, the simplest of the hydrocarbons. Other hydrocarbons are ethane, propane, butane, and pentane.

Another group of organic compounds are the alcohols. Alcohols are used as solvents and starting materials for synthetic processes. Rubbing alcohol is the common name for *isopropyl* alcohol. The ALCOHOL in

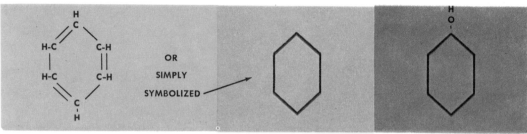

Benzene, C_6H_6, is the simplest of the benzene, or aromatic, group of organic compounds

A carbon benzene ring has a hexagonal formation

A benzene derived compound, phenol or carbolic acid

beverages is made by fermentation of sugars. An enzyme in yeast, *zymase,* converts the sugar to ethyl alcohol and carbon dioxide. Another alcohol, ethylene glycol, is widely used as an ANTIFREEZE in automobile radiators.

ETHER may be prepared by adding sulfuric acid to ethyl alcohol. It is used as a general anesthetic or as a solvent.

The *aromatic,* or benzene-ring, compounds are another important and large group. Benzene has the formula C_6H_6 and is not arranged atomically like the carbon compounds mentioned before. Its six carbon atoms are linked in a closed chain. Between alternate atoms there is a double bond of two pairs of electrons. Some benzene-ring compounds are fragrant substances found in plants; for example, balsams, resins, and perfume oils and flavorings. Still other benzene-ring molecules are made in animal and human cells; for example, hemoglobin in the blood and several hormones such as thyroxin and adrenalin all contain complex ring molecules.

Inorganic chemistry is used in geology, metallurgy, and mineralogy because it deals with inorganic materials such as gases in the atmosphere, water, rocks, minerals, metals and their salts, nonmetals and their compounds (i.e. sulfuric acid.) Organic chemistry is applied in physiology, biochemistry, and in the science of producing synthetic materials. Through organic chemistry man has been able to improve upon nature by creating synthetic dyes, synthetic rubber, drugs and medicines, synthetic fibers, and many other useful compounds. Organic chemistry has given man a better understanding of the way in which living matter functions under normal conditions and of the causes of disease.   J. R. S.

SEE ALSO: CHEMISTRY, HYDROCARBONS

Organic rock Organic rock is rock formed from the remains of plants and animals. COAL, composed of plant material, and limestone, composed of shells and skeletons of sea creatures, are examples of organic rock.

SEE: PALEONTOLOGY, ROCKS

Organism An organism is any living thing, such as any form of animal or plant. It consists of dependent parts which work together to form common life for the whole.

Oriole (OHR-ee-uhl) The oriole is a bird often seen where there are shade and fruit trees. Its deep nest, woven of fibers and grasses, hangs at the end of a branch. Orioles eat mostly caterpillars, beetles and some fruits.

The *Baltimore oriole,* familiar in eastern and central United States, is a colorful bird with its black head and orange and black wings and body. Its mellow, low-pitched whistle differs with each bird. The *orchard oriole* is similar to the Baltimore but browner and smaller. It lives in rural areas in eastern United States. *Bullock's oriole,* common in the farmlands of the West, is also like the Baltimore except for the orange on its head. The females of all species are dull yellow or greenish-yellow.   E. R. B.

Baltimore orioles weave a hanging nest

Orion, the Hunter

Chicago Natural History Museum
Eland, the largest antelope, is an oryx

Orion (oh-RYE-un) Orion is a large, bright CONSTELLATION which may be seen in winter. It is named after Orion, who was a great hunter. A row of three bright stars marks Orion's belt. Three fainter stars in a row represent a sword or a dagger hanging from his belt. Four more stars form a rectangle around the belt and sword. These mark his shoulders and knees.

Legends tell that Orion boasted he was the greatest hunter and no animal could kill him. A scorpion finally bit Orion and did kill him. The goddess Diana, a huntress, persuaded Jupiter to place Orion in the sky. Orion seems to be stalking the constellation, TAURUS, the bull. He is followed in his journey across the sky by Canis Major and Minor, his dogs. The scorpion is in the sky, too, but SCORPIUS is a summer constellation. This enemy of Orion is not visible when Orion is in the sky. Near the middle star in Orion's belt is a hazy cloud. This is the great Orion nebula, a gaseous cloud that reflects light from nearby stars.

BETELGEUSE, the bright red star on Orion's right shoulder, was supposed to be a ruby pin which held up his lion skin. Betelgeuse was the first star to have its diameter measured. Rigel, the bluish-white star diagonal to Betelgeuse, is pictured as the buckle on Orion's left shoe.   C. L. K.
SEE ALSO: NEBULA, STAR

Orion, dogs of see Canis Major and Canis Minor

Ornithology see Bird

Ornithopter see Aviation

Oryx The oryx is one of the largest members of the ANTELOPE family. Both buck and doe have long sharp horns. They inhabit open country in Africa. The best known are the *biesa,* the *fringe-eared* and the *desert* oryx.

Courtesy Society For Visual Education, Inc.
Osage orange tree and fruit

Osage orange (OH-sayj) An osage orange tree looks as though it is loaded with green cannon balls. These green balls or fruit, from three to five inches in diameter, are wrinkled and bumpy all over.

If the fruit or stem is cut, a bitter milky juice will flow. The branches have sharp thorns and are sometimes planted close together for a hedge. The ROOTS are colored a brilliant orange. The Indians and early settlers at one time used these roots as a dye for their clothing and blankets. V. V. N.

Oscillator An oscillator is an electric circuit which produces alternating voltage of required frequency. In RADIO transmitters, the electromagnetic waves produced by an oscillator serve as CARRIER WAVES. Audio oscillators vary frequency in test equipment and MUSICAL INSTRUMENTS.

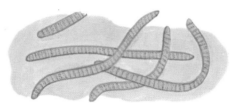

Oscillatoria

Oscilloscope

Oscillatoria (ah-sill-uh-TOH-ree-uh) Oscillatoria is the growth sometimes found on the outside of flower pots. It is a plant without roots, stems, leaves, or flowers. It is a blue-green alga, the most simple form of plant. It reproduces by simple cell division.

Oscillatoria produces long, slender cells without organized nuclei. A blue pigment and CHLOROPHYLL are often present, though not localized in PLASTIDS. This alga is found on moist banks and cliffs or in the water. It has a jellylike sheath, more visible in single-celled or colonial forms than in thread-like (filamentous) forms.

A species of oscillatoria is red and gives the Red Sea its name. P. G. B.
SEE ALSO: ALGAE; REPRODUCTION, ASEXUAL

Oscilloscope An oscilloscope is an electronic instrument which displays the image of an electrical signal on a fluorescent screen. The "heart" of the oscilloscope is a cathode-ray tube. Oscilloscopes are used to look at the waveform (shape) of an electric signal and to measure the strength and duration of very high frequency currents and voltages. When a serviceman fixes a television set, he looks at the waveform of the signal on the oscilloscope screen and compares it with a picture of what he should see.

An oscilloscope with *long persistence* has a screen coated with a special type of phosphor (the material which glows when bombarded with electrons) which will continue to glow at the spot the electrons have hit for a few minutes after the electrons have been removed.

It is sometimes necessary to compare two traces. This is most easily done using either a dual-trace oscilloscope or a dual-beam oscilloscope. The *dual-trace* oscilloscope has a single electron beam which traces out one signal and then switches to trace out another signal. The long-persistence screen of this type of oscilloscope displays both traces at the same time.

Dual-beam oscilloscopes, on the other hand, use two electron beams. Each beam traces out a different signal. Both signals are displayed simultaneously on the screen. A long-persistence screen is not necessary in a dual-beam oscilloscope. M. R. L.
SEE ALSO: CATHODE RAY, CATHODE-RAY TUBE, ELECTRICITY, ELECTRONICS

Osier see Willow

Osler, Sir William (1849-1919) Sir William Osler was a Canadian physician who became famous because of the improvements he made in the teaching and practice of medicine. As the first chief-physician of Johns Hopkins Hospital in Maryland, he introduced the practice of having young doctors serve long terms as resident doctors in the hospital. When Johns Hopkins School of Medicine opened, he sent students into the wards to study at the bedsides of patients.

Because of his concern for training good physicians, Osler is primarily remembered as a great teacher. He also made specific studies of the blood and heart, malaria, cholera, and tuberculosis. He was often called "the great physician."

Born to pioneer missionary parents serving the Church of England in Tecumseh, Ontario, Canada, William lived eight years in the rugged poverty of the north woods. The family then moved to Dundas where William and his brothers and sisters could secure an education. Because of his boyish pranks, William was withdrawn from the local elementary school and sent to a boarding school in Barrie. Although he continued to be mischievous, he proved himself again and again to be an excellent scholar.

When he was sixteen, young Osler went to Weston, a preparatory school similar to Eton in England. It was there that he met the two men who were to determine the course of his life: Reverend William A. Johnson, founder and warden of the school, and Dr. James Bovell, an outstanding physician and teacher of medicine in Toronto. After receiving his medical degree from McGill University in Montreal, he traveled and worked in Europe and Canada. In 1888 he assumed the position of professor of the principles and practice of medicine at Johns Hopkins University. He also was named Physician-in-Chief at the new Johns Hopkins Hospital affiliated with the University. In 1911 he was knighted and made a baronet.

One book written by Osler, *The Principles and Practice of Medicine,* has been used for many years as a medical textbook. He spent the last two years of his life cataloging his priceless medical library which he bequeathed to McGill University.   D. H. J.

Osmium (AHZ-mee-um) An Englishman named Smithson Tennant discovered osmium, element number 76, in 1804. He named it *osmium* after a Greek word meaning "smell" because its compound with oxygen had a sharp and irritating odor. It is a hard grayish-white or bluish-white metal.

Osmium and a similar metal, IRIDIUM, form an alloy which is very hard. This alloy, *osmiridium,* is sometimes used for fountain pen points and phonograph needles.

Osmium is a dense element, a member of the PLATINUM group. It is more than ten per cent heavier than gold.

The oxide of osmium, osmium tetroxide or peroxide, OsO_4, is important in synthetic chemistry. The atomic weight of osmium is 190.2.   J. R. S.

SEE ALSO: ELEMENTS

Osmosis (ahss-MOH-siss) Molecules, the tiny pieces which make up all matter, tend to move from where they are more concentrated to where they are less concentrated. This equalizing movement, called *diffusion,* occurs because the random motions of the molecules make them move around. If there are more molecules of one kind in a certain region than outside that region, more molecules will move out of that region than move into it. Osmosis is the DIFFUSION of water through a membrane that will not allow other, larger molecules to pass through it. Such a membrane is called *semipermeable.*

Many chemists and physicists include in osmosis the passage of any gas, liquid, or dissolved solid through a semipermeable membrane. Other scientists restrict the term to the passage of liquids and dissolved substances, such as food and minerals, through membrane. Most biologists, however, state that osmosis is the movement of water through a semipermeable membrane from where water is more concentrated to where it is less concentrated.

The classic experiment which shows osmosis uses parchment as the semipermeable membrane. The parchment allows water, but not molasses, to pass through.

The force by which water moves into the solutions is called *osmotic pressure.* Osmotic pressure depends upon the concen-

The classic experiment in osmosis uses a parchment membrane, thistle tube, molasses and water. The liquid rising in the tube is a solution of both fluids because diffusion occurs only one way—the water moves into the molasses

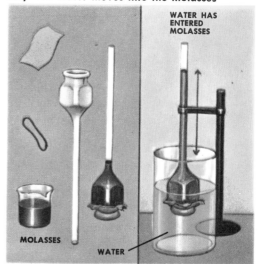

✳ **THINGS TO DO**

WHICH MATERIALS WILL GO THROUGH A MEMBRANE?

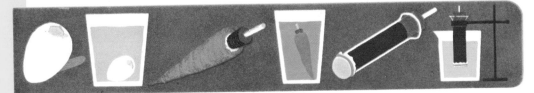

When two solutions are separated by a thin membrane, the stronger or more concentrated solution will pass through if the membrane is permeable to it. Set up several osmometers to determine which solutions go in which directions.

1   Carefully remove part of the shell at the large end of an egg. Do not break the membrane under the shell. Immerse the egg in a glass of water. What happens?

2   Hollow out the top end of a carrot or beet. Insert a one-holed cork into the hole and put melted wax around it to seal it closely to the root. Put a glass tube in the cork. Now place the carrot in colored water. What comes up the tube? Clear water or colored water?

3   Remove the bottom of a test tube by winding a wire around it and then holding this end over a flame. When the wire becomes hot it will break the end off the tube. Cover this open end with a cleaned piece of sausage casing. Fasten the membrane on tightly with a rubber band. Fill the tube with a molasses solution. Cap the tube with a cork and glass tube. Suspend the tube in a beaker of water from a ring stand. After several hours, observe the direction of liquid movement.

---

tration of water inside and outside the membrane and upon temperature. The greater the difference in concentrations and the higher the temperature, the greater the osmotic pressure. This pressure is frequently measured in pounds per square inch. Osmotic pressure is one of the important forces which makes sap in plants rise.

Living cells have a membrane surrounding them through which osmosis can take place, but this membrane can allow or not allow molecules to pass into and out of the cell much more selectively than a simple semipermeable membrane can.   J. K. L.

Osprey (AHS-pree) The osprey is a large bird, commonly known as the *fish hawk, bald buzzard,* or *fishing eagle.* The osprey is found throughout North America but prefers the South in the winter. The osprey dives feet first into the water and grips fish in its powerful talons. It is most often found along the coasts and near large lakes and rivers, but sometimes makes its home inland. It resembles the bald eagle but is smaller in size and has white underparts.

The osprey is about two feet long, with a wing-spread of four feet from tip to tip. It is a rich brown color, and its tail is banded with brown and white. The upper parts of the head and neck are whitish, and the legs have a bluish cast. The voice of the osprey is seldom heard but sounds like the peeping of baby chicks. Its nest looks like a bushel basket of sticks, built high in a dead tree, on a deserted building, or on the rocky ledge of a cliff.   M. R. L.

SEE ALSO: BIRDS OF PREY

The osprey is a fish-eating hawk

Ossification (ahs-ih-fih-KAY-shun) Ossification is the formation of BONE; the changing of CONNECTIVE TISSUE or of CARTILAGE into bone through progressive changes in the cells making up the tissue. As large mammals, such as man, grow, the skull becomes ossified.

SEE: SKELETON

Ostrich (AWS-trich) The ostrich is one of the few birds in the world which cannot fly. It has long legs which help it to run over the African grasslands, where it lives. It can run as fast as four-legged grazing animals, up to 35 or 40 miles an hour. Its diet is mostly vegetarian, including seeds and plants, but it also eats small mammals, reptiles and insects. Almost everything about it is big except its head. A male may stand five feet high at the back, and weigh over 300 pounds. The female is smaller.

The male's body is black and the feathers in the tips of its wings and tail are white. They can be pulled without hurting the bird. This is done annually to ostriches on farms in Africa and Europe and the feathers or plumes are sold for decoration. The head, legs and thighs are naked of feathers. It is the only bird with two toes.

Each male ostrich oversees several hens and nests. The female lays 12 to 16 eggs, each six to eight inches long and as heavy as 25 hen's eggs. They are simply covered with sand in the daytime and incubated by the male at night.

Ostriches thrive in captivity and have a life span similar to that of humans. E. R. B.

SEE ALSO: BIRDS, FLIGHTLESS

African ostrich family
Courtesy Society For Visual Education, Inc.

Chicago Natural History Museum
Sea otters of the Aleutian Islands

Otter (AHT-er) Otters are long, sleek, fur-bearing animals with long tails, short legs, and broad, webbed feet. They spend most of their time in water and are excellent swimmers, divers, and fishermen. These flesh-eating (*carnivorous*) mammals are closely related to WEASELS. There are two groups of otters, river otters and sea otters.

River otters grow to be about four feet long. Their grass-lined burrows may be found along the banks of streams and rivers. These very playful animals love to slide down muddy or icy hills. They dive and swim in the water, catching slippery fish with their sharp strong teeth. Otters also catch crayfish, snails, shellfish, frogs, and insects. River otters are active all year. Their bodies are covered with two layers of thick, water-repellent fur. The pale gray undercoat is short and soft, while the dark brown outercoat is long and stiff.

The otter's body is insulated by a layer of fat under the skin. In the early spring, two to three babies are born to each mother otter. They are cared for several months by the mother.

Sea otters are larger and have shorter tails than river otters. They live in the vast beds of seaweed or KELP in the North Pacific. Their range is from the coast of North America north of Oregon to the Asian coast north of the Kurile Islands.

Only one baby sea otter is born at a time. The mother sea otter often sleeps on her back and carries her dependent baby on her chest. Sea otters seem to enjoy floating on their backs. They dive to great depths to catch crabs, mussels, snails, sea urchins, starfish and other marine life. They bring the food up to the surface, roll over to their backs, crack open their dinner and use their chests as tables to eat on. D. J. A.

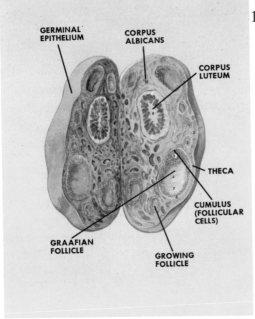

GERMINAL EPITHELIUM

CORPUS ALBICANS

CORPUS LUTEUM

THECA

CUMULUS (FOLLICULAR CELLS)

GRAAFIAN FOLLICLE

GROWING FOLLICLE

©Denoyer-Geppert Co.

Cut section of an ovary in a woman

Ovary (OH-vuh-ree) The ovary is the sex gland in a female. Within the ovary, germ or sex cells develop or mature into egg cells (*ova*) ready for fertilization.

There are two ovaries, each about one and one-half inches long and three-fourths of an inch wide in each female. When a baby girl is born, she has about 350,000 immature ova in the ovary, but only about 400 ever mature.

The maturing of ova is controlled by hormones secreted by the ovary and by another gland, the PITUITARY, located below the brain.

Germinal epithelium surrounds the ovary. Beneath it is the *cortex,* composed of fibrous and reticular connective tissue. It contains developing ova surrounded by follicle cells. A denser part of the cortex immediately under the epithelium is called the *tunica albuginea.*

The central part of the ovary is called the *medulla.* Developing ova are absent but there are smooth muscles, elastic fibers, and the branches of ovarian arteries and veins.

As a germ cell matures, it enlarges. The follicle cells divide by mitosis until a large follicle filled with liquid is formed.

This is known as the *Graafian follicle,* and the mature egg is attached to one side. The follicle ruptures or breaks, and the egg passes through the oviduct to the uterus.

The cells in the ruptured follicle, now known as the *corpus luteum,* secrete a yellowish hormone (*progesterone*) which fills the cavity. If the egg is not fertilized the follicle degenerates.   J. C. K.

SEE ALSO: HISTOLOGY, MENSTRUATION, MITOSIS AND MEIOSIS, OVUM, REPRODUCTIVE SYSTEMS

Oven bird see Warbler

Overtones Musical sounds have three characteristics: pitch, loudness, and quality of tone. The tone quality, often called *timbre,* is determined by the number, strength, and pitch of all the separate tones comprising the one principal tone. This principal tone is called the *fundamental*—that is, a tone of a single frequency or pitch. The other weaker tones, not heard as separate tones, are called *overtones* (or *harmonics,* if they are multiples of the fundamental). A tone with a frequency twice the fundamental is called the first harmonic.

No musical instrument ever produces a pure tone, that is a tone of a single frequency. It actually produces a mixture of tones. A tuning fork, mounted on a resonating box, will usually produce a pure tone, with only the fundamental present. A pure tone is dull and colorless. The richness of the tones of musical instruments and of the human VOICE is due to overtones. The more overtones, the richer the tone quality.

If the same note, say middle C, is played on the violin, clarinet and piano, the pitch or fundamental frequency is the same. However, the quality of the tone differs in each case, and the listener with a little practice can distinguish the instruments producing the given notes. The difference in quality between instruments is due to the number and strength of the overtones produced at each frequency.

When a musical sound is made, the lowest and usually the strongest frequency in the mixture is the fundamental. It is the fundamental tone that seems to be heard.

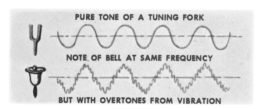

PURE TONE OF A TUNING FORK

NOTE OF BELL AT SAME FREQUENCY

BUT WITH OVERTONES FROM VIBRATION

The higher-pitched sounds are the overtones. These are generally weaker vibrations of higher frequencies which affect the tones heard.

A string on a certain instrument may give, in addition to the fundamental of 200 vibrations per second, an intense overtone of 400 vibrations per second, with a moderate intensity; another of 1200 vibrations per second with less; and very faintly, others of 1600 and 2000 vibrations per second. A string on a different instrument may give the same fundamental, and the notes of 400 and 800 vibrations rather faintly, but may make the higher pitched overtones relatively loud. These two instruments thus differ in tone quality. Whenever the qualities of two tones of the same pitch are different, the overtones in the two are different either in pitch or loudness, or in both.   D. L. D.

SEE ALSO: MUSICAL INSTRUMENTS, SOUND

Oviparous (oh-VIPP-uh-ruhs) Oviparous refers to an animal which reproduces by means of eggs in which the young develop inside the eggs and the eggs hatch after they have left the mother's body. Birds are oviparous.

SEE: EGG, REPRODUCTIVE SYSTEMS

Ovulation see Ovary, Ovum

Ovum (OH-vuhm) An ovum is the reproductive cell produced by the ovary. The production and release of this ovum or egg by the ovary is called *ovulation*. FERTILIZATION takes place when the ovum comes in contact with the male cell called the SPERM, and the two unite, forming a *zygote*. This divides by MITOSIS, grows and differentiates into a new individual *embryo*.

Many plants and animals come from fertilized ova or eggs.

SEE: EGGS; EMBRYOLOGY; GAMETE; OVARY; POLLINATION; REPRODUCTION, SEXUAL

Owl Owls are found all over the world. Most of them do their hunting at night and all are flesh eaters, preying mostly on small rodents, such as mice. They have large heads, hooked beaks and talons and large eyes set in flat feathered disks. Their calls vary, depending on the species, from screeches and hoots to whistles and low moans.

Night-flying owls often prey over the same territory hawks cover during the day. They are well adapted for night hunting. Their eyes are ten to 100 times as sensitive to low light as man's and their ears, large slits in the sides of the head, enable them to hear the slightest rustling. Their flight feathers are fringed for silent attacks. They plunge at their prey and strike with their hooked talons. They differ from other birds of prey in that they may swallow prey whole and digest the meat, casting up indigestible items in the form of pellets.

There are about 133 species of owls, ranging from as small as a sparrow to large as a rooster. A few owls, such as the pygmy and hawk owl, hunt by day. They are solitary birds, some living far from civilization and others preferring human habitations where rodents are plentiful.

The smaller owls nest in holes in trees or on the ground and the large owls build nests. The female lays white, round eggs, from one to 12 depending on the species. They hatch at intervals so the young vary in size.   E. R. B.

SEE ALSO: BIRDS OF PREY

Ox see Oxen

Some of the most common owls are the barn owl (left), horned owl (center), and screech owl (right)

Chicago Natural History Museum
Arctic musk ox

Oxen Oxen is a general term covering a group of hoofed animals belonging to the *bovine* family. They have some of the same body structures as cattle, sheep and goats. The only two wild oxen in North America are the bison and musk ox. The *kouprey* of Cambodia and the *gaur* (or *seladang*) of India are oxen of other countries.

Oxen generally have stocky bodies, cloven hoofs, large lateral horns and a long tail. Their stomachs have four chambers and are well adapted for digesting harsh grasses.

The *bison* is erroneously called BUFFALO in the United States. This wild ox is almost extinct in the wild state. Bison breed well in captivity. Their shaggy fur is brown to brownish black. The male may weigh up to 1700 pounds while the female is somewhat smaller. Both sexes have horns that are never shed. The hump-like shoulders, common in oxen, are quite pronounced.

The *musk ox* is smaller than the bison and the domestic ox of other countries. It weighs under 500 pounds. It gets its name from the strong musk odor it gives off when excited. Its shaggy hair is very long. As with bison, both the male and female musk oxen grow horns which are never shed, only new horny tissue is added annually. They are found roaming in groups around the Arctic region.

The *seladang* or *gaur* is a fast runner who spends its wild life in the forests of the Malayan Peninsula and India. It has horns measuring two and one-half feet long and stands about six feet high. The *Brahman ox (zebu)* has been brought to areas in southern United States from Africa. They are adapted to living and working in warm climates. H. J. C.

SEE ALSO: RUMINANT, UNGULATA, YAK

WHAT ELEMENT IS NECESSARY FOR THE PROCESS OF OXIDATION?

1 Light a match and insert it into an empty glass jar. The match continues to burn because oxygen is present.
2 Now put a ball of steel wool into the jar. Sprinkle it well with water. Cover the jar and permit it to stand for several days.
3 Observe the change occurring to the steel strands. The steel wool is chemically combining with something in the jar to cause it to rust.
4 Remove the cover of the jar and immediately insert a lighted match. What happens to the flame? Steel wool cannot oxidize nor can fire burn without oxygen or a similar substance such as chlorine.

Oxidation (ox-i-DA-tion) Oxidation is the process is which a substance combines with oxygen or with another substance such as chlorine. Oxidation may be rapid, as can be seen in a material burning in air, or slow, as in the rusting of iron. Regardless of the speed of oxidation, the process involves a substance uniting with oxygen to form an *oxide*.

Most metals combine readily with oxygen to form oxides. Some of the products, in order of quantity, are silicon dioxide, SiO_2; iron oxide, Fe_2O_3; aluminum oxide, Al_2O_3.

It was once believed that in the combustion process substance lost weight. The substance given off was called *phlogiston*. The theory involved substances that were "snuffed out" when burned in enclosed spaces. It stated that the saturation of the air by phlogiston made the burning object unable to release any more phlogiston to the

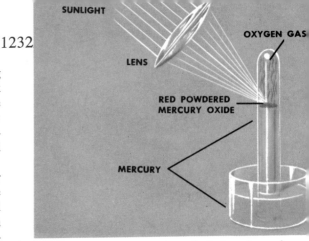

air. Many prominent scientists, including Joseph Priestley, who was one of the first chemists to produce oxygen, believed in the phlogiston theory. For example, Priestley called the oxygen he produced "dephlogisticated air" because he believed that he had removed the phlogiston from the air.

Later (in 1777) Lavoisier proved that air consisted mainly of two substances, one which suffocated a mouse (nitrogen) and the other which supported combustion (oxygen). He showed that materials undergoing oxidation actually gained in weight, disproving the phlogiston theory.   E. Y. K.

SEE ALSO: LAVOISIER, ANTOINE; OXIDE; OXYGEN; PRIESTLEY, JOSEPH

Lavoisier's experiment showed that a burned substance (mercuric oxide) can be made to reverse its action and release oxygen gas

Oxide Oxygen exists alone or is chemically combined with other elements. An oxide is a compound usually made of two elements; one is oxygen and the other usually a metal. Many useful mineral materials are oxides. Ordinary sand is silicon dioxide, SiO_2. Chinese white clay (kaolin) is aluminum oxide; and lime is calcium oxide.

Some oxides are nonmetallic compounds. Our body cells make a gas, carbon dioxide, and slow-burning fuel forms poisonous carbon monoxide.

Mineral oxides are used to obtain the metals with which they are combined in natural ores. The required removal of oxygen, called *reduction,* is technically difficult. In reducing common hematite iron ore (which is Fe_2O_3), carbon monoxide from coked coal is the reducing agent used:

$Fe_2O_3 + 3CO \rightarrow 2 Fe$ (iron) $+ 3CO_2$.

Aluminum is reduced from its ore, bauxite, by a different method. First, the BAUXITE is treated with soda lye to obtain pure aluminum oxide; this is melted with cryolite ($Na_3Al F_6$) and reduced by electrolysis, to yield pure molten aluminum.

Some of the nonmetallic oxides are very unstable. Sulfur dioxide, for example, is the choking gas formed when sulfur burns in oxygen or air. It will react with water to form sulfurous acid.   E. Y. K.

SEE ALSO: ELECTROLYSIS, OXIDATION, REDUCTION

Oxyacetylene torch see Acetylene

Oxygen (OK-si-jen) Oxygen is considered the most important element for life on this planet. Life can go on for a while without food or water, but not without oxygen. Oxygen is necessary also for fuels to burn.

Ancient philosophers did not know about oxygen as an element. They spoke of "something" in the air combining with fire. Zosimos, an Egyptian chemist, mentioned this as early as 250 A. D. Oxygen was not separated as a gas until 1772 when Karl Scheele of Sweden discovered it.

Independently Joseph Priestley had found oxygen but referred to the gas as "dephlogisticated air." He was surprised to find that a candle burned more vigorously in the gas.

The importance of oxygen was realized neither by Scheele nor by Priestley but by the French chemist Antoine Lavoisier. He identified oxygen as a material needed for combustion. Lavoisier's discoveries laid the foundation for modern chemistry.

About 20% of the ATMOSPHERE is made up of oxygen. It is a colorless, odorless, and tasteless gas. Its density is .00143 grams per cubic centimeter. Oxygen (symbol O) has atomic number 8. Its atomic weight is 15.9994. Until 1961, it was the standard for the atomic weights of all elements: $O = 16.000$.

Oxygen is found in air as a *diatomic* molecule, O_2. It occurs in many compounds called OXIDES. The most plentiful oxide is plain sand (silicon dioxide, SiO_2). Large amounts of oxides are found in rocks, as iron or aluminum oxides, and as silicates

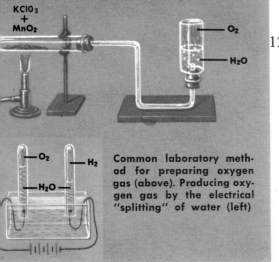

Common laboratory method for preparing oxygen gas (above). Producing oxygen gas by the electrical "splitting" of water (left)

(-SiO₃). Oxygen, next to silicon, is the most abundant element. About 50 per cent of the earth is made up of oxygen.

Oxygen also occurs in compounds called *peroxides,* which contain the peroxide ion. This ion is made of two oxygen atoms joined together by a *covalent bond.* The ion carries two negative charges. A peroxide commonly found in homes is hydrogen peroxide, H_2O_2. Hydrogen peroxide in water is used as a mild disinfectant and bleach. When hydrogen peroxide decomposes, it gives oxygen and water:

$$2H_2O_2 \rightarrow O_2 + 2H_2O$$

Oxygen is usually prepared in the scientific laboratory by the heating of potassium chlorate:

$$2KClO_3 \xrightarrow{\text{MnO}_2} 2KCl + 3O_2$$

Oxygen gas is liberated and collected by water replacement. Manganese dioxide is the catalyst in this reaction.

Oxygen is also produced by the electrolysis of water:

$$2H_2O \rightarrow 2H_2 + O_2$$

There are other methods of preparing oxygen. Commercially it is prepared by the liquefying of air. In the *Linde process* air is cooled until oxygen becomes a liquid at −183° C. A few years ago gaseous oxygen was kept in tanks under pressure but today liquid oxygen is kept in tanks as a space-saving measure.

Green plants produce oxygen during photosynthesis in daylight. Plants must use some oxygen from the air to carry on their own respiratory processes.

The ability of oxygen to support combustion, called *oxidation,* is its most significant property, and oxidation reactions always yield energy such as heat or light.

Tank oxygen is used in treating pneumonia and heart trouble. It is also used in flying, in submarines, in deep-sea diving, and in oxygen torches.   E. Y. K.

SEE ALSO: COMBUSTION; ELEMENTS; LAVOISIER, ANTOINE; OXIDATION; PRIESTLEY, JOSEPH; SPONTANEOUS COMBUSTION

Oxygen tent An oxygen tent is a piece of medical equipment used for people with illnesses in which the body cannot get enough OXYGEN from air. The condition in which the body tissues are without oxygen is called *anoxia.*

Oxygen tents are of various designs. Essentially an oxygen tent is a material which can retain an oxygen-enriched air mixture about a patient. It may be dome-shaped or box-shaped, with various arrangements of openings to allow for passing food and medication to and from the patient.

An oxygen tent enables a patient to get more oxygen per inhalation than he normally does. A tank of liquefied oxygen serves as the oxygen supply. If respiration is weak, each inhalation must be rich in oxygen to compensate for the small air quantity inhaled. Various conditions require differing mixtures.   D. J. I.

Oxygen tent

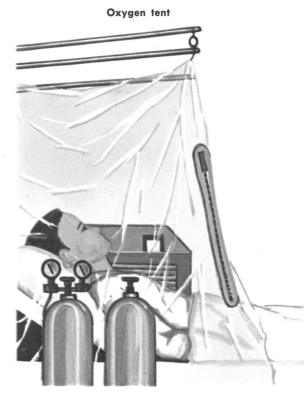

J. W. Thompson

Japanese oyster

Oyster The oyster is a small sea animal enclosed in two hinged shells called *valves*. Oysters belong to a group of mollusks called *bivalves* (two-valves). Varieties are used for food, mother-of-pearl, and PEARL production. Oysters are found mainly in waters off sea coasts.

The full-grown oyster's shell is the size of a woman's hand, appearing grayish colored and irregularly pear-shaped. One valve is larger and cupped, holding the animal's soft body. The other is like a lid on a box. The inside of the valves is made smooth by a secretion of the oyster. This is "mother-of-pearl." Its smoothness protects the soft, naked animal. The valves open and close slightly, controlled by adductor muscles, located on either side of the body. Oysters breathe by GILLS and eat minute plants and animals in the water. To remove an oyster, one must force the shell open by cutting the strong muscles at the hinge with a sharp knife.

Oysters develop from eggs, one oyster producing hundreds of millions of eggs in a season. This large number of eggs is vital, for quantities are eaten by fish, which also devour the larvae (small swimming forms which develop into adults. These swimmers travel about for two weeks until they anchor permanently. They continue to grow, arriving at full growth in three to four years.

Commercially, oyster "beds" are kept in favorable condition for oyster production and development. Since oysters live such perilous lives, "farmers" must do all they can to guard their investment by careful attention to oyster needs.   D. J. I.

SEE ALSO: MOLLUSCA

Salsify, with its oyster-flavored root

Oyster plant The oyster plant has narrow leaves and large yellow or purple flowers. There are several varieties which grow wild in Europe. The *salsify,* or purple goatsbeard, is grown in the United States for its edible, oyster-flavored root.

Ozone (OH-zohn) Ozone is a form of OXYGEN. It is different from ordinary oxygen in that the molecule consists of three atoms of oxygen instead of two. It is a bluish GAS that can be formed by passing an electrical discharge through oxygen. Thus LIGHTNING is a natural means of producing ozone. Ozone can be produced mechanically by passing air between highly-charged electrical plates of a special machine. Ozone is also formed by the arcs from electric motor brushes, and can be identified by the rather penetrating odor associated with running motors.

In the upper ATMOSPHERE, ozone is produced when ultraviolet sunlight strikes oxygen. Because these rays are harmful in great amounts, it is advantageous that they are absorbed. The ozone which is produced in the upper atmosphere is wafted downward by *convection* currents. Only minute quantities are in the atmosphere man breathes, however, and in small amounts this poisonous gas gives an invigorating touch to the air and can be tolerated.

Ozone is chemically active because the extra atom of oxygen is loosely held and combines readily with substances. It is used for certain cleaning and purifying processes.
                                        D. J. I.

Ozonosphere see Atmosphere

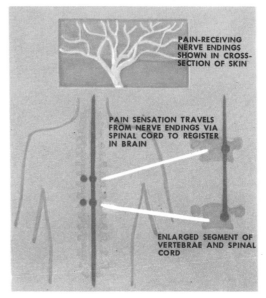

PAIN-RECEIVING NERVE ENDINGS SHOWN IN CROSS-SECTION OF SKIN

PAIN SENSATION TRAVELS FROM NERVE ENDINGS VIA SPINAL CORD TO REGISTER IN BRAIN

ENLARGED SEGMENT OF VERTEBRAE AND SPINAL CORD

Pathway of pain sensations through the spinal cord, and cross-section of skin showing finely-divided pain-receiving nerve endings

Pacemaker see Heart

Pachyderm A pachyderm is a thick-skinned, hoofed animal such as an ELEPHANT, RHINOCEROS, or HIPPO-POTAMUS. Cud-chewing animals (ruminants), such as cattle and goats, are also hoofed but are not pachyderms.

The pachyderm group is a popular group rather than a scientific one. Taxonomically most pachyderms are not even classified in the same order of mammals and are not closely related. For instance, the hippopotamuses are more closely related to cattle than to elephants, and yet cattle are not pachyderms. J. C. K.

Pacific Ocean see Ocean

Paddlefish The paddlefish, or duck-bill, is a freshwater fish found in the Mississippi River and its branches. It is scaleless, and sometimes reaches a length of six feet and a weight of 150 pounds. It is related to the sturgeon, and its eggs are often mixed with eggs of the sturgeon for caviar. Another species of paddlefish is found in large rivers of China.

Paddlefish

Chicago Natural History Museum

Pain Pain may be defined as suffering or distress in the body. Most animals, as well as people, can feel pain. Pain is one of man's oldest enemies, and man tries hard to avoid pain whenever possible. Pain is also a great friend of man, however, because it is the body's way of reporting DISEASE, INFECTION, or injury of certain body parts. A person who can feel no pain lives a life of constant danger. Such a person might even die because of an infection he did not find out about in time to see a doctor.

Most pain is detected in the body by thin, bare, and finely-branching nerve endings in the skin and internal organs of the body. These pain receivers are like a very finely-divided electric wire. Feelings of pain are carried as tiny electric impulses along the nerves up through the spinal cord to the brain. Pain is a very personalized sensation. Intensity of pain varies greatly in different persons and even in the same person at different times. No one can really know the intensity of pain felt by another person. Man has made great progress in his battle against pain. Doctors today have over 1,000 different pain killers, or *analgesics*. R. S. C.

SEE ALSO: NERVE CELL

✳ THINGS TO DO

CAN YOU MAKE A BLACK PAINT?

1   For making homemade black paint you need carbon or lampblack, turpentine, and linseed oil.

2   Lampblack can be obtained by holding a pyrex dish or bottle over a candle flame until the carbon forms on it. Scrap the film of black into a small amount of linseed oil.

3   Mix these materials thoroughly. Add a few drops of turpentine to make the paint thin enough to spread on a surface. The result will be a flat permanent paint. Shiny enamel paint is obtained by adding a few drops of varnish to the flat mixture.

Paint Paints have been used through the ages to decorate surfaces and to protect them from sun, water, or heat. Artists use paints to create beautiful pictures. Children use various paints to make murals and pictures.

One of the most important uses of paint in modern times is that of protecting surfaces. Wood is an excellent building material, but it quickly rots if left exposed to the weather. Special outdoor paint is used to paint wood exposed to sun and rain. Indoors, paint is used to beautify wall surfaces, to make them easier to keep clean, and to increase or decrease light reflected from the walls. Special purpose paints include anticorrosive paints to keep iron and steel from rusting; marine paints to keep boats shipshape; fireproof paints, used where fire is a hazard; luminous paints which glow in the dark; and poison paints, used to keep parasites from attacking wood.

All paints basically consist of a vehicle containing a pigment. The *pigment* is the coloring material of the paint. The pigment not only determines the color but also how opaque the paint will be. The less opaque the paint, the more paint needed to cover a given surface. The *vehicle* is the medium which holds the pigment. It is the vehicle which dries and forms a film, holding the pigment particles together and onto a surface. Oil and water are the vehicles most commonly used.

Oil paints consist of a pigment in an oil vehicle. The vehicle usually has both volatile and nonvolatile components. The volatile portion of the vehicle, usually a thinner such as TURPENTINE, makes the paint easier to apply and speeds drying by its evaporation from the paint. The dried paint film, however, contains none of the volatile portion of the vehicle. The nonvolatile portion of the vehicle is often called a *binder* because it binds the pigment particles together.

Water paints are those paints which use water, rather than oil, as the medium. They are used as house paints because they are economical, fast-drying, and easy to mix and apply. Calcimine paints and whitewash contain animal glue for a binder. Casein paints contain milk casein as a binder. The newer resin emulsion water paints (latex paints) use a synthetic resin as a binder. They are easier to apply than either calcimine or casein paints and may be applied with a roller.

Enamels are a type of paint in which the pigment is mixed with varnish, rather than with an oil. Enamel gives a high gloss finish and is much easier to clean than an oil paint, which is often referred to as *flat* paint. *Lacquer* is similar to an enamel but has a glossier finish and is harder.   D. L. D.
SEE ALSO: PIGMENT, VARNISH

Painted cup see Wild flowers

Palate The palate is the roof of the mouth. The front part, called the *hard palate* is bony and hard; and the back portion, called the *soft palate* is muscular and soft. Both are covered with MUCOUS MEMBRANE. They separate the mouth and the nasal cavity.

Paleolithic see Stone Age

Paleontologists may first make ground surveys of an area which is likely to hold fossils. Then, when a fossil is found it must be removed from the ground very carefully. The rock around it may be useful in dating the specimen

Paleontology (pay-lee-uhn-TAHL-uh-jee) Paleontology is the science that deals with *fossils*. Fossils are the remains of plant and animal life from thousands of years ago. Paleontology is often considered to cover just fossil animals, but a better division of this science is to use *paleozoology* for the study of fossil animals and *paleobotany* for the study of fossil plants. "Paleo" is from the Greek word *palaios,* meaning "ancient."

Fossils are useful as evidence of evolution. A collection of them may show the changes that a certain kind of animal has gone through. Fossil bones of early man found all over the world show the story of the changes from ape to modern man. These changes took almost two million years. As a general rule, paleontology usually does not deal with things less than 10,000 years old.

Paleontology is closely connected to GEOLOGY, the study of the earth's crust, including the sediment at the bottom of the ocean. Impressions such as footprints of past animals are often found in rocks. Though a fossil is rock, when the animal left an impression the surface was probably moist sand or clay. Physical changes on the earth's surface determine whether or not remains will be preserved as fossils.

Fossils tell the geologist much about the earth. He may want to know how old a rock is. If the rock contains fossils of animals that he knows lived only about 100,000 years ago, he can be fairly sure that the rock is about 100,000 years old. Such fossils are called *index* fossils.

HISTORY OF PALEONTOLOGY

The first notice and scientific interpretation of fossils was recorded by the Greek Xenophanes in 600 B.C. He observed fossils of mollusks inland, away from the sea, and thought that the sea had once covered that area. In Egypt one hundred years later, Herodotus observed shells in the desert and tried to interpret them.

Not until the beginning of the scientific renaissance in Europe, about 1400 A.D., did fossils again come to be considered as evidence of changes on Earth. Leonardo da Vinci was the first expert since the classical times of ancient Greece to recognize fossils without superstition. About the same time, they were mentioned in a scientific book by the geologist Agricola.

Modern paleontology started about 1800 from the work of two men—BARON GEORGES CUVIER and William Smith. Smith found that in different layers (strata) of rock, different fossils were found. His work started *stratigraphical* geology and, in large part, had a basis in the use of index fossils. Cuvier, however, studied fossils in the same way that zoologists and anatomists study living things. He tried to interpret the habits and environments of past animals from their fossil structures. The work of these two men brought about the first division of general paleontology into separate areas.

FIELDS OF PALEONTOLOGY

Paleobiochemistry: A very specialized field of paleontology is paleobiochemistry. This area of study is confined to studying fossils for remnants of organic compounds. Workers in this area of biochemistry have been able to identify amino acids in fossils up to 360,000,000 years old. These scientists know that the older the fossils are, the fewer amino acids remain.

When the fossil is recovered, it may be gently scraped or bathed in acid and fixed so it can be studied or displayed without damaging or destroying it

Paleobotany: The study of fossil plants and vegetation has become very important for a knowledge of environmental conditions in the geologic past. Paleobotany has been, and is, vital to a clear scientific description of the evolution of plant life on earth.

Evidence of the *angiosperms* (flowering plants which now dominate the earth) are found only in deposits made after the middle of the Mesozoic Era. The *thallophytes* (algae and seaweeds), on the other hand, have existed for more than 500 million years. There are eleven large groups of plants which are known only in fossil form, as the dinosaurs are known. The most dramatic plant fossils are the giant logs of petrified wood.

Collecting plant fossils is more difficult than collecting animal fossils because of the delicate plant structures that are so easily destroyed or carried away by water. Leaf deposits are often found in thin layers of fine sediment. Usually only impressions will be found because moisture caused the leaf to decay. Some fragments, though, will have been *carbonized* and are more easily preserved.

Paleoclimatology: Paleoclimatology is part of paleogeography. It deals with winds, precipitation, weather, and climate zones of past geologic ages. The study is based on rocks and organic remains.

For example, if fossils of what are now tropical plants are found in a far north region where such plants could not now grow, there may be two explanations. Either the climate of the region changed greatly, or the earth's crust itself shifted into a different climate zone. The way in which sediments hardened into rock also shows varying climatic conditions. Past conditions in the ocean can be interpreted by the presence of coral reefs and other fossil organisms. The mammoths found in Siberia is one of the greatest challenges to paleoclimatologists.

It is difficult to explain how such a huge animal as the mammoth could be frozen instantaneously, with undigested food still in its stomach.

Paleoecology: The ecology of fossil life is a more difficult study than the ECOLOGY of living things. Because of the vast geologic changes, the science has to be based on inferences. Its basic assumption is that plants and animals in the far past formed an interrelated and balanced society much as they do today. Most data are in the area of marine biology, because more fossils are found in marine sediment than are found on land or in fresh water.

Paleogeography is primarily concerned with the geography of the past and deals with fossils only in describing areas.

There are several other terms that fall into the general field of paleontology. *Paleoethnology* is the study of the races, cultures, and specializations of prehistoric man. *Paleontography* is the straight physical description of fossils.

COLLECTING FOSSILS

Searching for fossils can be an interesting hobby or career. They may be found accidentally, but it is necessary to have some general knowledge of geology and zoology to understand what they are. On discovering fossils, it is important for the amateur to note carefully the kind and location of rocks they were found in. The fossil can sometimes be identified with the help of the rock type. If the rock cannot be easily identified, the amateur should take careful note of the location so that an expert can identify it.

An experienced paleontologist may be able to compare the fossil find with other fossils and with living things. For this a knowledge of biology is vital.   J. F. B.

SEE ALSO: BALANCE OF NATURE, CLIMATE, EARTH, ECOSYSTEM, EVOLUTION OF MAN, FOSSILS, GEOLOGIC TIME TABLE, PETRIFACTION, ROCKS, SOIL TYPES, TRILOBITE

Chicago Natural History Museum
Corals of the middle Cambrian life

Chicago Natural History Museum
Marine invertebrates of the late Ordovician

Paleozoic Era (pay-lee-uh-ZOH-ick) The period of ancient life called the Paleozoic Era began about 500 million years ago and came to an end about 200 million years ago. Great changes in life took place throughout this era.

During this 300 million years many changes occurred, with a progression from the Age of Invertebrates to the Age of Fishes and the Age of Amphibians. During this era came the first vertebrates, land animals, insects, plants, forests, and seed-bearing plants.

The Paleozoic Era also saw a variety of climates. During long periods of warm dry temperatures, great deposits of salt were formed. There were also periods of warm humid climate in which vast coal-forming swamps came into existence. There were periods of very cold climate when huge glaciers covered the earth.

There were seven recognized periods that made up the Paleozoic Era. They are named after places where rocks of the period were first studied. Listed in order of occurrence they are: Cambrian, Ordovician, Silurian, Devonian, Mississippian, Pennsylvanian, and Permian. European writers refer to the Mississippian and Pennsylvanian periods together as the Carboniferous, or coal-forming, Period. The Appalachian revolution took place during the Paleozoic Era and resulted in the creation of the Appalachian Mountains near the close of the era.

There were many changes geographically during this period of ancient history. Large inland seas were formed when rising ocean waters flooded interior areas of North America. At other times uplifting occurred, the seas receded, and mountains may have been formed. These inland seas of the seven periods of the Paleozoic Era differed considerably in extent and location. There was no regular pattern or sequence to their origin and disappearance. Some existed for very long periods of time, while others were of shorter duration. Some formed at the start of periods, others in the middle or at the end. The three largest inland seas occupied broad shallow depressions known as the Appalachian Trough, the Cordilleran Trough, and the Ouachita Trough. The Appalachian Trough was located roughly where the Appalachian Mountain chain is today. The Cordilleran Trough occupied the Rocky Mountain area of today. The Ouachita Trough stretched from across Oklahoma to Texas and New Mexico.

This was an era of many changes. There were many beginnings, evolutional processes, and endings during the era known as the Paleozoic Era.   V. V. N.

SEE ALSO: GEOLOGIC TIME TABLE

Palladium (puh-LAY-dee-um) Palladium is a metallic element. It has a bright silvery luster. This rare, grayish element is less dense, a little harder, and more easily oxidized, than platinum. It is found in platinum, nickel and copper ores.

Pure palladium is used in the manufacture of mirrors and watch springs. It is also used in alloys with gold, platinum, and silver. These alloys are used for jewelry, dental equipment, picture frames, pocketbook trim, and scientific instruments.

Palladium (symbol Pd) has atomic number 46. It has an atomic weight of 106.4 (unchanged from oxygen). It was discovered in 1804 by William Wollaston.   M. R. L.

SEE ALSO: ALLOY, ATOM, ELEMENTS

From left to right: royal palm of Africa, flower of the date, palmetto—a small tropical American palm, and Travelers palm of Africa

Palm There are about 2000 kinds of plants in the palm family. They range in size from small house plants to trees up to 100 feet tall. They are found in tropical areas. The trunk usually has no branches. The small flowers are either male or female blooms. The fruit is a drupe or berry.

Palms belong in the *monocotyledon* subclass of angiosperms. The leaves may be pinnately compound as in the DATE palm, or palmately compound as in the fan palm. The stem may be spiny, smooth, or covered with stumps of old leaves.

Economically, palms are important to man. The COCONUT palm's rating is near the top. The natives have found over 800 uses for the *Palmyra palm*. *Royal palms* withstand strong winds and are popular ornamental trees in Florida. The *American oil palm* produces 2000 nuts annually for 50 years. The *cohune palms* of South America also yield an oil.

The pith of certain palms gives *sago* starch. The buds of *cabbage palms* are eaten. Leaves of the *hat palm* are dried, bleached and woven into hats. The *tagua palm* seed furnishes a vegetable ivory for buttons and dice. The epidermis of the *raffia palm* leaf is woven into baskets. Wax from *carnauba palm* leaves is used in varnish.   H. J. C.

SEE ALSO: MONOCOTYLEDON; PLANTS, TROPICAL; RAFFIA

Palmate venation see Leaves

Palsy see Paralysis

Pampas see South America

Panama Canal see South America

Pancreas (PAN-kree-uhs) The pancreas is a gland shaped rather like a fish. It is found in the abdomens of animals with backbones. The pancreas plays a double role in the body. It produces *enzymes* needed to digest all kinds of food. Small sections of the pancreas, called the *islands* (or *islets*) of *Langerhans,* produce a *hormone* that enables the body to use sugar.

The human pancreas is about six to nine inches long and an inch and one-half wide. It lies behind the stomach and a little below it. The right end of the pancreas is folded forward around a group of blood vessels. This hook-like piece is called the *head*.

The digestive juice is collected in a duct that leads from the pancreas to the duodenum.

INSULIN is the hormone produced by tissues in the pancreas. Unlike the digestive juices, it is a ductless *(endocrine)* secretion and enters the body through the blood vessels. It is called *insulin* from the Latin word *insula,* meaning *island,* because it is secreted by the islands of Langerhans. If they do not make enough of it, the body cannot burn sugar. This condition is called *diabetes mellitus.*   D. A. B.

SEE ALSO: ENDOCRINE GLANDS

The pancreas and its location

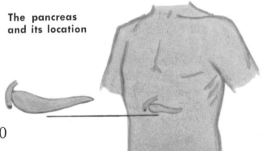

Giant panda

Pansies

Panda The giant panda is one of the rarest of large mammals. It looks like a giant black and white toy bear. Actually, it is not a bear at all but a relative of the RACCOON. It is very playful when young but can be dangerous when grown. It reaches full growth in about five years and then can weigh as much as three hundred pounds.

Another type of panda is called the *lesser* panda. It measures less than four feet from its nose to the tip of a ringed, raccoon-like tail. The Chinese call it *fire cat,* because of its rusty-red hair. When angry, it spits and hisses like a cat and can inflict severe injuries with its sharp teeth and claws.

Pandas are found only in mountains of western China. The lesser panda has long been known, but the giant panda was considered a myth until a hundred years ago. The first live giant panda was captured in 1937. Few have lived in captivity.   J. A. D.

Pandanus Pandanus is a large family of two hundred tropical trees and shrubs, called *screw pine.* The name comes from the spiral manner in which the leaves are arranged. They are easily raised as potted plants in homes or greenhouses. They need sandy loam mixed with charcoal and leaf mold, plenty of water, good drainage and partial shade in summer. Often the downward course of the roots will raise the plant out of the pot. Some of the roots raise above the soil and are called *prop roots.*

Pansy The pansy is probably one of the oldest cultivated plants. It is related to the VIOLET. For at least 400 years, the pansy, which is native to Europe, has taken to all cool, temperate climates of the civilized world.

The pansy is a low-growing plant, seldom more than six inches tall. It has heart-shaped leaves and large, irregular flowers that look like human faces. The blossoms may be purple, white, blue, yellow, brown or a mixture of these colors.

Pansies should be grown in partial shade and given plenty of moisture. When the air becomes dry during the hot summer months, the pansy plant is apt to fail even though it may be in the shade. Some pansies are annuals; some are perennials.   J. K. K.

Panther see Cat family

Papaya (puh-PAH-yuh) Papayas are herbs that are sometimes called *pawpaw trees.* Papayas grow in tropical America. They are about eighteen feet tall and look like palm trees. They have a cluster of huge leaves on top. Papaya fruits ripen in midwinter or early spring. They taste somewhat like muskmelons. They are yellow or orange and weigh as much as twenty pounds. Papaya fruits have a strong odor.

The unripe fruit is cooked like squash. The milky juice and black seeds inside the fruit are rich in papain. *Papain* is used in medicine and as a meat tenderizer. Papayas need sunshine, well-drained, rich loam, and frequent cultivation.   M. R. L.

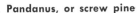
Pandanus, or screw pine

Papaya tree and fruit

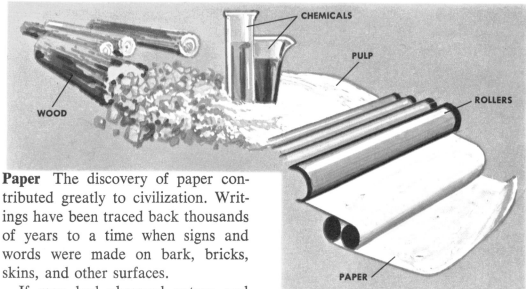

The main processes in paper-making

Paper The discovery of paper contributed greatly to civilization. Writings have been traced back thousands of years to a time when signs and words were made on bark, bricks, skins, and other surfaces.

If man had observed nature and watched paper-making wasps use wood pulp, he might have made paper earlier. The wasps chew the pulp and spread it in thin layers to form the walls of their nests.

Today there are about five thousand different types of paper with almost as many uses. The consumption of paper in the United States is enormous. Over four hundred pounds per person are used in a single year.

Paper is made from CELLULOSE or vegetable fibers. In the early days of paper-making, rags were the chief source of fiber for paper. Today the chief source of cellulose for paper is wood. When the forests were abundant, preferred woods were selected. Today, many kinds of wood are used for pulp, including pine, spruce, hemlock, fir, poplar, beech, birch, maple, and aspen.

Many successful experiments have been made to produce paper from fibrous materials other than wood. But while the supply of wood lasts, it seems to be the easiest and most economical pulp material. Paper has been made from hemp, turf, moss, potato skins, tobacco waste, coconut husks, bean stalks, cabbage leaves, bamboo, and many other vegetable materials. The important considerations for pulp material are the need for long enough fibers to make strong paper, the ease of changing the material to fiber form and eliminating impurities, availability of large supplies of low cost material, and economical means of getting the pulp materials to the mills.

If a sheet of medium-weight paper is held up to a good light, the paper can be seen to be made up of small fibers matted together. The logs that arrive at a pulp mill have to be reduced to these small fibers. One of the methods used is mechanical, the others are chemical. In the mechanical, or ground-wood method, pulp is produced by grinding the wood with grindstones under water. The chemical process takes wood chips that have come through a chipping machine, combines them in a digester, an enormous pressure cooker, with chemicals and cooks them to pulp. Different chemicals are used depending on the kind of wood used and the kind and grade of paper desired. There are sulfite (acid), sulfate (alkaline), and soda processes used in chemical methods.

The pulp, which is about 95 per cent water, is usually bleached and then goes to the paper machine. The pulp is spread onto a screen-like bed, which moves forward as it drains off some of the water and jostles from side to side to mat the fibers. The pulp is rolled between felt rollers to absorb moisture and pressed and dried as it goes through a series of rollers. The continuous sheet emerges and is wound in large rolls as finished paper to be used in manufacturing paper products.   C. L. K.

SEE ALSO: FOREST PRODUCTS, PAPYRUS, PRINTING

Red pepper, or capsicum, plant

Paprika Paprika is a spice made by grinding the dried pod of the red pepper, or *capsicum,* plant. It is a reddish powder, sweeter in taste than CAYENNE or chili pepper. It is often used for decorating foods such as mashed potatoes or creamed chicken.

The capsicum plant belongs to the NIGHTSHADE family and is not related to the *Piper nigrum* plant from which black and white pepper are made. The capsicum plant is an annual shrub bearing small white flowers and reddish oblong fruit which stands upright on the branch. These pods are called *pimiento.* J. M. C.

SEE ALSO: PEPPER, SPICE

Papyrus (puh-PY-ruhss) Papyrus is a tall reed-like plant that lives in wet places. It was used by the ancient Egyptians, Greeks, and Romans to make a writing material like paper. The word "paper" comes from the word "papyrus."

The Greeks peeled thin strips from the papyrus stem, pasted or pounded the strips together, smoothed them with shells, and rolled the sheets into scrolls.

Papyrus was also used for making boats, rope, sailcloth, and mats. The roots were used for fuel and the flowers for decorating the shrines of gods. Today, the plant is quite rare and usually found only as decoration in water gardens. J. M. C.

SEE ALSO: PAPER

Papyrus plant

Paracelsus

Paracelsus, Philippus Aureolus (pair-uh-SELL-suss) (1490-1541) Paracelsus was a Swiss physician and alchemist. An alchemist was a medieval chemist who attempted to prolong life indefinitely, to discover a universal cure for diseases, and to change common metals into gold. As a physician, Paracelsus preceded SIR JOSEPH LISTER in maintaining "All that is necessary [to heal wounds] is to prevent infection in wound diseases."

Paracelsus was born near Einsiedeln, Switzerland. He received his early education from his father who was a physician and chemist. He studied at the University of Basel, but left without getting a degree. Traveling to the mines in Tyrol, he studied the mechanical problems of mining, composition of minerals, and diseases of miners.

When he returned to lecture at the University of Basel in 1526, Paracelsus was met by intense opposition. His books in which he set forth his theories and methods of treating disease were burned by his enemies before he could begin his series of lectures.

He also lectured in German instead of Latin, the language of scholars, which was an inexcusable breach of their scholarship.

His opponents declared that his ideas had serious defects and that he did not have a degree. Finally, feeling became so heated that Paracelsus was forced to flee Basel. He wandered from place to place until 1541 when Archbishop Ernst invited him to live in Salzburg and offered him protection. However, his security lasted only a short time, for on September 24 of that same year Paracelsus met a tragic and brutal death at the hands of his enemies when he was thrown down a steep incline. D. H. J.

SEE ALSO: ALCHEMY, MEDICINE

WHY DOES A PARACHUTE MAKE AN OBJECT DESCEND SLOWLY?

1. Go outside in an open area and throw a ball as high as you can. Observe how fast the ball returns to the ground.
2. Now tie a network of strings around the ball. Attach four long strings to four sides of the ball by tying them to the net. Tie the other ends of the strings to the corners of a two-foot square of cloth. Wrap the lines and parachute around the ball.
3. Again throw the ball as high as possible. Does the ball descend at the same rate of speed? Any falling body must push aside the resisting air. Since the parachute encounters a much greater area of air, it falls more slowly.

Parachute The parachute was invented to allow men to escape from AIRCRAFT above the earth. Today it is also used for dropping cargo to places difficult to reach in other ways—cargoes of food and medicine and perhaps kits of fire-fighting tools. Fast planes may use parachutes to help in stopping or braking while landing.

An open parachute looks like a huge stickless umbrella. Closed or folded into a bundle, it looks like the pack of an overnight camper.

Any falling object has two main forces acting on it: the pull of *gravity* and the *resistance of the air*. GRAVITY, the stronger of these forces, accelerates a man in free fall to about 120 miles per hour when falling at lower altitudes. The broad-surfaced open parachute increases the air resistance, assuring a slower, safer rate of descent.

Once away from the aircraft, the falling parachutist pulls the *ripcord,* releasing a small *pilot chute* of about three-foot diameter. This

DO OBJECTS OF THE SAME WEIGHT FALL AT THE SAME SPEED?

1. You will need two sheets of ordinary typewriting paper approximately the same in size and weight for this experiment. Leave one as it is; wad the other tightly into a ball.
2. Stand on a chair for added height. Stretch arms and hands straight out in front, palms up. On one palm is the paper ball, on the other the flat sheet of paper. Quickly pull your hands away, letting both objects fall to the floor. Try timing the two descents with a stop watch.
3. What fact about the papers would account for the results you obtained?

E.M.N.

catches the airstream and pulls out the larger, *main chute* or *canopy* which may be 24 feet in diameter. Spaced evenly around the canopy's edges are about 36 long ropes or *shrouds,* connected to the harness worn by the parachutist. A hole or vent in the top of the canopy stabilizes the canopy's descent by letting some air escape. Fast modern craft, such as jet fighter planes, have ejection seats so that the pilot can, by exploding a gunpowder device, be thrown clear of his aircraft and then open his chute to come down safely.

The parachutes of today are made of NYLON which has great strength and flexibility.

The parachute idea has long intrigued men. Leonardo da Vinci in 1514 and Fausto Veranzio in 1595 worked out such devices on paper. But the first successful chute jump was made in 1797 by the French balloonist, André Garnerin. More than ten years earlier, the physicist Lenormand had practiced jumps from a high building.   R. J. J.

Paraffin (PAHR-uh-finn) Paraffin is a colorless, odorless, tasteless wax made from petroleum oil. It is used for sealing jars of jelly and for waxy coating of milk cartons.

SEE: HYDROCARBONS, PETROLEUM

Male (left) and female parakeets

Parakeet Parakeets are brightly colored birds found in warm areas of the Old World and South America. They are small (six- or seven-inch) relatives of macaws, cockatoos and PARROTS. Their strong curved beaks are well adapted for cracking seeds. Most nest in holes in trees or termite nests. One South American species, a gray-breasted parakeet, builds apartment houses of sticks.

Parakeets are more numerous in Australia than anywhere else. They are sometimes pests because they feed in flocks in grain fields or fruit trees. There are very beautiful species in Africa, India and Ceylon, such as the *blossom-headed parakeet* with its pink and violet head and blue and yellow tail. In Australia and New Zealand are large broad-tailed species which live on the ground.

The only North American species, the *Carolina parakeet,* has been extinct since 1920. These foot-long green and yellow birds were numerous along river bottoms until civilization changed their environment.

Parakeets are easily bred in captivity. The *budgerigar* ("budgie") or *shell parakeet* of Australia is a popular pet. In its wild state it feeds in flocks like sparrows near the waterholes of the dry Australian grasslands. When domesticated it can be taught to imitate speech, whistle and eat from a hand.   E. R. B.

Parallax Parallax is what seems to be a change in position of a distant object caused by a shift in the position of the observer. In observations of stars, parallax is the result of the earth's rotation moving the observer.
SEE: MATHEMATICS, STAR

Paramecium

Parallel Parallel refers to lines or planes which extend in the same direction and at the same distance apart at all points. Parallel lines or planes never meet, no matter how far extended. Some LEAVES have parallel veins.

Paralysis (puh-RAL-uh-siss) Paralysis is a condition of the body in which muscles fail to function. It may be caused by a birth defect, by disease, or by tumor growth.

Paralysis occurs in several ways. Since muscles react to stimuli from nerves originating in the brain or spinal cord, a disturbance or disability of any of these parts brings about a condition of paralysis.

Diseases of the BRAIN or SPINAL CORD prevent receiving, sorting, or sending stimuli to cause muscle reaction. Spinal MENINGITIS is an example of a disease caused by the inflammation of the spinal cord. In other types of paralysis, the nerves leading to or from the central nervous system have been disturbed so that they are incapable of transmitting stimuli as required. A third type of disability exists when the muscle cells themselves cannot perform normally.   D. J. I.
SEE ALSO: POLIOMYELITIS

One-celled paramecia, such as may be found in many ponds
Photo-micrographs by
National Teaching Aids, Inc.

Paramecium (pair-uh-MEE-see-um) The paramecium is a slipper-shaped, one-celled animal. This microscopic animal has tiny hair-like structures, called *cilia,* all over its surface. The best known kind, *Paramecium caudatum,* is widely used in schools for the study of PROTOZOA.

The fresh-water paramecia can be collected in the underwater weeds of ponds. These weeds, covered with pond-water in a glass jar, will decay after standing at room

✳ THINGS TO DO

HOW DO PARAMECIA REACT TO THEIR SURROUNDINGS?

1. Paramecia may be obtained from a supply house or from a homemade culture (see PROTOZOA). Place a few drops of the solution they come in on a glass slide. Put a few minute crystals of carmine in the edge of the drop of water.

2. Place the slide on a microscope and bring the paramecia into focus. A powerful hand lens will work almost as well if a microscope is not available. Observe the paramecia as they approach the crystals. The movement of the cilia causes them to roll, go forward and to back up.

3. Continue to experiment with different materials, starting each time with a fresh culture on the slide. Place a small chip of ice in one place in the drop of water. Which way will the paramecia turn? Cover one-half of the slide to eliminate the light. Do they prefer darkness? Connect a wire to each terminal of a dry cell. Touch the exposed ends of the wires together in part of the solution. A very slight current will be discharged. Can these little one-celled animals respond to an electrical charge? Paramecia, though lacking a nervous system, are still very responsive to their environment.

temperature for two to three days. The scum which forms on the surface will contain dozens of paramecia.

The paramecium's shape never changes. Its front end is blunt and its posterior pointed. About one-third of the way from the front is an oral groove lined with cilia. This groove ends in a *cell pharynx*. Bacteria, the paramecium's food, are swept into the mouth by the cilia in the groove and are enclosed in a bubble-like structure called a *food vacuole*. Digestion occurs in the vacuole as it moves in a set pattern through the cell. Undigested material is discharged from a point at the end of the cell called the *anal pore*.

The paramecium has two nuclei, the larger called the *macronucleus,* the smaller, the *micronucleus*. The micronucleus controls reproduction, the macronucleus, all other functions. *Trichocysts,* small glassy rod-shaped bodies just below the surface, are used for defense and for anchoring the animal. The cilia move food in and move the animal forward. Cilia are connected by threads inside the body, and beat in unison like many small oars. The paramecium avoids objects in its path by trial and error. When it strikes an obstacle, it backs up, changes direction and tries again. A contractile vacuole forms every ten to twenty minutes to expel excess water from the cell.

The paramecium divides crosswise, by mitosis, after the nuclei divide and a second cell pharynx buds off. *Conjugation,* a simple form of sexual reproduction, can also take place. Two paramecia lie with their oral grooves touching. The macronuclei of each disintegrate; the micronuclei of each divide twice, forming four micronuclei. Three disintegrate and one divides into stationary and migratory nuclei. The migratory nuclei are exchanged and unite with the stationary nucleus of the other cell.

The individuals separate and each divides to form four new individuals.   J. K. L.
SEE ALSO: MITOSIS and MEIOSIS; REPRODUCTION, ASEXUAL

Parasites A host is a person who allows guests to share his home and food. Although most guests are pleasant, some can be very selfish. Those which take·all that they can from their host are called *parasites*. Many plants and animals are parasites which feed upon other living plants and animals. They accept food and a home from their host. In return they offer only sickness and disease.

Houses for people are large enough to permit many kinds of plants and animals to live together. In one house there may be ants, geraniums, dogs, molds, moths, and people. To most parasites the body of the host is as large as a building. Parasites are always smaller than their host. Many cannot be seen except under a microscope. Thus, many thousands of parasites may live in one host.

Parasites often choose to live inside other parasites. A virus may live in a bacteria, which lives in a worm, which lives in a dog. One dog may be host to many kinds of parasites.

The word *parasite* really means "alongside food." Parasitism is concerned mainly with the problem of obtaining food. Certain plants and animals have found it easier to become parasites than to compete for food. Organisms which feed upon other plants and animals do not always find quantities of food. Parasitism flourishes among viruses, non-green plants, and animal groups.

PARASITIC PLANTS AND ANIMALS

A true parasite feeds only upon living plants and animals. Plants which feed upon dead or decaying matter are called *saprophytes,* while animals which feed upon dead organisms are called *scavengers*. A few parasites, like the blue-green mold on the orange, are able to live upon either dead or living hosts. Green plants, which contain chlorophyll, like the mistletoe, are able to manufacture part of their own food. Since they cannot manufacture enough food, they become *semi-parasites* upon larger plants.

There are parasitic members of nearly all

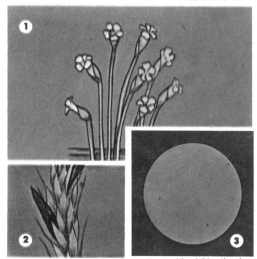

Courtesy Society For Visual Education, Inc.
1—Cancerroot, a parasitic plant, lives on the roots of other plants
2—Ergot on rye is also caused by bacteria
Photo-micrograph by National Teaching Aids, Inc.
3—Pneumonia bacteria is a parasitic plant that may live in man

phyla of both plants and animals. Many plant parasites are found among the *bacteria, slime molds,* and *true fungi*. Diseases of man, such as tuberculosis and pneumonia, as well as rots and galls of plants are caused by bacteria. Several molds cause infection of animals. Aquarium goldfish are often killed with water mold, while man may develop skin diseases caused by black mold. The fungi cause damage to higher plants by producing rusts, mildews, smuts, and rots. Such diseases as potato blight, Dutch elm disease, and apple scab result from attachment by these parasites. In man, ringworm and athlete's foot, caused by the same organism, are fungous diseases.

Animal parasites attack almost every species of animal. Parasitic species number in the tens of thousands. The greatest number of parasitic animals are found among the *protozoan, flatworm, roundworm* and *arthropod* phyla. In man, yellow fever, sleeping sickness, and amebic dysentery are caused by members of the *Protozoa*. The fluke, tapeworm, trichina, and filaria are a few of the parasitic worms that cause disease to many higher animals. By sucking cell sap, some roundworms cause wilting and gall in plants. Lice, mites, and ticks are well-known parasites among the arthropods. With greater powers of locomotion, higher animals are better equipped to compete for food. Only a few, such as the LAMPREY eel, adopt parasitic habits.

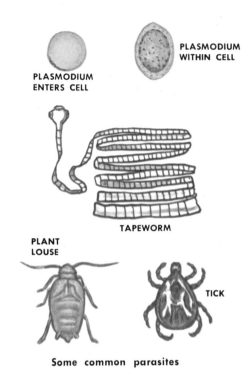

PLASMODIUM ENTERS CELL

PLASMODIUM WITHIN CELL

TAPEWORM

PLANT LOUSE

TICK

Some common parasites

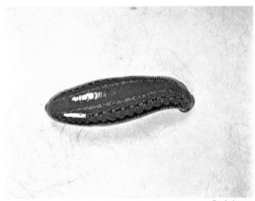

Buchsbaum

The leech has suckers which cling to skin

METHODS OF ATTACK AND DEFENSE

A soldier in the army must have special equipment to invade the enemy camp. In the same way, all parasites must have special body parts to enable them to live as unwelcome guests within the host. Each species has its own equipment for attack.

Those which attach themselves to the outer surface are called *outer* or *ectoparasites*. Animals like the leeches, mites, and lamprey eels, which cling to skin or hair, have developed suckers and hooks. Many have cutting, biting, or sucking mouth parts. Plants like the molds, fungi, dodder, and mistletoe have rootlike structures called *haustoria* which pierce the outer tissue of the host and draw nourishment from the inner cells.

Plants and animals which live inside the body of the host are called *inner* or *endoparasites*. They must have defenses against digestive juices, antibodies, white blood cells, and acids. Those like the viruses, bacteria, and fungi which move into the cells and feed directly upon the cell protoplasm develop thick outer coverings. Parasitic worms have thick cuticles, while many have additional hooks and suckers. Endoparasites often produce enzymes which break down the tissue and provide a pathway for movement.

Since the body changes in function, many parasites are no longer able to live independently. Many adults lose important body parts. The tapeworm, for example, loses its digestive, muscular, and nervous systems. One parasitic barnacle loses its shell so that it no longer resembles a barnacle.

Since parasites do not have to worry about locomotion, digestion, or protection, they are able to concentrate all their efforts upon reproduction. Most of them have well-developed reproductive systems and are able to produce quantities of young. One fluke for example may produce thousand of eggs. However, parasites must be prolific since many of the young never reach the proper host.

MOVEMENT FROM HOST TO HOST

Many animal parasites are able to move freely, either in the larva or the adult stage. For example, the larva of the hookworm is free to move to find a host, while the adult is completely parasitic. But organisms like the bacteria, viruses, and molds must rely upon wind, water, or an intermediate host like the mosquito to transfer them from host to host. These organisms lack the power of locomotion.

Many parasites need to have two or more hosts in order to complete their life cycles. Since they alternate in order from one host to the next, this method is called *alternation of host*. They rely upon both food chains and physical agents like wind, air, and water.

The wheat rust has two hosts. Carried by the wind, the spores are passed to the barberry, where they undergo development. The Chinese liver fluke has two intermediate hosts. The adult, which lives in the liver of man, sheds eggs into the intestine. These are passed with the feces to the ground. After being eaten by a snail, they are able to develop into larvae which swim through the water, find a fish, and settle in the muscle tissue. Man is the third host, if he eats raw or undercooked fish.   E. P. L.

SEE ALSO: BACTERIA, BALANCE OF NATURE, BLIGHT, FILARIA, FUNGUS, HOOKWORM, LIVER FLUKE, MOLDS, PINWORM, PROTOZOA, TAPEWORM, TRICHINA, VIRUS

Parasympathetic see Autonomic nervous system, Nervous system

Parathyroid (par-uh-THY-royd) The parathyroid is a special gland in the body. There are actually four parathyroid glands. Two pairs of these tiny pea-shaped structures rest on the back of the THYROID gland. The parathyroid glands secrete a hormone called *parathormone*.

Parathormone controls the amount of calcium and phosphorus in the blood and the way in which these minerals are used by the body. Normally there is a balance in the body between the level of calcium and phosphorus. When there is too little parathyroid hormone, there is a rise in the level of phosphorus in the blood and a drop in the level of calcium. If blood calcium is markedly decreased, a condition called *tetany* occurs. In such cases, the muscles of the body become irritable and contract, producing spasms throughout the body. The muscles of the larynx may be involved and obstruct the passage of air from outside into the lungs. The muscles controlling breathing go into spasm. Death results in severe cases. Accidental removal of the parathyroid glands during surgery can produce the same effect.

Oversecretion of the parathyroids is called *hyperparathyroidism*. It may be caused by tumors of the glands or by other disturbances of calcium-phosphorus metabolism. The blood level of calcium rises and the level of phosphorus falls. In such a condition there is a loss of calcium from the bones. This calcium loss causes a weakening of the bone structure. Bone pain, fractures, bone deformities, kidney stones, and nephritis often result.   G. A. D.

SEE ALSO: ENDOCRINE GLANDS

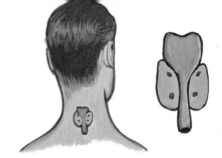

Parathyroid glands around the thyroid

Paré, Ambroïse (pah-RAY, ahm-BRWAHZ) (1510-1590) Paré was a French barber-surgeon who became the greatest surgeon of the Renaissance. He later became known as the "father of modern surgery."

A barber-surgeon was just what the name implies. He cut men's hair and shaved them, but he also drew blood and performed all kinds of surgery from treating cuts to amputating limbs. However, the barber-surgeons were despised by medical surgeons and barely tolerated by the people themselves. Paré's humble birth committed him to this position. He was unable to attend a university to study Greek and Latin, subjects absolutely necessary to the training of a physician of that period.

During Paré's lifetime France was at war against Italy, Germany, and England, and later against the French Huguenots at home. After a three-year appointment at the Paris Hospital, he joined the French army and saw military service for the next thirty years. He performed so many operations of every sort on so many men that he developed new techniques and methods of treating wounds. He invented artery forceps and other types of surgical instruments.

In 1554 Ambroïse Paré received the greatest honor of his life. He was made a member of the College of St. Come, the most important surgical society of France at the time.   D. H. J.

Paregoric (par-uh-GORE-ick) Paregoric is the name for a preparation containing a small amount of OPIUM, ANISE oil, benzoic acid, honey, dilute alcohol, and camphor. It is used in the treatment of DIARRHEA and as a pain reliever.

SEE: NARCOTICS

Paris green see Arsenic

WHITE-CRESTED COCKATOO

SULFUR-CRESTED COCKATOO

LEADBEATER'S COCKATOO

MACA

TRUE PARROT

CAROLINA PARAKEET

Australian News & Information Bureau

Chicago Natural History Museum

Parkinson's disease Parkinson's disease is a condition which affects the NERVOUS SYSTEM. The symptoms of the disease are stiffness of muscles, slowness of movement, and tremors of resting muscles. These rhythmic tremors occur as the limbs rest after excitement or exertion.

The disease is a progressive one. At the onset the tremors are mild, but as time goes on the tremors become more severe and obvious. Those suffering with Parkinson's disease experience increasing difficulty in writing, in dressing, in maintaining balance, in turning around, and in rising from a seated position. It is only in the later stages of the disease that the patient's speech shows obvious change.

Parkinson's disease occurs most often among those between 50 and 60 years of age. Men are afflicted with the disease more frequently than women. It may be caused by poisoning, strokes, head injury or more commonly by ARTERIOSCLEROSIS, or hardening of the blood vessels of the brain. Drugs are often used in the treatment of the disease. They are useful in lessening the rigidity of muscles and controlling the tremors to some degree. In some cases surgery has been attempted but at the present time its effectiveness is uncertain. G. A. D.

Parrot Parrots and their relatives, the macaws, parakeets and lories, make up a large family. They are brightly colored birds ranging from warbler to eagle size, with strong, hooked beaks and hawk-like heads. The upper jaw moves up so that the beak can work like pliers, crushing the parrot's food.

The 316 species of parrots live in the tropics all over the world. At one time parrots lived in colder regions and disappeared from North America only recently. They travel in pairs or gangs through the tops of tropical forests, shrieking to each other when food is found.

Parrots can be divided into two groups depending on whether their thick, fleshy tongues are fringed or blunt. The former eat nectars and fruit juices and the latter eat seeds and nuts. One branch of parrots, the lorikeets, crush blossoms and lick up the sticky nectar with their tongues.

Parrots use their feet as hands to eat. Two of the four toes are turned backward. They are either left or right-handed. They are good climbers, using their beaks to help.

Most species nest in holes in trees but a few build stick nests. The male helps the female incubate the eggs for three weeks and the young hatch out blind and naked. Most species feed their young on partly digested food.

Men have made pets of parrots since ancient times. They are the best talkers in the animal kingdom and are good at voice mimicry. As pets, they may live from 50 to 80 years. At one time when it was found they carried *psittacosis,* or parrot fever, their popularity declined but now an antibiotic is available which will cure birds of this disease. E. R. B.

SEE ALSO: ANIMAL DISEASES, MACAW, PARAKEET

Parrot fever see Animal diseases, Parrot

Parsley

Parsley In modern cooking, parsley is mainly a flavoring and decorative herb. Sprigs of its leaves give a delicate taste and a lacy, green garnish to soups, salads, and meat or cheese dishes. This leafy sweet herb is grown in several varieties. Many have been grown since ancient times in Mediterranean countries.

Besides plain parsley, two other popular varieties are *paramount* and *moss curled*. *Hamburg* variety has an enlarged root looking like a parsnip but tasting like celery.

Agricultural department food bulletins state that parsley is a good source of vitamins A and C and a fair source of niacin. It is rich in iron, but one is not likely to eat large enough amounts to supply much of that element for the body.   D. A. B.

Parsnip The parsnip is a root vegetable. It looks like a carrot but is yellow-white in color. It has a tangy sweet, celery-like flavor. It grows best only in cool temperate climates, and its flavor improves when it is left in the winter soil or stored in a cold place for awhile.

Parsnip seeds can be planted in rich soil, in the spring. They germinate slowly. The leaves have a dark-green, celery-like appearance. By fall, they may grow to be over one foot tall. Chemicals may be sprayed to ward off animal and plant pests.

Care should be taken not to confuse the parsnip plant or its roots with the poisonous weed, water hemlock (*Circuta*), which has a similar appearance and odor.   D. A. B.
SEE ALSO: LEAVES

Parsnips

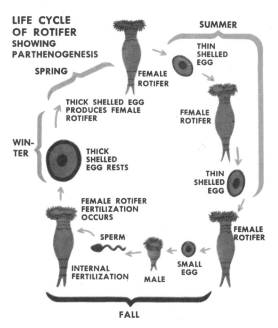

LIFE CYCLE OF ROTIFER SHOWING PARTHENOGENESIS

A rotifer's life cycle illustrates parthenogenesis

Parthenogenesis (pahr-thuh-noh-JENN-uh-siss) Parthenogenesis is a type of reproduction in which a new organism develops from an egg which has not united with a sperm. In animals, it occurs naturally in *rotifers,* a type of worm, in BEES and APHIDS, and in water fleas. Some algae and fungi also reproduce parthenogenetically. Eggs of many invertebrates and of frogs have been developed without fertilization through artificial stimulation of the eggs by pricking, shaking, and changing the kind of solution they are in. Occasionally parthenogenesis occurs naturally in all major groups of animals except the vertebrates and echinoderms and in all plants except mosses and liverworts.

Parthenogenesis is the sole means of reproduction only in a few aphids and parasitic insects. In other groups males are produced periodically, usually in the fall. They fertilize eggs which are capable of surviving the winter. These eggs in turn produce females which reproduce parthenogenetic females until the next fall.

A slightly different parthenogenetic reproduction occurs in bees. The queen bee is the sole egg-producing female. It mates once with a drone and stores the sperm in its body. The fertilized eggs which it produced develop into queen bees or workers (infertile females). It also lays unfertilized eggs which have half the number of chromosomes of the female bees. These develop parthenogenetically into the male drones.   J. K. L.

SEE ALSO: REPRODUCTION, ASEXUAL; REPRODUCTIVE SYSTEMS; ROTIFERA

Particle see Nuclear particles

Particle detector Charged atomic or NUCLEAR PARTICLES are detected when passed through a particle detector. The charged particles create an electrical disturbance which can be observed, as in the Wilson CLOUD CHAMBER, or recorded, as in the Geiger-Müller counter.

SEE: GEIGER COUNTER

Partridge see Fowl, Grouse, Quail

Parturition Parturition is the act of giving BIRTH to young. It begins with contractions of the uterus which force the infant out of the uterus and through the vagina, and it ends with the delivery of the placenta.

SEE: REPRODUCTION, SEXUAL

Pasqueflower see Wild flowers

Passion flower see Plants, tropical

Pasteur, Louis (1822-1895) Louis Pasteur was the French chemist who became known as the "father of bacteriology." He was the first scientist to discover how to prevent the spread of diseases caused by INFECTION. He proved that the microscopic organisms found in liquids after a chemical change (a process known as FERMENTATION) come from the air. He also discovered that they could be killed, thus preventing the

Louis Pasteur

spread of disease. The process he discovered to kill these germs in milk and dry wines by heating the liquid to a point just below the boiling point and then cooling it rapidly is called *pasteurization.*

Louis Pasteur was born at Dole, France. He was the son of humble parents. His father was a tanner; his mother, a gardener's daughter. As a boy he was in no way unusual. His teacher described him as "a good average pupil" and one who "never affirmed anything of which he was not absolutely sure." With money his father somehow had managed to save, Pasteur attended the Ecole Normale in Paris to study chemistry. Later he did advanced work in chemistry at the Sorbonne.

In 1849, Pasteur was invited to serve on the Faculty of Sciences as the professor of chemistry at Strasbourg, and it was there that he began his research on fermentation. There he first showed that certain organic chemicals made by plants exist in two light-polarizing varieties. The improvements he eventually brought about in winemaking are said to have saved France enough money to pay its indemnity to Prussia at the close of the Franco-Prussian War. In Strasbourg, also, Pasteur met Marie Laurent, the daughter of the Rector of the Academy. They were married in May, 1849; and for the rest of his life, she remained his partner, sharing his misfortunes as well as his successes.

In 1854, Pasteur became the Dean of the new Faculty of the Sciences at Lille. Although his administrative duties combined with his teaching responsibilities made a heavy load, he consented to make a thorough study of a disease threatening to destroy the silkworms in France. For five years he carried on intensive research, and eventually discovered the parasite causing the trouble. This gift to France saved the entire silk industry of the country.

Courtesy Society For Visual Education, Inc.

Milk is put into sterilized bottles (left) after being pasteurized by this machine

Pasteur's second great claim to fame (after pasteurization) is his work in medicine, especially his development of a vaccine against rabies. While experimenting with chicken cholera, he stumbled upon the principle of using killed or weakened viruses to make animals resistant to diseases. This principle is called *immunization*. He next applied the idea to anthrax, a disease that attacks cattle and sheep. Then he began looking for the germ that causes rabies. The disease, sometimes called *hydrophobia,* was known to be transmitted by the bites of animals that were sick with it. A dog that had rabies was called a "mad dog," and was terribly feared because the disease was usually fatal. Pasteur developed a vaccine against it, and his first human patient, nine-year-old Joseph Meister, recovered.

Even more dramatically, 16 out of 19 Russian peasants who had been bitten by a mad wolf were saved by Pasteur's injections, despite the fact that the treatment was not started until 19 days after they were bitten. They had had to come all the way from Russia. In recognition, the Czar donated 100,000 francs toward the building of the Pasteur Institute. This institution, built by contributions of people in every land, is a living monument to Pasteur. He served as its director from 1888 until he died in 1895.   D. A. B.

SEE ALSO: MEDICINE, PASTEURIZATION

Pasteurization (pass-ter-ih-ZAY-shun) After milk leaves the farm and goes to the dairy, it goes through a process called pasteurization. This process destroys dangerous disease-causing microorganisms.

Pasteurized milk has been heated and held at a given temperature for a certain length of time. This can be accomplished in two ways. The milk may be heated to about 143 degrees Fahrenheit and held at that temperature for thirty minutes, or it may be heated to 160 degrees Fahrenheit and held for about sixteen seconds. The process destroys most microorganisms and spares the flavor of the milk which higher temperatures would affect. The same process is also applied to wines.

Microorganisms, too small to be seen without a microscope, are the cause of tuberculosis, typhoid fever, dysentery, undulant fever, diphtheria, scarlet fever, and septic sore throat. Pasteurization prevents the spread of disease through the milk supply.

Pasteurization does not kill all the microorganisms present in milk. Many bacteria still live, but these are not harmful to the body. Milk is tested from samples taken from each source. The city or county health department is responsible for this task, and milk is graded according to the bacteria count and number of coloform organisms in each milliliter.

Unpasteurized milk may still be sold in some communities, but it must be used more quickly than milk which is pasteurized. Almost all milk sold in stores is Grade A pasteurized. Lower grades of milk are used in making powdered milk or cheeses as the bacteria will be destroyed by cooking or chemical treatment.   V. V. N.

SEE ALSO: BACTERIOLOGY; DAIRY PRODUCTS; PASTEUR, LOUIS

Patella see Skeleton

A pathology laboratory may make a variety of tests on samples of blood, urine, saliva and other body fluids or tissues to aid the physician in making a diagnosis of a disease

Pathology (puh-THAHL-uh-jee) Pathology is the branch of medical science which considers the changes of function and the changes of structure brought about by disease.

General pathology is that division of pathology which studies those abnormal processes caused in different organs of the body by diseases. An example of such a change is that found in an inflammation showing redness, swelling, heat, and pain.

Humoral pathology, an older science introduced by HIPPOCRATES (460 B.C.-355 B.C.) attributed the cause of disease to an abnormal condition of the blood. *Cellular* pathology, which was formulated about 1840, considered the cell as the basis for all living phenomena. Today pathology recognizes both the humoral and cellular concepts.

Other subdivisions of pathology are *pathologic physiology,* which deals with disturbances of function in disease; *morphologic* pathology which deals with the study of structural changes in disease; and *special* pathology, covering special diseases.

The study of pathologic physiology received its first great impetus about 1830 to 1840 from Karl Rokitansky, professor of Pathological Anatomy in Vienna. Rokitansky had tremendous experience, having performed 30,000 autopsies during his lifetime. He emphasized, however, that medicine wished to understand the living, rather than dead, organs. Because of his background he was a genius in presenting a pathologic description of diseased parts, in promoting an understanding of the *pathogenesis* (development) of disease, and, then, in correlating anatomy with the symptoms of the disease.

Rudolph Ludwig Virchow (1821-1902) was the father of cellular pathology. Because the humoral theory had held sway for almost 2000 years, introduction of cellular pathology was courageous as well as progressive. Virchow's thesis stated that the seat of disease should be sought in the cell. This concept not only replaced the older humoral theory, but it did not restrict study to gross material, and required a more thorough investigation of microscopic, cellular changes. Virchow taught in Berlin until 1849, but his political utterances demanding improved health conditions antagonized Bismarck, who was the outstanding Prussian politician of his day; and he was forced to leave.

By correlating studies of tissue and organs removed during surgical operations and studies of disease in the living body, the pathologists learn something of the life processes.

Fever, for instance, is a pathologic change caused, in most cases, by the presence of poisonous substances called *toxins* in the blood acting upon the heat centers within the brain. These substances may be bacterial poisons, metabolic products, end products of protein digestion, or ferments. Toxins are also produced by injury, by direct exposure to heat as in sunstroke, by starvation, or even by hysteria. Any infectious process within the body may produce fever.

The changes in body tissue brought about by the toxic substances just named result from increased oxidation and body waste. During a fevered condition the amount of nitrogen in the urine is in excess of the amount in food taken into the body. The specific gravity of the blood is increased, and the alkalinity of the blood is reduced by various acids produced in tissue destruction. The hydrogen ion concentration of the blood is reduced. If the fever is excessive or protracted, the muscles, heart, liver and kidneys are the seat of fatty degeneration (seen with the microscope) and coagulation. Necrosis, or death of the tissue cells, occurs within these organs. By knowing of these changes brought about by varying disease phenomena, corrective steps can be taken to stop the process and restore health.

The trained pathologist must be not only a practical clinician; he must also have a basic knowledge of human and comparative anatomies, of histology, physiology, embryology, biochemistry, and bacteriology. The knowledge of his field thus serves the future of clinical medicine.   H. K. S.
SEE ALSO: MEDICINE, PHYSIOLOGY

Pavlov, Ivan Petrovich (1849-1936) Ivan Pavlov was a Russian doctor (physiologist) who is now remembered for his work on conditioned reflexes in dogs. He discovered that if he always rang a bell each time he fed a dog, the dog would continue to react to the bell even when food was withheld. He was awarded the Nobel Prize for his work on digestion.

Born in Ryazan on September 14, 1849, Ivan Pavlov, the son of a priest, attended Ryazan Seminary for four years and then the University of St. Petersburg where he studied science and then medicine. After receiving his M.D. degree in 1883, he traveled to Germany to work under two leading physiologists. Two years later he returned to St. Petersburg where he began his experiments at the Military Medical Academy. Pavlov's work was in three basic areas: circulation of the blood, action of the digestive glands, and formation of conditioned reflexes. His research on techniques causing neuroses in dogs laid the foundation for scientific study of mental illness in humans.

Pavlov achieved world-wide fame as his writings were translated into German, French, and English.   D. H. J.
SEE ALSO: PSYCHOLOGY

Pawpaw see Papaya

Garden pea plant and pod

Pea The garden pea is an annual, climbing herb. The green or yellow seeds formed in pods are used as a vegetable. *Pea* also refers to a large family of plants (*Leguminosae*) which includes locust trees, mesquite shrubs and peanut plants.

Garden peas have hollow stems, white flowers which are self pollinated and fruit classified as LEGUMES. The roots develop nodules containing nitrogen-fixing bacteria. Field peas are hardy plants used mainly for stockfeed. The pigeon or cajan pea is gaining popularity as food for poultry, humans and livestock.

The pea is the plant that MENDEL experimented with in doing his well-known work in breeding and genetics.   H. J. C.

Peach The peach tree bears fruit that has one large seed. The tree grows until it is about twenty-five feet tall. The leaves are long and narrow. The flower, of a pinkish hue, is the state flower of Delaware.

The peach tree, a member of the rose family, is native to China and has been culti-

Peaches, ready for picking
U.S. Department of Agriculture photo

vated for over 4000 years. It produces best in regions where the winters are mild and the temperature rarely goes below ten degrees below zero. Many peach trees grow in the wild state.

Botanically the fruit is classified as a DRUPE. The outer fruit wall is fleshy with a stony endocarp surrounding the seed. The pit is grooved. Peaches produced are *free stone* or the *cling* variety. The *Elberta peach* is most widely grown. The tree starts to bear fruit after three or four years of growth. The flower and fruit appear on the new branches each year. A volatile and fixed oil are extracted from the seed. Brandy is made from the fruit.

Leaf curl, brown rot, scab, peach borer and oriental fruit moth are the most serious pests of this plant.

Nectarines are a variety of peach. The fruit is smaller, more solid and the exocarp is smooth.   H. J. C.
SEE ALSO: FRUIT

Peacock Peacock is the name for the male peafowl. The peafowl is related to other fowl, such as quails, pheasants, and chickens. Almost all zoos have peacocks, many wandering free, because they are easily domesticated and very beautiful.

The peacock of India and Malaya is a large green and blue bird with long naked legs and a small crested head. A distant cousin discovered recently in the Congo is glossy black with a white tuft in its crown.

Wild peacocks live in groups in open forests, roosting at night in trees. The male courtship display consists of raising the upper long tail

Peacock, the male peafowl

coverts into a fan which reaches the ground on both sides. The feather surfaces are covered with many thin layers of horn which reflect and refract light, making the colors iridescent. Yellowish spots add to the beauty. These tail coverts develop in the male's third year. Each male has a harem of two to five smaller and duller females. The buff-colored eggs are laid in a crude nest on the ground.   E. R. B.
SEE ALSO: FOWL

Peafowl see Peacock

Peanuts see Legume, Nuts

Pear leaves, fruit and flower

Pear The pear tree has been grown for over 4000 years. It is a member of the rose family. In the United States, most pears are grown in the northwestern states. These trees cannot stand extremes of temperature change as apple trees can, therefore they are rather limited to certain regions.

The leaves of the pear tree have serrated margins. The flower has five petals and five carpels and is generally white. The flower is perfect, meaning that both male and female parts are present. The fruit is classified as *accessory* since much of the wall is the fleshy receptacle. The grittiness of the fruit is caused by the presence of minute stone cells or *schlerenchyma* tissue.

Propagation is done by seeds or grafting. The dwarf pear is grafted onto a slow growing rootstock such as quince. Besides using the fruit as food, man extracts oil from the seeds. A drink called *perry* is made from the fruit juice.   H. J. C.

Pearl A pearl is a gem made by certain animals that live within shells. These animals are *mollusks*. A pearl is formed when a grain of sand or other small object gets between the hard outer shell and the inner coat, called the *mantle*.

Formation of a pearl

Admiral Robert E. Peary

The mollusk surrounds the irritation with *nacre,* a secretion from the mantle. This is the same substance that lines the oyster's shell and is called *mother-of-pearl.* Many thin layers of nacre give a pearl its luster. The result is a sore spot for the oyster but a beautiful jewel for man.

The biggest pearl oysters are found in the South Seas. The Persian Gulf yields a yellowish pearl. Some may be pink, bluish, gray, or black. The coasts of Australia, Venezuela, Malaya, Mexico, and lower California are other important sources of pearls. Many mollusks produce pearls, but only two types produce precious pearls. These are the genera *Meleagrina* of the tropical seas and *Unio* of fresh water streams.

The average pearl takes about seven years for its development. Its value is determined by its size and luster. The largest pearl found was about two inches in diameter. *Cultured* pearls are real pearls but the original nucleus was inserted by man. They are not as costly as true pearls.

Unfortunately, pearls are perishable. Sunlight and skin acids are injurious to them. Pearls should be kept clean and wrapped in moist coverings when not in use. With care, they last over a hundred years.   J. A. D.

SEE ALSO: GEM, MOLLUSCA

Peary, Robert Edwin (1856-1920)

Robert Peary was the American explorer who discovered the North Pole. From soundings taken, he also discovered that the sea around the North Pole was not as shallow as was popularly believed up until that time.

Peary was born in Pennsylvania, but his family soon returned to Maine, where his ancestors had lived. He attended Bowdoin College where he took the civil engineering course. He worked first as a land surveyor in Maine and then as a draftsman for the U.S. Coast and Geodetic Survey. He passed the difficult examination for civil engineers in the U.S. Navy and took up his lifelong career in engineering, from which he took leaves of absence when he went on his Arctic explorations. He first worked on ship canals and dry docks. When a canal was being planned across Central America, Peary was sent to survey the possibility of a route across Nicaragua. He is often credited with being one of the first engineers to recommend that the canal be dug through the Isthmus of Panama, as it later was.

His first four Arctic journeys were in Greenland. His wife went with him on several of these expeditions, and their first child, Marie, was born in Greenland, further north than any but Eskimo children had ever been born before. Peary was not the first man to cross Greenland, as another explorer, Nansen, beat him by a small margin, but he made many useful discoveries. He established the fact that Greenland is an island; he found and brought back three enormous meteorites; and he made friends with the Eskimos and learned to use their methods and clothing.

With the knowledge gained from the Greenland explorations, Peary set his sights on reaching the North Pole. His plan was to sail a ship as far north as it could go along the Greenland coast, and push on with dogs and sledges. Twelve years, three expeditions, two ships and seven frostbitten toes later, he achieved his goal. At his side when he planted five flags at the North Pole were his Negro assistant Matthew Henson, who accompanied him on nearly all his trips, and four Eskimos. And behind their achievement stood Robert Bartlett, captain of the ship *Roosevelt,* and all the men who had been working in relays to break trail, build igloos, and bring up supplies so that Peary and his adventurous companions could not only get to the North Pole, but also come back to civilization alive.

Another explorer, Frederick A. Cook, claimed to have reached the Pole first, but after a Congressional investigation, it was decided that Cook had probably not reached it at all.   D. A. B.

Sphagnum moss is the common moss of peat bogs

J. W. Thompson

Peccary, or javelina

Peat During the early stages of the Earth's development, plants such as mosses and ferns grew thickly in many swamps then present. As the plants died, their remains sank to the bottom and new plants grew on top of them. Great masses of half-decayed brown, spongy material formed. This is peat. If there had been more pressure and heat from the great amounts of sand and clay that were gradually piled on the peat, the peat would have changed into coal.

The wet marshy ground where peat is found is called a *peat bog*. The water in a peat bog is acid and preserves plants that fall into it. Botanists are able to identify plants that grew in peat bogs centuries ago. The most common type found is the large sphagnum.

Most of the peat deposits were formed during the Carboniferous Age. Mosses, giant ferns and ancient conifer-like plants became bogged down in stagnant swamps. When these were covered with clay, they were more or less hardened into peat, lignite or harder COAL.

Peat has many uses. It is used as a FUEL even though it leaves ten times more ash than most other fuels. It holds water well and so is used for surgical dressings, soil conditioners and a propagating medium. H. J. C.
SEE ALSO: MOSS

Pecan see Hickory, Nuts

Peccary (PEK-ar-e) The peccary is a hoofed, tailless, piglike animal with tusks that turn downward. It is a vicious fighter, and usually travels in herds. The two species, the collared peccary and the white-lipped peccary, are found from Texas to Paraguay.

Pectin (PEK-tin) Pectin is a carbohydrate found in ripe fruits and some vegetables. It dissolves in boiling water and forms a jelly when cooled. Commercial pectin can be bought in stores and used to make jellies. It also has various uses in medicines.

Pedigree A pedigree is a record of a family. It may be of a family of plants, animals, or humans. A person's pedigree is called a *family tree*. It tells the name of parents, grandparents, and ancestors back through the centuries, and gives information of cities and counties where they were known to have lived. Anyone can make a simple family tree.

In animals and plants, pedigrees are of great value in breeding certain desirable characteristics into the offspring. These records of ancestors help to improve varieties of plants and breeds of animals because they tell breeders the kind of offsprings the male and female will have. Two fast horses may produce a winning race horse. A male and female Airedale dog with proper proportions and markings may produce a champion puppy. More perfect and valuable fruits, vegetables, trees, and flowers may be developed when records are kept of the original plants. Pedigrees are a record for controlled breeding, an important science based on Gregor Mendel's laws of heredity.
J. K. K.
SEE ALSO: BREEDING; HYBRIDIZATION; MENDEL, GREGOR

The peewee resembles other flycatchers, such as the yellow-bellied.

Peewee The peewee is a member of the flycatcher family, often confused with the phoebe. It is hard to see and can be most easily distinguished by the sad way in which it says its name.

The adult is from six to six and one-half inches long, dark olive-gray above with a grayish-white breast. The wings are marked with whitish bars. It prefers to live in dry woods, often nesting in orchards. When it is feeding, it perches in the tops of trees and dives for flying insects.

The peewee breeds in eastern North America and winters in South America. The nest is broad and flat and beautifully made. It is covered so that it seems to grow out of a branch.   E. R. B.

SEE ALSO: FLYCATCHER

Pegasus (PEGG-uh-suss) Pegasus is a group of stars that seemed to ancient people to outline the shape of a horse. This CONSTELLATION covers a large area of the sky. It can be found by locating the *Square of Pegasus*. Four bright stars mark the corners of this large square. The square represents the body of the horse. A line of stars ending in a triangle composes his neck and head. The horse is usually upside down. The stars that represent its forefeet usually point upward in the sky. Pegasus does not have any hind legs marked by stars.

Pegasus can be found most easily in autumn and winter. It is near the royal family of constellations—Cassiopeia, Cepheus, Andromeda, and Perseus. In fact, one of the stars of the square is part of the constellation of Andromeda.

Pegasus

According to legend, Pegasus was the winged horse which sprang from the head of Medusa when Perseus killed Medusa. Either Minerva or Neptune tamed Pegasus and gave him to Bellerophon. Pegasus carried his master to Lycia, where Bellerophon slew Chimera, a monster. Jupiter was displeased and sent a gadfly to sting Pegasus. The horse threw Bellerophon and flew up into the sky.

C. L. K.

Peking man see Evolution of man

Pelagic (puh-LAJ-ick) Pelagic is a term which is used to describe the part of the ocean away from the shore. This is the open sea which lies above the *abyss* or *depths*. The pelagic zone usually refers only to the part of the ocean as far down as sunlight penetrates.

SEE: CURRENTS, OCEAN; GRAND BANKS; MARINE BIOLOGY; OCEAN; PLANKTON; SARGASSUM

The major life zones of the ocean (not drawn to scale)

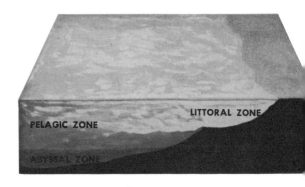

PELAGIC ZONE   LITTORAL ZONE   ABYSSAL ZONE

F. A. Blashfield
White pelicans

Pelican

The pelican is a large fish-eating bird. It looks strange because of its short legs, crested head and hooked, pouched bill. It uses its pouch to help it catch food. All four toes of a pelican are webbed.

Pelicans live in groups in warm areas all over the world. Some kinds hunt together and are often seen flying in formation, gliding or beating their wings in unison. The white pelicans inhabit fresh-water inland lakes. The brown pelican hunts in salt water from the southern coast of the United States to southern South America.

Pelicans breed on islands in huge communities. They make nests in trees or on the ground near water. The nests are of sticks or pebbles and sand. From two to four eggs are laid and incubated by both parents, who are easily frightened away from the young. The babies take food from deep in the parent's gullet   E. R. B.

Pellagra see Vitamin deficiency

Peltier, Jean Charles Athanase (1785-1845)

Peltier was a French physicist now remembered as the man who completed a discovery made by T. J. Seebeck. This discovery, made in 1834, revealed that an electric current produces either heating or cooling at the junction place of two different metals. The direction in which the current is traveling determines whether cooling or heating is produced.

In 1961, production of small-sized electric refrigerators using the cooling effect discovered by Peltier was announced. A clock-maker by trade, Peltier was born at Ham, France, on February 25, 1785. He died in Paris on October 27, 1845.   D. H. J.
SEE ALSO: ELECTRICITY, REFRIGERATION

Pelvis

The pelvis is the bony ring formed by the two hip bones and the *sacrum* and *coccyx* of the vertebral column. It is also the abdominal cavity which is enclosed by these bones.
SEE: SKELETON

Pendulum (PEN-juh-luhm)

A pendulum can be made by tying a weight, such as a stone, to a string. If the string is held and the weighted end is pushed, the string and weight will swing back and forth. A pendulum is used in certain clocks, in earthquake detectors, and in determining geological mineral deposits.

A simple pendulum has a weight, or *bob,* suspended from a fixed point by a light weight line. The bob swings back and forth in a path called the *arc.* The time it takes for a pendulum bob to swing from one end of the arc to the other and back again is called the *period of the pendulum.* If the length of the line remains the same, the period of the pendulum is affected only by changes in gravity—not by the width of arc.

Certain basic laws apply to a pendulum's period. A pendulum's period is not affected by the weight of the bob unless extreme air resistance exists. A pendulum's period increases as the length of line increases. The pendulum's period is directly proportional to the square root of the length of the pendulum's line. It is inversely proportional to the square root of the ACCELERATION due to gravity (g). In other words, short pendulums have short periods and swing rapidly. Pendulums with long lines have long periods

The changing length of the pendulum's string produces the different periods on the pendulum's swing

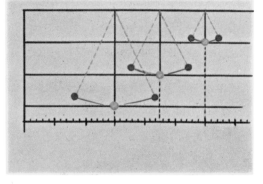

and swing slowly. In a pendulum clock, if the clock runs too rapidly, one lengthens or lowers the pendulum bob. If the clock runs too slowly, one shortens or raises the pendulum bob.

The *Foucault* pendulum, developed in 1851 by Jean Foucault, uses a large iron ball as the bob, connected to a 200-foot line. The arc of a Foucault pendulum seems to rotate very slowly as the ball swings back and forth. Actually it is not that the arc is rotating, but rather the earth is rotating under the arc of the pendulum. If one were able to look at the pendulum from a fixed point in space far away from the earth, one would see that the direction of the arc remains fixed in space but the earth makes one rotation under the arc each 24 hours. If a circle below a Foucault pendulum is marked in hours and minutes, the pendulum will give the time of the day. P. F. D.

SEE ALSO: CLOCKS, GALILEO, GRAVITY

Penguins are adapted to live in the icy Antarctic

Penguin The penguin is a large bird, often as much as four feet tall. It cannot fly but is well adapted for swimming. It can also stand erect and walk well.

The short tail, webbed feet and scale-like feathers help to make the penguin a fast swimmer. It propels itself with its wings both underwater and on the surface, using its legs as a rudder. Even its eyes are adapted for underwater vision. It feeds on fish and mollusks.

Penguins range in color from black and white to bluish gray and some kinds have bright orange or yellow markings. It molts all at once and the feathers grow back in about 14 days.

All but one of the 15 species of penguin live in the cold seas of the Southern Hemisphere. They are found on islands off Africa, Australia, New Zealand, in the Arctic Ocean, and on Antarctica. One col-

ony of about 250 birds lives on the Galapagos Islands, near the equator.

The penguin courtship begins early in the winter. Birds tend to keep the same mates year after year and return to the same nesting grounds. Some species nest in holes and under rocks and others on the surface. Often the males are left to incubate the eggs, not eating for weeks as they do. Since penguins live closely together in colonies, the adults often share the care and feeding of the young. The adults of some species swim out for food, and, as they return, feed the first and hungriest babies they find. In other species, the adults carefully find their own young. The fledglings reach down their parents' throats for partly digested food. In an Emperor penguin colony, it is not unusual to see a huge nursery of young birds guarded by one adult male. The young require several months to grow to full adult size. E. R. B.

Penicillin Penicillin was the first ANTIBIOTIC to be used successfully in the treatment of bacterial infections. Antibiotics are substances which are formed by living organisms. They are produced by MOLDS, soil organisms, and BACTERIA. Antibiotics interfere seriously with the organisms which produce disease. Penicillin has been used to treat many diseases that once were a great threat to life.

In 1928, SIR ALEXANDER FLEMING made a very great discovery. He found that a simple mold could destroy disease-producing bacteria. He noticed that a large colony

Laboratory-grown penicillium mold

Abbott Laboratories

of *staphylococcus* bacteria became transparent and hence dead, when they grew near a contaminating mold. This observation was the key to the discovery.

Fleming cultivated the mold in liquid broth, and noticed that during growth a substance was formed which inhibited the growth of some organisms. He called this penicillin, for the mold was *Penicillium notatum*.

Fleming then showed by experimentation that the extract containing penicillin was not poisonous to animals.

Since penicillin is a product of a mold, other species of molds were investigated for the presence of substances with similar properties. Thus a large number of antibiotic agents were discovered.

At present, several different forms of penicillin are known, and have been synthesized in the laboratory.   J. R. S.
SEE ALSO: BACTERIOLOGY

Peninsula (puh-NINN-suh-luh) A peninsula is almost an island. It juts out from a larger land mass. The Malay Peninsula in southeast Asia is typical with its narrow land connection. Many peninsulas have very broad bases where they connect with the continent. Some geographers think the continent of Europe is like a huge peninsula of Asia.

Penis see Reproductive systems

Pennsylvanian see Geologic time table, Paleozoic Era

Penumbra see Eclipse

Peony (PEE-uh-nee) The peony is one of the showiest of modern garden flowers. The kind most popular is a hybrid of the *common peony* of southern Europe and the *Chinese peony*.

Peonies belong to the *crowfoot,* or *buttercup,* family. There are over 300 varieties of the *bush peony*. It is a herbaceous PERENNIAL that reaches a height of about three feet. The flowers usually appear during June. They have single or double blooms ranging in color from white to red to purple. The petals are waxy. The large leaves possess deep grooves or divisions. The roots are fleshy and store food material for new growth each year. The stem has a red to green color. When peony bushes are separated and transplanted to a new location, flowers will not appear for a year or two while the plant rests.

Some peonies have woody stems and are called *tree peonies*. They grow about five feet tall with many branches and a great number of blossoms. The woody tree peonies are native to Pacific coastal areas of Asia and North America.   H. J. C.
SEE ALSO: HYBRIDIZATION

Peperomia (peh-puh-ROME-yuh) Peperomia is a tropical plant raised for its attractive leaves. The leaves are a bright, shiny green with interesting markings and colors. Some leaves have brown, purple, or dark red markings, and others have light colored stripes between the veins.

Peperomia comes from the moist forests of Brazil. It is a member of the PEPPER family. *Peperomia* is a Greek word meaning "pepper-like." It is an annual or perennial herb, depending on the variety.

Peperomia is a small-growing plant used in greenhouses, as a pot plant, or in hanging baskets. It should be shaded in summer, and requires lots of moisture and regular applications of liquid fertilizer.

The plants of this group are succulent with thick, fleshy, slightly oval leaves, three to six inches long. Its tiny flowers are crowded on a dense, slender, usually curving spike.   M. R. L.
SEE ALSO: PLANTS, SUCCULENT

Double peony

F. A. Blashfield

Peperomia

Pepper, the spice   **Red, or chili, pepper**   **Green and red pepper**

Pepper Pepper is the name for several plants and products. The best known is black pepper, a spice for flavoring food. It comes from a tropical vine native to the East Indies, Thailand and India. Twice a year the vine bears fruit in the form of green berries, which turn red. They are picked, dried in the sun and turn black. Then they are ground into fine, black pepper powder. The whole berries are called *peppercorns*. To get the best flavor, the peppercorns should be ground in a pepper mill at the time they are to be used.

White pepper is ground from the same ripe berries, after the dark outer rind has been removed.

Red pepper, not related to either black or white, is the dried, crushed pods of a large variety of hot chilies.

Green and *red* peppers found in vegetable markets are from entirely different plants, and their history has always been confused with the common table spice. They are called *sweet* or *bell peppers* and are berry-like fruits, related to the tomato and used fresh or cooked in salads, soups, and stews. The red bell pepper is simply the ripened green bell pepper. They were first found in the West Indies by a botanist of the Columbus expedition, who took samples back to Europe with him.   J. K. K.

SEE ALSO: CAYENNE, PAPRIKA, PIMENTO

Peppermint A favorite member of the MINT family, peppermint is an HERB used for medicines, perfumes, soaps, and for flavoring foods and candy.

There are two common varieties of peppermint, black and white. The black has dark green leaves, square stems, and purple blossoms tinged with red at the tips of long spikes. The white is a similar plant but shorter and with lighter green leaves. The oil taken from the leaves of the white peppermint is the best quality.   J. K. K.

Pepsin see Enzymes

Peptic ulcer see Ulcer

Perception see Eye

Perch Fish of the perch family live in fresh water—ponds, lakes and streams —of North America, Europe and Asia. They eat eggs, larvae, insects, and other fish. Perch are good to eat.

In the spring, perch lay their eggs in a long string which sticks to shallow-water plants. A single perch can produce an amazing number of eggs.

The *yellow perch* is more bronze or golden than yellow. It has five to nine dark bars down its sides, a white belly, and red-orange lower fins. The *wall-eyed pike,* or *pike-perch,* sometimes grows to three times the size of the average foot-long yellow perch. Its color varies from olive green to bluish-gray. The *European perch* is quite like the yellow perch.   C. L. K.
SEE ALSO: FISH

Peppermint plant

Yellow perch
Chicago Natural History Museum

Percussion (per-KUHSH-uhn) Percussion is the act of striking an object with a sharp, quick blow. The blow may be delivered by the hand or some instrument especially designed for the purpose of striking the object.

More commonly, percussion is related to the production of musical tones or rhythms. Many musical instruments employ the principles of percussion. The *drum* is considered a percussion instrument and is used for keeping the tempo or "beat" of the music. *Cymbals, tambourines,* and *castanets* are other examples of the same type of percussion instrument. The *piano* and *xylophone* are percussion instruments also, but they are capable of producing melodies as well as keeping the tempo.

Along more purely scientific lines, percussion is used to describe a point on an object such as a PENDULUM. When a blow is delivered to exactly that point, it will cause rotation only around the place of suspension. This point is known as the *center of percussion.* An example of this effect is shown by a baseball and a bat. If the batter hits the ball directly on the center of percussion, there will be no shock transmitted to the batter's hands as would be the case if the ball were hit any other place on the bat.   A. E. L.
SEE ALSO: MUSICAL INSTRUMENTS

Perennial (puh-RENN-ee-uhl) A perennial is a plant that lives longer than two years. A BIENNIAL lives two years. An ANNUAL lives one growing season.

Woody perennials include trees and shrubs. They have stems that live for many years. Each year, a new season's growth is added and the stem increases in diameter. Most woody perennials lose only their leaves after the growing season, and *evergreens* retain even their leaves or needles, sometimes for three years. *Herbaceous perennials* have stems that die down to the ground after the growing season. Plants such as RHUBARB, LILY, ASPARAGUS, and many GRASSES live through the winter and use stored food from underground parts, such as tubers, rootstocks, and bulbs, to produce new shoots that grow the following season.   M. R. L.
SEE ALSO: ANGIOSPERMS, ANNUAL RING, BULB, TUBER

Some perfume flowers—(from left) lavender, jasmine, violets

Perfume (PURR-fyoom) Perfume is a substance with a pleasing odor. It is made by blending oils, alcohol, and other materials.

Perfume has been in use since ancient times. In ancient Egypt, it was considered a symbol of immortality and was often placed in the tombs of the Pharaohs. The Bible frequently refers to the use of perfume. Perfume has grown in popularity through the ages, and is a favorite with women who like its good scent on their skin and clothing. It is used in soaps, shaving lotions, shampoos, cosmetics, and hundreds of other products.

The finest perfumes are expensive because of the high cost of the essential oils and fixatives used in their preparation. They are made in nearly all countries, but France is considered the leader of the perfume industry. Fragrant flowers such as lavender, carnations, jasmine, orange blossoms, and violets are raised in France and made into famous French perfumes. The finest rose perfume is made in Bulgaria. Most of the spice scents come from tropical sections.

Gland cells in the nectaries of flowers produce fragrant oils. These oils, or *attars,* are the essential oils that are blended with other ingredients to make perfumes. The essential oils are removed from flowers either by steam DISTILLATION; by allowing lard to absorb the oil; or by dissolving the flower oils with petroleum ether. It takes many thousands of pounds of flowers to produce an ounce of essential oil. This is one reason for the high cost of perfumes.

Fixatives are used in perfumes to make the scent last and to blend the many separate odors into one fine scent. Animal products such as ambergris, civet, and musk are fixatives. They must be properly treated, aged, and blended before use. Natural fixatives are very expensive and add greatly to the cost of perfume. Synthetic musk has been successfully made and used.   M. R. L.

Pericardium The pericardium is the closed membranous sac which envelops the HEART of vertebrates and some other animals. It holds the clear, serous liquid with which the heart is bathed. It consists of an outer and inner coat.

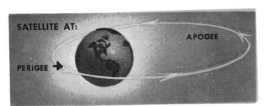

Perigee Either a natural SATELLITE (the moon) or a man-launched satellite (*Echo I*) moves in a curved path about the earth. Such a satellite's ORBIT is never a perfectly circular one, nor is the earth ever exactly at the orbital center. Therefore, at some time during each revolution, the satellite will reach a point when it is *nearest* to the earth. This near point is called the *perigee*.
SEE: APOGEE, ORBITAL SYSTEMS

Period see Geologic time table

Periodic table see Elements, Mendeleev's Periodic Table

Peripatus (puhr-RIP-uh-tuss) These shy little animals look like a caterpillar because they have short, stubby legs and a wrinkled body. But they are not insects. They have a long, soft, body and are often called "walking worms". But they are not worms.

These animals are not easy to find. They live in warm countries, like Africa and South America. Although all of them live on land, they must live in a damp place. They find shelter under stones, logs and tree roots in wet, tropical forests and come out only at night or during a rain.

Buchsbaum

Peripatus resembles a worm with legs

The peripatus seems to feed only upon dead animals. It is able to catch insects, termites and worms in a very interesting way. From two large salivary glands on its head, it spits out a sticky secretion like rubber cement. As this secretion dries, it entangles the prey.

Scientists often place the peripatus in a separate phylum with the name *Onychophora*, meaning "claw bearer." Although there are only about eighty different species, these animals were the first to have a true leg. From 14 to 40 pairs of fleshy legs turn downward and lift the animal off the ground. The peripatus provides a missing link between the segmented worms (annelids) and the jointed-legged arthropods.

Like the annelids, they have a segmented head, fleshy, unjointed legs, and a similar excretory system. Like the arthropods, they have feet with curved claws, and a well-developed head which bears two long antennae. Like the insects, they breathe by means of tracheal tubes.

The male peripatus has three or four fewer legs than does the female. Most females retain the embryos inside their bodies until they are ready to be born. Since pregnancy for the peripatus lasts for over a year, the female may carry two litters of young in its body at the same time. At birth, the peripatus is about one-half inch long. However, it grows to a length of about five inches.   E. P. L.

SEE ALSO: ANIMALS, CLASSIFICATION OF; ANNELIDA; ARTHROPODA; EVOLUTION

✳ THINGS TO DO

MAKING A PERISCOPE

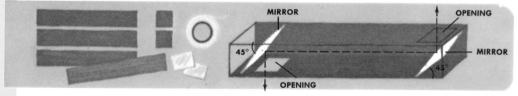

If you are too short to see over people's heads in a crowd then make this instrument. It will also enable you to peek around corners without your being noticed.

1 Cut four strips of balsa wood measuring three inches by one foot. These will form the sides of the tube. Cut two more pieces measuring three by three inches for the ends.

2 Cut out a two-inch square near the end of two side strips. Tape pocket mirrors at a 45 degree angle to the two sides with holes. Follow the illustration carefully. Tape the remaining sides, the top and bottom pieces to form a completely closed box.

3 It is now ready for use. Hold the tube upright and look through the bottom opening. Since light travels in straight lines the mirrors will reflect the object down to your eyes.

Periscope (PAIR-uh-skope) A periscope is an OPTICAL INSTRUMENT which enables a person to obtain a view otherwise impossible to see. Periscopes allow a SUBMARINE crew to survey objects on the surface of the water. A simple periscope can be made by mounting two mirrors on an angle within a tube or a narrow box. A person can look around a corner or over a fence with this homemade periscope.

A submarine periscope consists of a long, stainless steel or bronze tube. The optical lenses and prisms are sealed at the top by a glass window so they are watertight. When the periscope is raised above the surface of the water, light enters through the window. The light, striking a right-angle prism at the top, is totally reflected downward through several lenses to a second prism or a mirror. At this level the light is again totally reflected to the eyepiece, and thus to the observer.

Periscopes are also used for other military purposes. Warships and gun turrets may contain range-finding periscopes designed to protect the operator from enemy fire. Tanks use periscopes, as do foot soldiers in trenches.

Periscopes are employed to observe radioactive materials. This is one way scientists can see over or through protective walls. Scientists can examine the inside of the stomach with a periscope-type instrument called the *gastroscope*.   P. F. D.
SEE ALSO: LENS, MAN-MADE; PRISM; TELESCOPE

Peristalsis (per-uh-STAL-siss) Peristalsis is a type of movement, occurring in the hollow organs of animals, which causes the contents of the organ to be pushed out. Peristalsis occurs when the *circular* and *longitudinal muscle fibers* of the organ contract in rhythm. It occurs in circulatory, reproductive, and excretory systems but is most apparent in the digestive tract, where food is churned, mixed, and moved by peristalsis.

Circular fiber contraction makes the organ narrower and longer, while longitudinal fiber contraction makes it wider and shorter. The contractions begin at the top and run consecutively down the organ. If peristalsis is reversed in the upper digestive tract, vomiting occurs.   J. K. L.
SEE ALSO: DIGESTIVE SYSTEM

Peritoneum see Abdomen, Peritonitis

Peritonitis (per-uh-tuh-NYE-tiss) Peritonitis is a very serious disease. It is an inflammation of the *peritoneum*. The peritoneum is the largest *serous* membrane of the body, and lines the abdominal cavity. It has two layers, an inner surface layer that is smooth and moist, and a rough outer layer which is attached to the inner layer. If this membrane becomes infected, peritonitis results.

Peritonitis may be caused by bruises or wounds, or by damage to the membrane by such diseases as TYPHOID FEVER, a chronic ULCER in the stomach, dysentery, appendicitis, cysts, tubercular or cancerous growths. It is either acute or chronic.

Acute peritonitis is not easily diagnosed because the patient may have INFECTION for a long period before it becomes acute and definite symptoms are produced. At first, pain is generally felt in one small local area. Later, the pain spreads and becomes worse, especially when the body is moved. Shivering and an enlarged, sore and tender abdomen are symptoms. Finally, profuse perspiration and chills indicate serious trouble.

Chronic peritonitis is sometimes the result of a case of acute peritonitis, and may take a very long time to cure. It is more often caused by deposits of tubercular or cancerous materials, or by ulcerations of the stomach. Symptoms are dull pain that increases with movement, poor appetite, a wasted appearance, and dry skin.   M. R. L.

Periwinkle (animal) The periwinkle is a little SNAIL with a thick spiral shell. The shell is yellow, black, brown, or red with dark bands.

Periwinkles can be eaten and are used as fish bait. They are common in European waters and are now found on the Atlantic coast.

The periwinkle's head sticks out of the shell and its eyes are at the end of tentacles. When the animal moves, it swings from side to side on a foot that is divided lengthwise.

J. W. Thompson
The periwinkle is smaller than a man's thumb

The snail's tongue is twice as long as its body. The periwinkle clings to rocks where it lays its eggs and eats plants.   P. G. B.

Periwinkle (plant) see Vinca

Permeability (per-mee-uh-BILL-uh-tee) Permeability is a measure of how easily fluids can penetrate and flow through a solid. Solids are permeable because they have networks of pore spaces through which fluids can flow.

Permeability is an important property of building materials and textiles. The permeability of sedimentary rocks like sandstone and limestone, through which flow water and oil into wells, has been the most carefully studied.

Magnetic permeability is a property of a substance which tells how much it becomes magnetized when placed in a magnetic field. The higher the magnetic permeability of a substance, the more highly magnetized it becomes when placed in a magnetic field.

Permeability is also a property of semipermeable membranes. In this case, permeability is a measure of how rapidly a substance on one side of the membrane can diffuse through the membrane to the other side. The membranes around plant and animal cells are *selectively permeable*. These membranes will allow certain ions to pass through but will not permit other ions to pass.   E. R. B.

SEE ALSO: MAGNETS, OSMOSIS

Peroxide see Oxygen

Perpendicular Perpendicular means exactly upright or at right angles to a line. A line perpendicular to another line or plane forms a 90 degree angle with that line or plane.

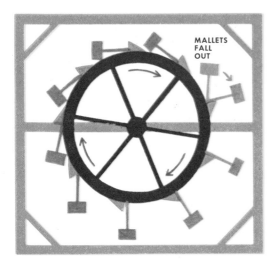

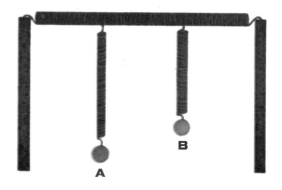

(Above) Spring-type perpetual motion machine. (Left) In the 1200's, a Frenchman planned a machine which used gravity to turn it forever. Mallets fall away from the rim on one side pulling it out of balance and making it turn. It will not start itself, and the energy used to start it turning is used up by friction

Perpetual motion machine Perpetual motion is an idea which people from ancient times tried to build into some kind of machine. The idea was that a properly built machine would run forever without having any constant supply of energy from outside itself. Thus, it would run itself while producing its own power to continue running.

The scientific view today is that a real perpetual motion machine is a practical impossibility. The reasoning is as follows.

Any machine starts to operate when supplied with some definite amount of energy of the proper type (for which the machine was designed) and of the proper "energy order-level." High-level energy forms include those mechanical motions of an engine drive-rod or a steady current of electricity or of a hot object sending its heat (molecular motion) into a colder object. The colder object has the lowest order of energy of the whole series named.

As the machine starts up, the moving parts rub together and wear away. Thus they waste some of the original high-level motion and spread it about as worn machine fragments and low-level heat. In short, friction and heat loss are the two ever-present conquerors of perfect use of energy and thus of perpetual motion. The *second law of thermodynamics,* states that the heat in a material cannot be completely changed into

mechanical energy—except if the machine could work at absolute zero ($-460°$ F., $-273.1°$ C.). ABSOLUTE ZERO temperature has never been reached.

The planets and natural satellites, such as the moon, do seem to travel about their central bodies perpetually, for they move in the near-vacuum of space and undergo little or no friction. The main friction-like forces on satellites are those made by space debris—meteors, or comets. Such debris— or large-sized collisions—might sometime end the perpetual motion of even these bodies.

One of the many proposed perpetual motion machines is that sketched above, right. It has three springs, one of which is supported by two upright rods. The other two have metal spheres at their lower ends.

The system is started by introducing energy into sphere A; that is, it is set to vibrating up and down. Eventually sphere B will vibrate and A will come to rest.

This process will repeat itself for quite some time. Then why will it fail in perpetual motion? There will always be some air friction; and even in a vacuum, there will also be the internal friction and heat loss of the molecules in the springs themselves. Without adding more outside energy then, this machine will finally run down.

The perpetual motion idea has been valuable since it has led men to build better machines—with better lubrication and finer parts, such as ball bearings. A. E. L.

Perseus

Perseus Perseus is a beautiful group of stars in the Milky Way. The CON-STELLATION was named for a mythical Greek hero, the son of Zeus, who beheaded the wicked Medusa. A glance from Medusa would have turned him to stone, but he was aided by Mercury and Minerva. The ancient Greeks believed the constellation to be Perseus holding the severed head of Medusa.

Though not easy to find, Perseus is visible with a small telescope. It is seen in the northern sky in December and January, and reaches from Cassiopeia to Taurus. The star *Algol,* visible to the naked eye, is actually a double star. The light shed by Algol is variable, caused by the revolving of the dim STAR around the bright star every three days, producing a partial eclipse.

A telescope will reveal many variously colored star clusters in the constellation. About August 10th the famous meteor shower, the *Perseids,* can be seen.   C. L. K.

Persimmon The persimmon tree has pale orange fruits. They are juicy berries about two inches in diameter. The leaves are long and narrow. The flowers are white. Persimmons belong to the EBONY family.

The American persimmon grows from 50 to 100 feet tall, has a spreading, rounded head, and drooping branches. The plumlike fruits are about an inch in diameter, colored yellow and pink. The taste of the persimmon is mouth-puckering until fully ripe.

The Japanese persimmon or *kaki* is a smaller tree, rarely reaching more than 40 feet in height. Its fruit is larger and redder

Persimmon bark, fruit and flower

than that of the American persimmon. A decorative tree with large, shining, blackish-green leaves and yellowish-green flowers, it is easily injured by frost, and the foliage is easily sunburned. The fruit of the Japanese persimmon is the one most frequently marketed.   J. K. K.

Persistence of vision Persistence of vision is the ability of human eyes to retain an image of what they have just seen for a short period of time after the object has disappeared from sight. A person can "see" a light for a second or two after the light has been turned off.

If an electric light bulb is placed behind an electric fan moving at high speed, the light seems to shine continuously although the fan blades are covering it for short intervals. This persistence of vision explains why still pictures shown rapidly appear to move. Motion pictures are actually numerous still pictures shown so rapidly that they seem to blend into one continuous moving picture.   E. R. B.
SEE ALSO: MOTION PICTURES

Perspective Perspective is the science or art of drawing an object on a flat or curved surface so that the object appears to have depth and be at a distant point from an observer. The visual rays from the object appear to converge at the observer's eye.
SEE: EYE; EYE, BINOCULAR; LENS, MAN-MADE

Perspiration see Sweat glands

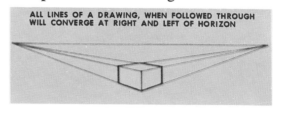

ALL LINES OF A DRAWING, WHEN FOLLOWED THROUGH WILL CONVERGE AT RIGHT AND LEFT OF HORIZON

Petrel

Petrel The petrel is a small seabird with long wings. It has the ability to fly for long periods of time and to sleep on water. Some return to land only to breed.

SEE: FALCON

Petrifaction (pet-ruh-FACK-shun) Petrifaction is the process in which materials such as wood become rock formations. This happens through a replacement of the original substance by minerals of various types. The best known examples are the Petrified Forests found in Arizona. These are classified as a kind of FOSSIL.

The word *petrifaction* explains what has occurred. *Petri-* means "rock," and *-faction* refers to "make." Thus petrified wood becomes "rock made from wood."

Wood started petrifying millions of years ago when conifer trees lay decaying. Minerals including silica, pyrites, and dolomites in water solution penetrated the cells of the wood. The minerals, separating from the water, left all spaces filled with solid rock. These logs have thus been preserved in forms very much as they originally appeared. Branches and leaves have, of course, disappeared.

These petrified logs are three and four feet in diameter and some are over 100 feet in length. Their colors run through grays and browns with variations of shading as well as patches and streaks brought about by various combinations of minerals. D. J. I.

SEE ALSO: PALEONTOLOGY

Petrified Forest, in Arizona
Courtesy Society For Visual Education, Inc.

Petroleum (puh-TROW-lee-uhm) The formation of petroleum, or crude mineral oil, took place long ago when great seas covered most present-day land masses. As the seas came and went with the shifting of the earth's surface, organic materials from plants and animals were buried with sediments from oceans and rivers. These sediments were subjected to great pressure and bacterial action, thus slowly becoming petroleum.

As a result of folding of the earth's crust, pockets or reservoirs of gas, oil, and salt water formed in the rock layers—valuable resources awaiting man's discovery. The earliest known use of petroleum was during Biblical times when surface-seeping pitch was used to seal the seams of ships. Often men dug for salt water to get edible salt, and found black oil instead. Knowing no use for the oil, the wells were abandoned.

In the mid-nineteenth century, a salt-maker, Samuel Kier of Pittsburgh, bottled and sold petroleum as medicine. Samples of this "rock oil" reached Professor Benjamin Silliman of Yale University in 1855. He analyzed it and separated out light-weight fractions that burned in lamps better than the commonly used spermwhale oil.

The chief oil-producing countries are: The United States, Venezuela, Russia, Saudi Arabia, Kuwait, Iraq, Indonesia, and Iran.

The most important early product of oil was *kerosene,* and the lighter *gasoline* which would explode in kerosene lamps was thrown away. Today, the chief products are: NATURAL GAS, gasoline, kerosene, lubricating oil, FUEL oils, asphalts, and oil coke.

Much of the oil recovered from oil deposits today is found off shore along the sea coasts where special drilling rigs are set up.

Crude oil recovered from the ground is separated in the gas-oil separator. Then it is sent through a network of pipelines throughout the country to be refined.

With the tremendous demand for different oil products there are over 4000 oil fields producing over 2½ billion barrels annually. There are over 30 billion barrels of proved United States petroleum reserves. E. Y. K.

SEE ALSO: OIL WELL, ORGANIC COMPOUNDS

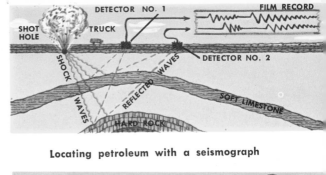

Locating petroleum with a seismograph

American Oil Co.

In giant oil fractionating towers, crude oil is made into high-octane gasoline

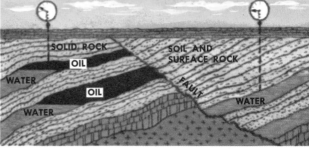

The gravimeter can help in locating petroleum deposits. When used over a fault, as shown above, gravity registers stronger on the raised side of the fault as dense rock is closest there. Below is shown the gravimeter registering less gravitational pull as it is used over a salt dome, because salt is lighter than surrounding rock

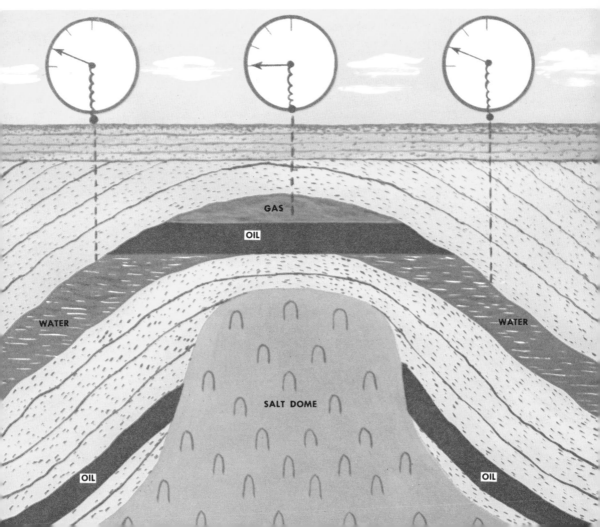

Petroleum jelly Petroleum jelly, or *petrolatum,* is a semi-solid substance obtained by refining the greases which result from the distillation of PETRO-LEUM. It is used as a protective dressing, a base for ointments, a lubricant for metals, and a leather-softener.

Petrology see Rocks

Helen J. Challand

Pink petunias

Petunia The petunia is one of the favorite flowers of home gardeners. The velvety, funnel-shaped blossom of the petunia may be white, pink, reddish, violet, purple, or sometimes striped. Some hybrids, or mixed varieties, have ruffled edges. The petunia is a member of the NIGHTSHADE family.

The petunia is a hardy annual and a satisfactory flower for beginners to grow. Seeds should be sown early indoors or in a cold frame. Some gardeners say the smallest and slowest-growing seedlings often produce the best colors. The many leaves and the stems of the plant are covered with hair-like structures.

Petunias like a rich soil and plenty of sunshine. They are not only a popular flower for the backyard garden, but they are widely used for window boxes, porch boxes, and hanging baskets.   J. K. K.

Pewter Pewter is an ALLOY of tin and lead, in the proportion of four to six parts of tin to one part of lead. Sometimes copper, antimony, or zinc are used instead of lead.

SEE: METAL

Caventou and Pelletier of France separated quinine from cinchona bark about 1820

Pharmacology (fahr-muh-KAHL-uh-jee) Pharmacology is the science that deals with the action of medicines and other chemicals on animals and man. It is different from *pharmacy,* which is the preparing and mixing of medicines of known action.

Pharmacology is a young science. It recently has become important not only to doctors and druggists but also to research biologists studying newly-produced chemicals.

Many nineteenth century biochemists helped build this science of drug action. Two of the most prominent contributors were Francis Magendie and Otto Schmiederberg.

In ancient times and until the last century, knowledge of how DRUGS cure disease was unreliable. The sciences of biology and chemistry were still undeveloped. Superstition and magic influenced early alchemists and herb collectors. They wrote thick· "books of medicines" called *pharmaco-poeias,* and these books recommended many drugs that were either worthless or harmful, when examined by the standards of modern pharmacology. For example, powdered dandelion root was listed in pharmacopoeia books, and was claimed "to cure colds, kidney stones, and deep fevers."

On the other hand such medicinal plants as the medieval herb-extract of foxglove plants, called DIGITALIS, has been shown to contain the curative chemical *digitalin;* and this purified drug is now prescribed for certain heart ailments. A similar backing up of the use of an old herb discovery of the South American Indians—the bark of the cinchona tree containing quinine—has led

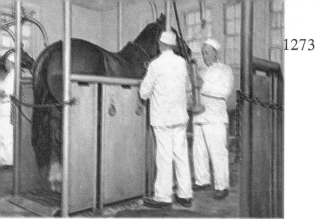

The development of biological serums started about 1894 with the use of diphtheria toxin

About 1920, Fourneau of France produced many compounds to fight specific diseases

to the modern use of purified quinine to treat malaria. Quinine has been further studied by pharmacologists, and a successful man-made drug, atabrine, has been created which is even better than quinine for treating malaria.

THE BRANCHES OF PHARMACOLOGY

Four branches of the science are recognized: *Pharmacodynamics* deals with finding how chemicals act on men's bodies, or first on those of laboratory animals.

Chemotherapy includes two studies: (a) how drug chemicals can destroy invading germs, and (b) how to restore normal health to unbalanced organs and glands. The *antibiotic* drugs (sulfa chemicals, etc.) are such gifts of chemotherapy to the conquest of many human bacterial diseases. Some antibiotics act, not directly to kill germs, but indirectly by stimulating body cells to fight germs. Some act in both ways. Another product of chemotherapy is the hormone *insulin,* an extract of the pancreatic glands of cattle, which has saved the lives of millions of people sick with diabetes.

Clinical pharmacology is practiced by research doctors in hospital clinics. After the pharmacodynamic action of a new drug has been determined, that chemical becomes ready for testing on volunteer patients. In the clinic the researcher makes tests to learn if safe doses will cure or relieve the disease which it was intended to help.

The fourth branch of drug science, *toxicology,* is studied to determine how especially poisonous (toxic) chemicals act on living things. The study includes the search for antidotes and for other ways of preventing injury by poisons. As example, there is the recently-discovered chemical that is taken as a pill to relieve the painful skin rash of poison ivy.

MEDICINE DOSAGE BECOMES MORE SCIENTIFIC

Doctors have long been concerned about how to find the correct dose of a medicine. Pharmacologists have recently created an ingenious way to test and record drug doses.

Suppose that an entirely new chemical with some curative effect is discovered. The drug scientist first tests and records all the doses which were administered to laboratory animals and later to human volunteers. Then he reports to the waiting world of drug manufacturers and physicians just what the best doses and effects are. To do this, he reports the *effective dose response* (ED), meaning that dose required to produce one-half (50%) of its observed curing effect. For example, for ASPIRIN to relieve a fever due to a cold, might be reported: "Aspirin, anti-febrile, ED_{50} dose 2.5 grains every 2 hours, per 150-pound adult body weight." The full dose for an adult this size would be 5 grains. (A grain is equal to 0.0648 grams.)

This manner of stating dosage allows for individual differences in drug sensitivity.

METHODS OF DRUG STUDY

Good drug-action research usually follows certain accepted methods. Laboratory animals are given measured doses of a promising chemical. The bodily effects on the animals are accurately observed. Then perhaps certain bad effects of the drug cause the researcher to seek a related but slightly changed chemical. Often the researcher will go to a fellow organic chemist and ask for a similar chemical that has only one atom or a small molecular group of atoms changed. The new chemical is then given in measured doses to animals. This process may continue for many months until a drug is finally found that is satisfactory. It is then

Since the discovery of penicillin, the synthesis of antibiotics has become vitally important

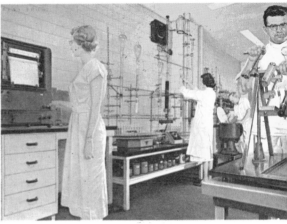

Continuous research in pharmaceuticals is the most important task of pharmacologists

ready to be tried on volunteer clinical patients. In this very way, the old herbal drug, salicylic acid, was rejected for the much-improved acetylsalicylic acid, which is commonly known as ASPIRIN.

NUCLEAR ENERGY ISOTOPES

Since World War II, pharmacology has found a powerful new discovery tool in radioisotopes. For example, radio-carbon-14 and radio-iodine, which are both products of nuclear energy reactors, can be chemically added to drugs and fed to laboratory animals or to man. These radioactive chemicals become *tracers,* so-called because their paths in the body can be followed by the detecting electronic radiation counters or by photographs. Thus an animal that is fed radio-iodine will later show a "hot" radiation area right in the iodine-hungry thyroid gland area of its neck.

The curing values of most medicines is owed to pharmacologists. The earliest discovered antibiotic, PENICILLIN, was first detected only as a crude, green mold (*Penicillium notatum*) by Sir Alexander Fleming in 1928. Only after he and many pharmacologists studied this mold for more than ten years was the pure chemical, penicillin, finally given to the world.   D. A. B.

SEE ALSO: MEDICINE, PHYSIOLOGY

Pharynx (FAIR-ingks) The pharynx is the section of the alimentary tract of some invertebrates connecting the mouth and esophagus. In vertebrates, it is the tube back of the nose and mouth where air crosses the path of food going to the esophagus.

SEE: ADENOID, DIGESTIVE SYSTEM, RESPIRATORY SYSTEM

Phases of the Moon see Earth; Moon, phases of

Pheasant The male pheasant is one of the most colorful of all game birds. The female is not as pretty. Hunters like the pheasant both for its colorful feathers and for its flavorful meat. It is protected by game laws.

The ring-necked pheasant is the most popular in the United States. It is a hybrid, a cross between the Chinese ring-necked variety and the common English pheasant.

Pheasants can run with great speed on their long legs. They can fly for short distances but only with effort because their wings are short. Their wings are, however, wide and the bird can glide for great distances. The male has a beautiful multicolored tail.   V. V. N.

Male ring-necked pheasant

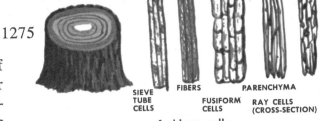

SIEVE TUBE CELLS FIBERS FUSIFORM CELLS PARENCHYMA RAY CELLS (CROSS-SECTION)

Four types of phloem cells

Phenols The phenols are a group of organic compounds which have one or more HYDROXYL groups (OH) attached directly to an aromatic-ring system. The simplest is phenol (C_6H_5OH). They are used in disinfectants, plastics, and preservatives.
SEE: ORGANIC COMPOUNDS

Philodendron

Philodendron The philodendron is a common house plant. It is an interesting VINE, because it grows rapidly and is decorative whether it is trained to climp up or to trail down.

The leaves of the philodendron are large, bright green, and somewhat heart-shaped. It does not need much sun and is an excellent plant to place in a north or west window. It needs much moisture. Stems that include a node may be placed in a container of water, and they will root. It is wise to add a small amount of house plant food to the water.

The philodendron, if properly cared for, will live a long time. Its large leaves should be washed from time to time.   J. K. K.

Phloem (FLO-emm) Inside a plant are groups of cells which carry on a particular job for the plant. Phloem makes up conducting tubes for the purpose of carrying the manufactured food to all parts of the plant. Phloem cells are found around the outside of XYLEM cells, the other kind of conducting tissue.

There are several kinds of cells in phloem. *Parenchyma* are large thin-walled storage cells. *Fibers* have thick walls to give the plant support and strength. *Sieve tubes* are elongated cells which retain their cytoplasm but lose their nuclei. They appear to need companion cells to help them function. The constant flow of solutions through the sieve cell may weaken the cross-walls and cause them to be perforated as a sieve.

Phloem tissue in trees makes up the inner part of the BARK. It is separated from the xylem tissue by a sheath of meristematic cells called *vascular cambium*. The cambium constantly divides and forms new phloem and xylem cells every year.   H. J. C.
SEE ALSO: PLANT TISSUES

Phlox (FLOCKS) Phlox is a flower that will bloom all summer. The dwarf kind, no more than six inches tall, can be found in many rock gardens. Another higher variety is used as a border herb. The blooms are most commonly white or pink to purple.

This annual or perennial plant grows in a creeping manner or in an erect position. The leaves are alternate in arrangement with a smooth margin. The petals of the flower are fused to form a tube with the outer edges scalloped. The flower is perfect, meaning it has both male and female reproductive structures. Many hybrid varities now come fringed or star-shaped in a wide range of flaming colors.

In late fall or early spring, the mature plant should be dug up, the rootstock cut into several pieces and replanted over a wider area. This is referred to as multiplication of a flower bed by division. If phlox is permitted to reseed itself, the offspring will revert to the wild state.   H. J. C.

Phoebe see Peewee

Globe phlox

George J. Ball, Inc.

Phosphate Phosphate is the name given to the large series of chemical compounds which have as part of their formula a phosphate component. Of all the phosphate compounds, the most common are the ammonium, calcium and sodium salts of phosphoric acid. Any phosphate has PO₄ in its formula.

The most familiar phosphate compounds are inorganic and are used in large quantities in many industries. For example, *diammonium phosphate* is used as a fireproofing agent for textiles. *Monoammonium phosphate* is used in baking powders. *Monocalcium phosphate* is used as a dietary supplement in animal feeds, and the various sodium phosphates are used as laxatives, as buffering agents, and in detergent mixtures. M. S.
SEE ALSO: PHOSPHORUS, SALT

A lantern fish has organs which produce a phosphorescent glow

Phosphorescence (foss-for-ESS-sense) Phosphorescence is the condition in which certain organic or mineral matter and certain plants and animals give off light without the presence of heat. Also known as "afterglow," phosphorescence has been known to persist for a period of only a few seconds up to several days.

The scientific explanation of phosphorescence is that the substance absorbs radiant light energy which increases the energy of some of the electrons in the substance. When the electrons slowly return to their original state, they emit this extra energy in the form of light. If the radiation of a substance fades immediately after the light is stopped, the process is called *fluorescence.* If light continues, however, the process is called *phosphorescence.*

In ancient times, phosphorescence was, of course, seen and recorded as it appeared in nature. However, the earliest record of serious investigation and experimentation of this phenomenon comes from Bologna, Italy, where a cobbler and alchemist named Cascariola conducted extensive research with a barium compound.

The delayed luminescence of phosphorescence is the result of the object being subjected to an exciting light source. The time during which phosphorescence persists is known to decrease with an increase in temperature of the substance. The principles of phosphorescence are being applied in many new areas of research, using especially the highly phosphorescent ruby.   D. A. B.
SEE ALSO: BULB, ELECTRIC

Phosphorus (FOHS-fuh-ruhs) Phosphorus is an element that is found in four different pure forms. Each form has different characteristics. Chemically it is a non-metal, related in its properties to the elements nitrogen and astatine.

Phosphorus was first isolated in 1669 by H. Brandt. It is the first element whose date of discovery is known. Brandt isolated phosphorus from animal urine. Phosphorus occurs in compound form in all fertile soils. It is necessary for all plant and animal life. In man it is found mainly in bones, teeth, muscles, and nervous tissues.

The most common form of phosphorus is a yellow waxy solid. This form is originally white, almost colorless, but turns yellow when exposed to light. Yellow phosphorus melts at 111.6° F, is extremely poisonous, and must be stored and cut underwater to prevent fire. When moist yellow phosporus is exposed to air, it burns, forms phosphorus pentoxide, and gives off a glow from the heat generated. This glow is a chemical change and is unrelated to phosphorescence. The only similarity between phosphorus and phosphorescence is in the word root *phosphor* which means "light bearer."

Red phosphorus, another form, is widely used in making safety MATCHES. Red phosphorus is produced by heating yellow phosphorus or exposing it to a bright light. It is

A glow and heat are produced when phosphorus is exposed to air

not poisonous and must reach 500° F to burn. Red phosphorus is used in making bronzes and medicines and in gas analysis.

There are other forms of phosphorus, named for their colors, black, scarlet, and violet. Scarlet phosphorus is produced by dissolving yellow phosphorus in phosphorus tribromide and heating it to 357° F. The solid scarlet phosphorus then settles out. Violet or metallic phosphorus is produced by heating red phosphorus in contact with lead for ten hours at 932° F. The phosphorus dissolves in the lead and upon cooling it separates as violet phosphorus.

Phosphorus for commercial purposes is obtained from rock PHOSPHATE, a phosphorus-rich mineral. Rock phosphate is purified by heating with sand and carbon. France and the United States are the largest producers of rock phosphate. Phosphorus is the eleventh most abundant element.

Phosphorus (symbol **P**) has an atomic number of 15. Its atomic weight is 30.9738 (30.975, O = 16). J. K. L.

SEE ALSO: ATOM, ELEMENTS

Photochemistry Photochemistry is the study of chemical changes involving light. It studies those processes in which light causes chemical changes. Also it studies the reverse processes in which chemicals react to emit light. *Photo* is from Greek meaning "light."

Photochemical processes of the first type are illustrated by what happens to a film when a picture is being taken, and by the whitening of dark-colored clothing or hair when exposed to sunlight. Examples of the second type are illustrated by the flashing of a firefly and the burning of candles or oil and gas lamps.

In nature, an important, photochemical change occurs in green plants. CHLOROPHYLL in the cells of green plants uses light to combine ordinary water and carbon dioxide chemically to make sugar. This photochemical process is called PHOTOSYNTHESIS.

Photochemistry is basic to making and developing of photographic FILM. A clear plastic film is coated with gelatine containing tiny grains of silver bromide. When the film is placed in a camera and light is focused on it through the shutter and lens, the silver bromide undergoes chemical changes in those spots where light strikes it. The grains in these spots are said to be *sensitized*. Chemical developers reduce the sensitized grains of silver bromide to metallic silver. Chemicals called *fixers* are next used to remove the silver bromide which was not sensitized.

BLUEPRINT paper is photochemically similar to film. But for blueprints, paper is coated with iron-ammonium citrate and ferrocyanides. Light changes these pale iron salts to deep blue ferric ferrocyanides. Developing an exposed print only requires washing it in water.

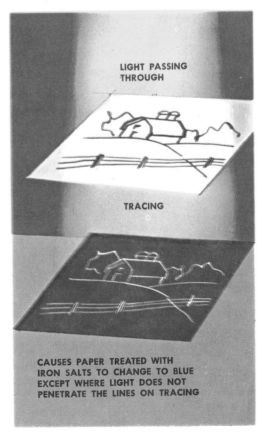

LIGHT PASSING THROUGH

TRACING

CAUSES PAPER TREATED WITH IRON SALTS TO CHANGE TO BLUE EXCEPT WHERE LIGHT DOES NOT PENETRATE THE LINES ON TRACING

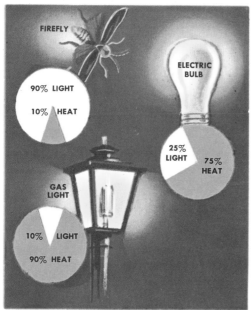

The firefly has a much more efficient photochemical process of light than does any of the light sources which man has been able to devise. Much less heat is produced for the amount of light given off

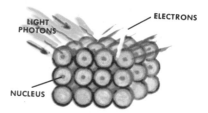

The outermost electrons of heavy metal atoms have weak binding force. They can be knocked loose by light and utilized as photoelectrical energy

CHEMICAL PRODUCTION OF LIGHT

The oldest known photochemical change is that of burning fuels. Candles and gas or oil lamps are such light-giving devices. Even the best modern kerosene lamp is photochemically wasteful, since nine-tenths of the chemical energy in the original fuel is changed to heat and less than one-tenth to light. Even an electric light bulb wastes about 75 per cent of the original electrical energy as heat.

The reverse photochemical change has been difficult for man to produce. In nature, the firefly (lightning bug) has long been admired by scientists. In his laboratories, man has never yet found chemicals that give light matching the efficiency and coldness of the firefly's light.

Besides fireflies, many other living things perform photochemical feats. Fox fire is the glowing of decaying fallen logs, caused by bacteria that decompose the wood. Several kinds of sea animals produce light. The scallops (*Pectens*), clam-like animals that propel themselves by flapping their shells, have rows of phosphorescent eye spots lining the outer edges of their shells. When a scallop rests with its shell agape, small prey are lured into the scallop's vise-like shell body.   D. A. B.

Photoelectricity

Photoelectricity Photoelectricity is the study of how light and electricity work together. It has made possible the "electric eye" which automatically opens the doors of the supermarket, counts the number of articles made each hour in factories, and measures the brightness of distant stars. Even cameras now adjust themselves with its aid.

Light sometimes acts as though it were a stream of particles instead of waves. The brightness of the light is determined by the number of these particles, or PHOTONS, in the beam, while the energy of each individual particle determines what is called the *color* of the light.

Metals, like all matter, are made up of atoms. These, in turn, consist of a dense, positively-charged nucleus surrounded by a cloud of electrons. It is the electron's negative charge which binds it to the nucleus by electric-field attraction.

Since the atoms of most metals are relatively large, the outermost electrons are relatively far from the nucleus. As a result, the binding force upon these outer electrons is quite weak. When metal atoms are linked together to form a solid, the outer electrons can move freely anywhere in the solid and are called conduction electrons. If a photon of light is absorbed by a conduction electron, the additional energy may be enough to drive that electron out of the metal surface. When electrons are driven out continuously by light falling on a metal surface, a voltage can be applied between the surface and an electrode and the photoelectrons collected.

One of the major types of phototubes includes a semi-cylindrical CATHODE that has its inner surface coated with a light-sensitive alloy of cesium and silver. The anode is a

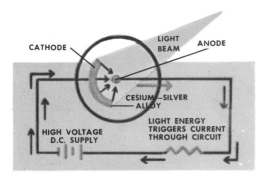

piece of wire arranged to collect any electrons driven out of the cathode.

As normally used, the cathode is connected to the negative side of a high voltage DC power supply, while the anode is connected to the positive side of the supply. A resistor is also connected in series with one of the electrodes. As long as the phototube is in the dark, it acts as an open circuit; no current can pass between its electrodes. However, when a beam of light strikes the sensitive cathode, the photons knock electrons from its surface. Being negatively charged, these electrons are strongly attracted to the positively-charged anode wire. These moving electrons thus form the current that flows around the entire circuit.

The picture below shows the simplified wiring diagram of an actual photoelectric relay, such as is widely used in industry. For simplicity the usual rectifier power supply has been replaced by batteries.

As long as the phototube remains in the dark, no current flows through the relay MAGNET coil. The spring holds the relay contacts open. But as soon as a light strikes the phototube, a current flows through the phototube and through the resistor. The voltage drop across the resistor causes the upper end of this resistor to become positive with respect to the lower end. This positive voltage overcomes the opposing effect of the battery. Thus the grid of the triode becomes positive and allows electrons to pass from its cathode to its plate and around through the relay coil. This current magnetizes the core of this coil and closes the contacts so that it starts any piece of apparatus connected to the terminals moving. This apparatus may be a door-opener motor or any common piece of electrical machinery.

When the light is removed, the phototube ceases to conduct. The triode grid again becomes negative; the current stops, and the magnet coil releases the contacts.

In recent years scientists have also found that light photons can change the electrical conductivity of a semiconductor junction. *Semiconductors* are such materials as SILICON and GERMANIUM and are used in transistors. By suitable chemical treatment during manufacture, silicon can be made in two

A broken light beam breaks current through a relay switch which falls to activate a motor circuit. The circuit will lower the drawbridge

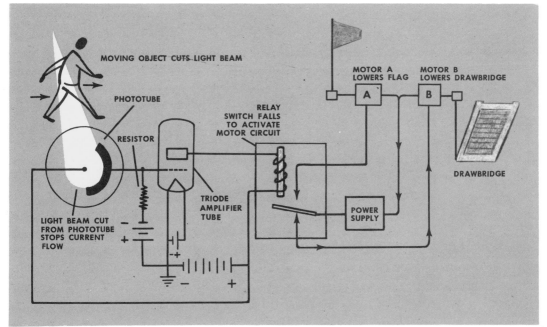

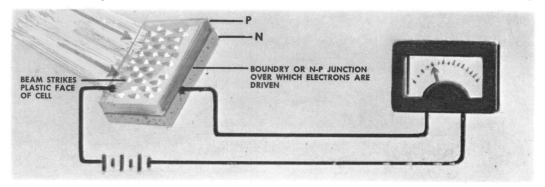

A system may be designed to operate a meter which measures the brightness of light

forms: (1) an "N material," and (2) a "P material." A single crystal of silicon is treated in both ways so that a boundary forms between them. This boundary is called a "P-N" semiconductor junction.

When a P-N semiconductor junction is connected, only a small current can flow across it in the dark, because the battery acts to prevent the free electrons in the N material from moving across into the P material. But when light photons strike the junction, they give some electrons enough additional energy to overcome the opposition and cross over. Thus the current through the semiconductor will tend to increase in proportion to the brightness of the light striking it. This is the principle of the phototransistor and of other semiconductor light-sensitive devices.

The N-P-N junction transistor in a semiconductor photoelectric relay is normally in a practically nonconducting state, as is the phototransistor when in the dark. Light photons, striking the P-N junction of the phototransistor, cause it to pass current into the base of the N-P-N unit, which then also conducts strongly enough to magnetize the relay coil and close the system contacts.

In addition to an "off-on" switching operation as described, the photoelectric device can also measure light of smoothly varying intensity. The photographer's light meter makes use of a copper-oxide, or similar photovoltaic cell. Here the photons give their energy to loosely-bound electrons and develop a proportional electrical voltage, just like a battery, between a copper plate and an overlying thin layer of copper oxide. This voltage, proportional to the intensity of the light, operates a sensitive millivoltmeter calibrated in light intensity. A similar device controls the lens opening in the automatic camera. An electron phototube and amplifier, similar to that first described, is used by astronomers to measure the light from distant stars.

As interesting as these and many other applications of photoelectricity seem, the science of photoelectricity has revealed more of the nature of light and of matter than would have been possible with the knowledge and equipment available before.   C. F. R.

SEE ALSO: AUTOMATION, ELECTRICITY, ELECTRONICS, LIGHT, PHOTOCHEMISTRY, TELEVISION, TRANSISTOR, VACUUM TUBE

A photoelectric circuit can be utilized to do tasks around the home

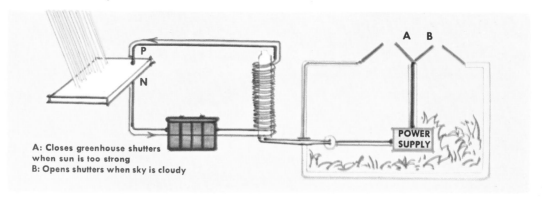

A: Closes greenhouse shutters when sun is too strong
B: Opens shutters when sky is cloudy

Photography Photography is the process of producing images on a surface. Basic to the entire process is the chemical reaction of certain substances to light. Light rays affect things in different ways: skin turns red, colors often fade, grass and flowers grow.

About 150 years ago, chemists discovered that silver salts (combinations of silver and bromine or silver and chlorine) were affected by light. They found that if they put a coating of silver salt on a glass plate, or transparent paper, the light would affect the silver salts so that an invisible change took place where the light hit. If this paper or plate were then bathed in a special solution, the change could be made visible where the silver salt changed into silver. The untouched silver salt could then be dissolved in another solution and only the parts changed by light would remain.

One of the earlier processes, becoming popular around 1839, was introduced by a French inventor, L. J. M. Daguerre. He made use of silver plates or copper plates coated with silver, on which photographs were produced. These photographs were called *daguerreotypes,* and were sometimes called *tintypes.*

THE PHOTOGRAPHIC PROCESS

Light source: Light from the sun or a flash bulb falls on the object to be photographed. The object reflects some of the light rays and absorbs some of them. The lighter colors reflect more of the light rays.

Camera: The pattern of reflected light rays from the object is focused by the camera's lens on a film coated with silver salts. The camera must be light-tight so no other light rays can enter.

Film: A latent (invisible) image of the object is impressed upon the film by the reaction of the silver salts to the light rays.

Negative: Three solutions are needed in a darkroom. The picture, or visible image, is brought out when the film is placed in a *developer* solution; another solution stops any further development; a third solution, or *fixer,* dissolves the silver salt which has not been affected by light. In these three solutions, a "negative" picture is made. The white objects look black, the blacks are clear.

TAKING PICTURES THROUGH A MICROSCOPE

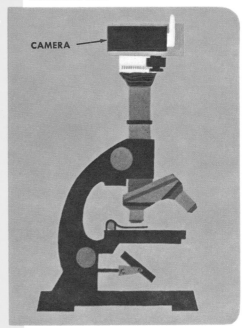

CAMERA

1 Place a microscopic slide under the objective on the stage of the microscope. Direct as much light as possible upon the specimen to be photographed.
2 Using electricians' tape, seal the lens opening of the camera directly over the eyepiece of the microscope.
3 Set the range finder on infinity. While taking the picture be careful not to jar the instruments.
4 Microphotography takes patience, experience, and a knowledge of general photography.

Prints: Light must pass through the negative to shine on paper coated with silver salt in the same manner as the film. Again a latent image is formed, which is then developed and fixed. The black objects now look white, as in the original, and the clear areas, where the light penetrates and hits the paper, are dark. If the negative is placed directly against the printing paper, the process is called *contact printing.* This is used for much amateur photography. Enlargements are made by projecting the light through the negative onto the printing paper some distance away.

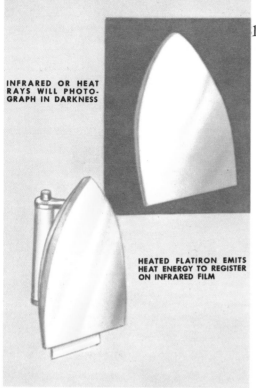

INFRARED OR HEAT RAYS WILL PHOTO-GRAPH IN DARKNESS

HEATED FLATIRON EMITS HEAT ENERGY TO REGISTER ON INFRARED FILM

VARIATIONS IN THE PHOTOGRAPHIC PROCESS

Art: By special lighting, light filters, camera lenses, exposure times, developing and printing techniques, a great many different effects can be created in photography. The subject matter may be so emphasized that artistic relationships and interesting compositional arrangements are achieved.

Photoengraving: A negative is made by taking a picture of a drawing or photograph. An image is produced on a coated metal plate, which is then etched by acid, the acid affecting the parts of the plate unaffected by light in the PRINTING process. When inked and printed, the etched-away areas are the light areas.

Photomicrography involves taking pictures of the images produced by a microscope.

Astronomical photography uses lenses of large diameter and long exposure times to capture the faint light from distant stars.

Underwater photography requires special water-and-pressure-proof cameras and special lighting for depths below twenty feet.

Spectrography is photography using infrared, ultraviolet, and X-ray films which have been sensitized to wave lengths shorter or longer than those of the visible spectrum.

High-speed photography employs a very bright flash, powered electronically, extremely short exposure times, and very sensitive "fast" film. Such rapidly moving objects as revolving wheels and the beating of insect wings can be photographed at high speed, then slowed down for viewing.

Aerial photography uses multiple lenses and high-speed shutters to take pictures of the ground for map making.

PHOTOGRAPHIC THEORY

In ordinary negative processing, the most common developers are *hydroquinone* and *monomethylparaminophenol* (trade names Elon, Metol). Developers are able to distinguish between the exposed and unexposed silver halide and convert the exposed halide to silver. Fixing solutions of *sodium* or *ammonium thiosulfate* (hypo and ammonium hypo) then dissolve out the unchanged silver halide.

It is possible to treat the film in the camera so that the final result is a positive instead of a negative. This is called *photographic reversal* and is used in some motion picture and color photography. Here the film is placed first in the developer, then in a solution of *potassium dichromate* acidified with sulfuric acid, which will dissolve the developed negative silver image, but not affect the undeveloped silver halide. After exposure to light, a positive image is produced from the remaining silver halide by developing it a second time. Thus the same film that was in the camera becomes the positive. In MOTION PICTURES, light shines through the moving positive film to reproduce the original scene—enlarged—on a screen.

Color photography involves the use of a special film containing three separate layers which record the red, blue, and green wave lengths of the visible spectrum. Because all colors can be made of mixtures of red, blue, and green, they are called *primary* colors. Color film can be developed by the reversal process, producing positive transparencies which are viewed by projection. Another kind of color film is developed so that the negative shows the opposite color values; red looks blue-green, blue looks yellow, green looks magenta. The printing process reproduces the original colors.   H. W. M.

SEE ALSO: LENS, MAN-MADE; OCEANOGRAPHY; PHOTOCHEMISTRY; PHOTOMETER; SPECTROSCOPE; TELESCOPE; X-RAY

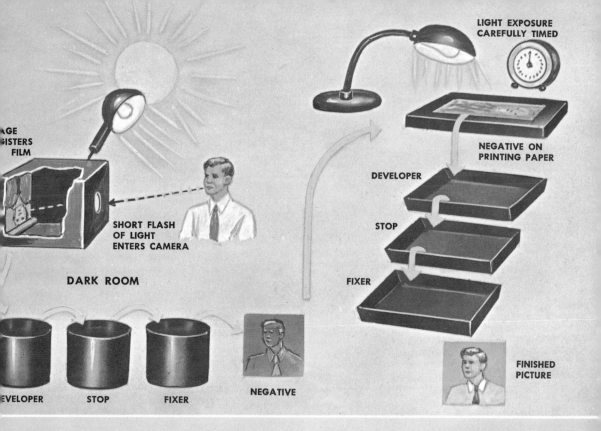

LIGHT EXPOSURE
CAREFULLY TIMED

IMAGE
REGISTERS
FILM

NEGATIVE ON
PRINTING PAPER

SHORT FLASH
OF LIGHT
ENTERS CAMERA

DEVELOPER

STOP

FIXER

DARK ROOM

DEVELOPER   STOP   FIXER

NEGATIVE

FINISHED
PICTURE

For still camera
A. Improper setting
   for high speed

B. Proper setting
   for high speed

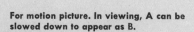

For motion picture. In viewing, A can be
slowed down to appear as B.

TRANSPARENT
COLOR SLIDE

RED

PRIMARY COLORS
PRODUCE COLOR
IMAGE

BLUE

YELLOW

X-RAY PHOTOGRAPH OF A JEEP

Marvin English

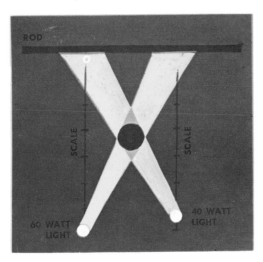

ROD

SCALE

SCALE

60 WATT LIGHT

40 WATT LIGHT

The shadow photometer requires the movement of light source until shadows are equally illuminated to compare their illuminating power

Photometer (foh-TOHM-eh-ter) The photometer is an OPTICAL INSTRUMENT used for measuring the intensity of a light source, such as a light bulb. The eye is not capable of directly comparing two light sources, but it can compare the brightness of two similar surfaces. If the color of the two surfaces is the same, the eye can detect quite small differences in brightness.

Probably the best known device for measuring the intensity of a luminous source is the *Bunsen photometer*. This device actually compares the illumination from the source of unknown intensity to one which has a known CANDLE POWER output.

Difficulty arises if the eye tries to make a comparison between two sources of different color. Lamps of different color may be compared by using a *flicker photometer*. This device enables the observer to view one side of the screen and then the other in relatively rapid succession. A frequency will be found where the flicker due to color difference will disappear and the color seemingly blends into a single hue. The flicker due to illumination will still appear, however. If the screen is moved, a position can be found where this flicker will also disappear. The illumination can be calculated, using an equation. A rotating prism is used to view both sides of the screen alternately. A. E. L.
SEE ALSO: COLOR, LIGHT

Photon (FOH-tahn) A photon is the elementary bundle or packet of electromagnetic energy absorbed or emitted by an atom or a molecule. Electromagnetic energy travels as a set of waves. But the emission or absorption of the electromagnetic energy occurs only in units called *quanta*. A quantum of energy is the energy carried by a single photon.

When an atom loses energy by passing from one state to another, it must satisfy the principle of conservation of energy. The energy lost is taken up by some other atom or given off in some form of radiation.

Niels Bohr, a Danish physicist, adopted the *energy packet* idea from Max Planck, a professor at the University of Berlin. There were certain phenomena, such as the photoelectric effect, which indicated that light did not always behave as a wave. The packet theory states that energy can be emitted or absorbed only in small but definite amounts, called quanta or photons. A. E. L.
SEE ALSO: PHOTOELECTRICITY, QUANTUM THEORY

Photosphere (FOH-tuh-sfihr) Photosphere is the name given to that part of the SUN which is seen by the naked eye. It seems to be a surface, but is actually a huge layer of GAS about five hundred miles deep. It appears brilliant white, becoming brighter toward the center.

The brighter parts of the sun are distinctly *granular* in shape because of millions of granules constantly moving at such a rapid rate that their form is changed every half minute or so. Along the edges are seen larger irregular areas called *faculae,* heated gases rising into the atmosphere.

The gases of the photosphere are glowing constantly and reach a temperature close to 6000° C. Because they are burning so brightly, they seem to be the actual surface of the sun. It is in the photosphere that deep areas called *sunspots* develop. D. E. Z.

PHOTOSYNTHESIS

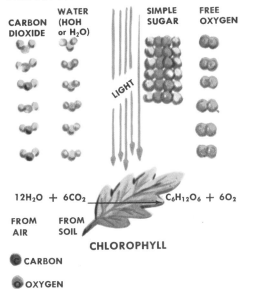

CARBON DIOXIDE | WATER (HOH or H_2O) | LIGHT | SIMPLE SUGAR | FREE OXYGEN

$$12H_2O + 6CO_2 \longrightarrow C_6H_{12}O_6 + 6O_2$$

FROM AIR   FROM SOIL

CHLOROPHYLL

- CARBON
- OXYGEN
- HYDROGEN

Photosynthesis (foh-toe-SIN-thuh-sis) A plant is like a little factory. It will take several things, put them together with the help of light, and end up with something new. Making food by plants is called photosynthesis. This word can be broken into two words: *photo* meaning "light" and *synthesis* meaning "put together." Only green plants can take water from the soil, carbon dioxide from the air, and with the help of light, make sugar. Since plants do not use all of the oxygen for food-making, it is given off. Animals need plants for food and oxygen.

Photosynthesis is a chemical change which occurs in all green cells. Only green plants are able to take the sun's energy and put it into a stored form for use by other plants and animals. Scientists know most of the materials and steps involved in this wonderful process yet are still unable to accomplish this in the laboratory. There is a secret about green plant cells that man has not discovered as yet. The equation for photosynthesis is as follows:

$$12H_2O + 6CO_2 + \text{light}$$
$$\rightarrow C_6H_{12}O_6 + 6O_2 + 6H_2O$$

water + carbon dioxide → sugar + oxygen + water

The electromagnetic energy contained in sunlight is converted by photosynthesis to chemical energy stored in the sugar mole-

✳ THINGS TO DO

DO LEAVES MAKE FOOD?

1   Remove a leaf from a plant that has been in the sunlight for several hours.

2   Partly submerge a small container of alcohol into boiling water. Alcohol should not be heated directly over a flame. When the alcohol is boiling put the leaf into it.

3   The chlorophyll will be removed. When the leaf is white spread it on the surface of a dish.

4   Put several drops of iodine on the leaf. If starch (food) is present, it will become a deep blue.

cule. The sugar can then be converted into starch and stored.

The rate of photosynthesis is dependent upon several conditions. A greater amount of water available will increase the rate of photosynthesis. Food-making occurs best in a temperature range from 68° to 110° Fahrenheit. The amount of carbon dioxide present in the air is important. The air contains one-half per cent of carbon dioxide and a plant can use up to five per cent concentration, therefore this is a limiting factor. The amount and nature of the light controls photosynthesis. Food production is most active in about one-tenth of full sunlight. Too much light tends to destroy some of the products of photosynthesis.

Food manufactured in the leaves or other green parts of a plant is transported to various parts and stored for future use. Most annual plants store food in their seeds. Biennials and perennials also store food in their roots, stems, and leaves.   H. J. C.

SEE ALSO: BALANCE OF NATURE, CARBON CYCLE, LEAVES, PLANT

Phototropism see Tropism

Phylogeny (fi-LOJ-eh-neye) Phylogeny is the history of the development, or EVOLUTION, of a species, family, or larger group of animals or plants from the simplest form to the most complex.

SEE: ANIMALS, CLASSIFICATION OF; EVOLUTION OF MAN; PLANTS, CLASSIFICATION OF

Physical states and changes Physical states and changes involve the study of matter. All MATTER takes up space and has weight. All matter has three physical states: solid, liquid and gas. Heat, or the lack of heat, changes matter from one state to another. Water can exist in three different states. Water in the form of ice in a refrigerator is in its solid physical state. Water coming from a faucet is in its liquid physical state. Water boiling in a tea pot turns to steam, its gaseous physical state. Through all these physical changes, the substance itself—water—remains the same.

Matter can neither be created nor destroyed by ordinary means. The physical states of matter can be changed or matter can be combined with other forms of matter to make new substances. When matter changes its physical state, the scientist refers to it as a *physical change*. When kinds of matter combine with one another to form a new material, the scientist refers to it as a *chemical change.*

All matter, solid, liquid or gas, is alike in two ways. A block of wood, a glass of water, or air, all occupy space. Air, and other gases, may appear not to take up space. However, if a drinking glass is turned over and pressed down in a bowl of water, water will enter the glass only part way because the air in the glass does occupy space. The space occupied by a material is called its *volume.* All material has weight. Solids, such as a brick, or liquids, such as water in a bucket, obviously have weight. That air has weight is shown by the difference in weights of a deflated and an inflated basketball.

Solids are different from liquids and gases

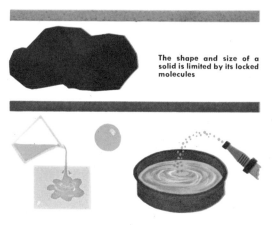

The shape and size of a solid is limited by its locked molecules

The shape of liquid can be spherical if outside forces do not interfere, otherwise it will take the form of the container it occupies

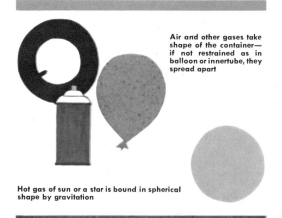

Air and other gases take shape of the container— if not restrained as in balloon or innertube, they spread apart

Hot gas of sun or a star is bound in spherical shape by gravitation

in two ways. Solids have the characteristics of keeping a definite shape and having a definite volume. A pencil or a brick do not change shape by themselves, nor do they change the amount of space they occupy.

Liquids, like solids, take up a given amount of volume. A glass of milk occupies a certain amount of space, but if the milk is poured into a pan, it takes the shape of the pan. A liquid, not having a shape of its own, takes the shape of the container it fills. Therefore, a liquid has volume, but no constant shape.

Gas has no form of its own. Air in a covered drinking glass takes the shape of the glass. A gas does not occupy a definite amount of space. Air in a bottle, if uncorked, spreads into the room. A gas, then, is matter in a state in which it has no definite shape nor volume. Gases will expand to fill any container.

Very often matter in one state is com-

Special apparatus, such as a molecular still (left), perform operations in molecular research. Substances to be irradiated are placed inside a nuclear radiation chamber (right) with a highly radioactive sample. The chamber is an aid to physicists in their study of radiation

bined with matter in another state. Mixing sugar into lemonade combines a liquid material with a solid material. In a solution these things happen. First, the liquid in a solution is clear and free of particles. Secondly, the dissolved material can pass through the finest of filters which allows the liquid to pass. The dissolved material cannot be filtered out. Thirdly, the dissolved material spreads evenly throughout the solution medium.

Some solid materials added to a liquid do not go into solution, but are suspended in the liquid. Starch and water when combined do not form a solution. Rather, a suspension of the starch particles occurs.

Changes from one physical state to another can occur by heating or by taking away heat. When a solid is heated enough, it changes to a liquid. For example, a piece of aluminum melts when heated to 1220° F. Liquids, when heated enough, change to gases. Water changes to steam at 212° F. Liquids may also evaporate at low temperatures. For example, water evaporates from wet clothes hanging on a line.

Cooling the materials of each state of matter reverses the physical changes. Gas will turn to a liquid, and liquid, when cooled enough, will become a solid.   P. F. D.
SEE ALSO: ATOM, CHEMICAL CHANGE, CHEMISTRY, EVAPORATION, GAS, HEAT, LIQUID, MOLECULAR THEORY, PHYSICS, SOLID, SOLUBLE, SOLUTION

Physics (FIZZ-icks) Physics is the science dealing with matter and energy. MATTER is anything which occupies space and has weight. ENERGY is the ability to do work. There are many kinds of energy such as light, sound, electrical, heat, and mechanical energy. Physics is an exact science which requires careful measurement of many quantities.

MATHEMATICS is an important tool in the study of physics. The science is concerned with the natural laws which govern the environment of man and theories about the behavior of matter. The pull of GRAVITY which causes weight is an illustration of the Universal Law of Gravitation, an important law in physics. Theories may change when experiments give new evidence about the nature of matter. Atomic theory illustrates how a theory may be modified. At first, atoms of matter were thought to contain only a few particles. Now atomic theory must account for over twenty different particles which have been discovered.

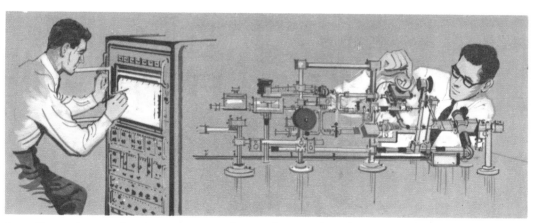

Recording and measuring instruments are designed to study substances under varied conditions. Specialized instruments and equipment enable the physicist to determine the nature of matter

Physics usually covers the subjects of mechanics, heat, sound, light, magnetism, electricity, and modern physics. MECHANICS involves a broad area of knowledge, especially the topics of motion, force, energy, solids, liquids, and gases. Mechanics includes a study of many fundamental quantities and their measurement. These include the concepts of mass, weight, density, and volume. Some of these are *vector quantities* which have not only numerical value but a definite direction. Weight, the pull of gravity on an object, is directed toward the earth and illustrates a vector quantity. MASS refers to the amount of matter in an object and is not a VECTOR, or directional, quantity. Mass would not change even if gravity changed. Studies of potential and kinetic energy are part of mechanics. *Potential* energy is stored-up energy, such as water in a dam. The energy becomes *kinetic* when the water flows over the dam to run a HYDROELECTRIC POWER plant.

HEAT, another form of energy, includes study of its nature and behavior. The quantity of heat a body contains is measured in calories or British Thermal Units. Temperature indicates the intensity of heat but not its quantity. In terms of the MOLECULAR THEORY of heat, temperature is the average kinetic energy of the molecules of matter, but the quantity of heat is the total kinetic energy. Studies of RADIATION, conduction, and convection are included as methods of heat transfer.

The physics of SOUND concerns how sounds are produced and transmitted. Energy is required to make objects vibrate and send out sound waves. Sound waves are longitudinal, and in air, air particles vibrate back and forth in the same direction as the sound wave travels. The study of sound includes the special properties of musical sounds—pitch, loudness, and quality.

LIGHT as a form of energy requires two theories to fully explain its behavior. The *wave theory* of light holds for light as a transverse wave motion, an electromagnetic wave, which travels with a velocity of 186,-000 miles per second. The *quantum theory* explains how atoms absorb and emit light energy. The energy is given off or taken up in small bundles rather than in a continuous manner.

ELECTRICITY is another broad area of physics. It includes a study of electric charges, magnetism, and current electricity. Electricity is used in many electrical devices such as motors, generators, batteries, transformers, and electronic equipment.

Rapid advances in physics in recent decades have occurred in atomic and nuclear physics. This area includes electrical discharge in gases, electromagnetic and spectral series, and X-rays. Research in NUCLEAR ENERGY, radioactivity, and atomic disintegration has brought dramatic results. The atomic bomb demonstrated how tremendous amounts of energy may be released when a small amount of matter is converted into energy.

There are also specialized areas in physics dealing with physical properties of living matter. BIOPHYSICS is the study of living things using the methods and tools of physics. The theories and facts of physics are so basic they are involved in almost every other science. L. M.

WILLIAM HARVEY   ISAAC NEWTON   BENJAMIN FRANKLIN   ANTOINE LAVOISIER

Physiology Physiology is the study of how living structures work. For example, in order to keep alive, all living things get ENERGY from food. They grow and reproduce new living forms just like themselves. They react to the world around them, and try to adjust to changes. As plant and animal life becomes larger and more complicated, the different parts of a body must be coordinated so they work together. Physiology studies these processes.

Because the scientist must first understand how a thing is made, before he can understand how it works, a physiologist studies the various parts of the living structure—its ANATOMY. He studies the functioning of the structure. He may study how an individual NERVE CELL sends an impulse, how the muscles of the body move together, or why a plant produces flowers at certain times of the year. But to have an understanding of the building materials of living things and the natural laws governing them, a physiologist must also know the basic PHYSICS and CHEMISTRY of the non-living world, as well as the biophysics and biochemistry of living structures.

For example a boy or girl eats food and grows bigger. The physiologist checks digestion, circulation, elimination, metabolism, respiration, and excretion to find out what is happening to the food inside the person's body.

DIGESTION

When food enters the mouth, it is chewed by the teeth into small pieces, mixed with saliva produced by the salivary glands, and passed down the esophagus into the stomach. Once in the stomach, an acid mixture of enzymes begins the digestion of the food

THREE CENTURIES OF DISCOVERY IN PHYSIOLOGY AND IN FIELDS THAT HELP IT

1600 Fabricius (Italy) studies human anatomy and writes book *About Venous Valves;* (teacher of Harvey)

1628 William Harvey (England) publishes *Motion of the Heart and Blood*

1650 Robert Boyle (Ireland-England) invents air pumps and studies lung-pressure

1656 Thomas Wharton (England) is first to study gland physiology

1661 Malpighi (Italy) describes mechanism of breathing; later studies kidney secretion

1670 Borelli (Italy) studies the physics of animal movement

1687 Isaac Newton (England) publishes his *Principles* that lay the foundation for all exact sciences

1688 Leeuwenhoek (Holland) discovers capillaries with his microscope

1733 Stephen Hales (England) writes about blood pressure

1752 Benjamin Franklin (U.S.A.) shows that lightning is electricity; shows some electrostatic actions on the body

1774 Joseph Priestley (England) discovers oxygen

1777 Spallanzani (Italy) studies how foods digest —in test tubes

1780 Antoine Lavoisier (France) refines Priestley's ideas about air and oxygen; and shows similarity of burning and breathing

by chemical action, and the mechanical churning of the muscular stomach wall aids in this digestion. When the food has been broken down into a thick, soupy liquid, it passes through an opening into the small intestine a little at a time. In the small intestine the most important part of digestion begins. First, the acid solution is made slightly alkaline. Separate ENZYMES, which are specific in their action, are secreted by the cells of the intestinal wall and pancreas. These enzymes break down starches into sugar, fats into glycerol and fatty acids, proteins into amino acids. The liver forms a substance to break fat into small droplets. Secretions from pancreas and liver reach the small intestine through ducts. The coordination of all this enzyme activity is controlled by hormones circulating in the blood.

CIRCULATION

When all the large molecules of food have been reduced to small molecules by digestion, the particular substances that the body needs to build new tissue are available. First, however, these small molecules must be taken inside the cells throughout all parts of the body, for it is within each small cell that new tissue is made. From the digestive tract the blood receives the small molecules that can be used as building blocks for new tissue, and transports them through the body. They travel through the network of blood and lymph vessels, and are propelled by the pumping action of the heart.

ELIMINATION

The part of the food that cannot be used by the body passes from the small intestine into the large intestine and rectum. It is discarded as feces after such important substances as water and vitamin K have been restored to the body.

METABOLISM

Once the small molecular building blocks are brought within the cells of the body, the formation of new tissue begins. Hormones circulating through the blood regulate the amount and kind of tissue formation and the places in the body where new tissue will be formed. The chromatin material in the nucleus of each cell provides the pattern of tissue formation and the enzymes that make it possible.

When a person is little, the growth hormone of the PITUITARY gland stimulates a high rate of protein synthesis and, conse-

quently, rapid growth. As he reaches PUBERTY, the long bones of the body and the masses of muscle tissue are conspicuous areas of growth. When he becomes an adult, the amount of new tissue formed is normally only enough to keep pace with the damage produced during the wear and tear of living.

RESPIRATION

In order to make new tissue, there must be energy provided by the body to link together the small building blocks into those particular large molecules needed by the body. There are definite chemical reactions that take place in the cell and provide this energy. These reactions require oxygen, which is obtained from the air by respiration. To bring oxygen to the cell, the boy's lungs, aided by the muscular action of the diaphragm and the chest muscles, breathe in air. Once again, it is the pumping action of the heart that drives the oxygen-bearing blood through the body to reach each individual cell. The respiratory muscles are controlled by the brain, and function automatically without the boy's being consciously aware of doing this work. Indeed, many parts of the body function automatically in this way, and free large areas of the brain for observing and evaluating the outside world.

EXCRETION

The creation of energy and the synthesis of new tissue results in wastes that must be removed from the body. If these wastes remain in the body, they poison it. The liver detoxicates nitrogenous wastes, and these products are then carried by the blood stream to the kidney for removal as urine. The water balance of the body is a crucial physiological necessity, and this balance is maintained by the functioning of the kidney and supervised by endocrine hormones.

ADAPTATION

The delicate physiological balance (*homeostasis*) needed by the body for it to function properly is a never-ending study. As the biochemical reactions proceed within the body—the processes of digestion, respiration, muscular activity, or secretion of hormones—new products accumulate, and old reserves of raw material are used up. There are continuous changes going on inside the body, and adjustments must be made continuously to preserve the conditions neces-

LUIGI GALVANI   CHARLES DARWIN   LOUIS PASTEUR   MARIE CURIE

sary for life. These adaptations are, for the most part, set into motion by the nervous system and the endocrine secretions.

Outside the body, changes are also influencing the physiology. If the aroma of food reaches the hungry boy's nostrils, he gets ready to eat. If he is riding his bicycle and loses his balance around a curve in the road, the nervous system and muscles cooperate to keep him from falling and injuring himself. If it suddenly becomes cold, the nervous system alerts the boy to put on warmer clothing. If infectious germs enter the body, the defenses of inflammation, reaction, and *phagocytosis* go to work.

These physiological processes proceed in every living organism, whether it is a one-celled body or a complex many-celled body. The simpler the organism, of course, the less elaborate the mechanisms necessary to sustain life.

For example, a one-celled alga plant is able to take in food and release wastes by means of its semipermeable cell membrane. Simple diffusion circulates the particles within the cell. In the earthworm there are many cells, and although the animal is relatively small in size, it still requires a special network of tissues to distribute nourishment and remove wastes. The human body has evolved complex organ systems to insure nutrition, waste removal, and physiological harmony.

Indeed, all the systems involved in physiology are so complex that research proceeds continually to discover the secrets of life that still elude man's understanding.   B. B. G.

SEE ALSO: ADAPTATION, CIRCULATORY SYSTEM, DIGESTIVE SYSTEM, ENDOCRINE GLANDS, EXCRETORY SYSTEM, HISTOLOGY, HOMEOSTASIS, METABOLISM, MUSCLE SYSTEM, NERVOUS SYSTEM, NUTRITION, REPRODUCTIVE SYSTEMS, RESPIRATORY SYSTEM, SENSE ORGANS, STRESS

1791 Luigi Galvani (Italy) discovers the effect of electricity on muscles

1796 Edward Jenner (England) successfully uses first vaccine and immunizes people against smallpox

1810 Franz Gall (Germany) offers first theory of brain action: led to now discredited phrenology

1821 Magendie (France) experiments on nerves acting on muscles and glands

1833 Wm. Beaumont (U.S.A.) army surgeon works with patient who has an opening to the stomach and advances physiological ideas about digestion

1839 Schleiden and Schwann (German biologists) offer evidence that cells are basic life units

1846 Long and Morton (U.S.A.) use first safe anesthetic, ether

1857 Claude Bernard (France) as a young student physiologist discovers how animal starch (glycogen) works in the liver and the muscles

1858 Charles Darwin and Alfred Wallace (England) advance the idea of organic evolution; in 1859, *Origin of Species* is published

1868 Lister (England) follows Pasteur's ideas about bacteria causing diseases; and introduces antiseptic surgery—later to be replaced by aseptic surgery

1876 Louis Pasteur (France) writes about fermentation and develops finished evidence that germs cause certain diseases

1882 Koch (Germany) identifies the germs causing tuberculosis; works out new methods of bacterial experimentation

1895 William Roentgen (Germany) discovers X-rays

1899 Pierre and Marie Curie (France) discover radium

Auguste and Jean Piccard

Piccard, Auguste (1884-1962) Auguste Piccard was the twin brother of Jean Piccard. He was a Swiss physicist who foresaw SPACE TRAVEL by means of rockets. In 1932 he prepared the way for interplanetary travel by ascending 53,152 feet into the stratosphere in an airtight gondola suspended beneath a BALLOON.

In 1953 he broke another record, this time by descending 10,330 feet under the sea in a steel sphere attached to tanks filled with gasoline. These tanks were pulled down into the water by weights controlled by electromagnetic current. When the current was turned off, the tanks brought the sphere to the surface of the water.

Piccard was born in Basle, Switzerland, in 1884. He was graduated as a mechanical engineer from the University of Basle and the Institute of Technology at Zürich. D. H. J.
SEE ALSO: BATHYSPHERE AND BATHYSCAPHE, OCEANOGRAPHY

Piccard, Jacques see Bathysphere and bathyscaphe

Piccard, Jean (1884-1963) Jean Piccard was a Swiss physicist who, in 1934, ascended 57,549 feet into the stratosphere at Dearborn, Michigan. Three years later he tested the possibility of using a number of large balloons to carry an open gondola into the atmosphere. The one hundred balloons he used were six feet in diameter.

Unlike his brother Auguste, Jean came to the United States in 1916 where he

taught at the University of Chicago for three years. Returning to his native Switzerland, he taught at the University of Lausanne until 1926 when he returned to the United States to accept a post as instructor at the Massachusetts Institute of Technology. In 1931 he became a citizen of the United States, and five years later he joined the faculty of the University of Minnesota. Jean Piccard was born and educated in Switzerland.   D. H. J.

Pickerel see Pike

Pickle see Cucumber

Pickling Pickling (in metallurgy) is the removal, by the use of acids, of the scale, or OXIDE layer, which forms when metals are heated for rolling or forging. Pickling (in food processing) is preservation with BRINE.
SEE: METAL

Picric acid see Carbolic acid

Piezoelectric effect When crystals of certain materials are subjected to a mechanical STRESS, they generate electromotive force. If these crystals are subjected to an alternating electrical stress, they vibrate. The relationship between the mechanical and electrical properties of the CRYSTAL is the piezoelectric effect.

Quartz, rochelle salts, and tourmaline all exhibit the piezoelectric effect. Quartz crystals are used to control the frequency output of transmitters or any other equipment where exact frequency control is required. Rochelle salts are used in microphones; tourmaline may be used in pressure gauges.
                                        D. A. B.

SEE ALSO: PHOTOELECTRICITY

The stress produced by a hammer hitting a crystal may produce enough electricity to light a small bulb

Some of the types of hogs raised for meat in the United States

Common pigeon, or rock dove

Pig The pig family includes both wild and domestic hogs. The word *pig* is usually used to refer to a baby hog. The mother hog is called a *sow* and the father, a *boar*. Hogs are also called *swine*. Farmers raise large quantities of hogs mainly for their tasty meat.

Pigs have a round, heavy body, short legs, and a short tail. Their feet have an even number of hoofed toes. Short bristles grow from their thick skin. Their tough snouts are used for lifting, pushing and digging. Wild pigs are especially strong and fierce. Pigs, or their relative, the PECCARY, are found in almost all temperate areas except Australia. Pigs will eat almost anything.

Hogs were tamed by man as early as the STONE AGE. They may be found on farms in all parts of the world. Man has learned to use almost every part of the hog's body. He eats its flesh (bacon, ham, pork, sausage, spareribs) as well as its stomach, kidneys, liver, ears, brain, skin, snout and jowls. Its fat is rendered (extracting by melting) for lard, skin is tanned for leather, and bristles are used for brushes.

There are many different breeds of hogs. Selective breeding has developed one that produces a maximum of lean meat and a minimum of fat (lard).

Pigs are good breeders. A sow may have two or three litters a year. Each litter may include eight to 25 or more little pigs. A sow may have as many as 28 nipples, more than any other animal. A piglet grows to marketable size, about 200 pounds, in about six months.   D. J. A.

SEE ALSO: HOOF, UNGULATA

Pig iron see Iron

Pigeon At one time, there were supposed to be more pigeons on earth than any other type of bird. Pioneers told stories of how millions of migrating pigeons would darken the sky for hours and the noise of their approach could be heard for miles. The weight of so many pigeons roosting together would break trees and branches throughout the forests. Although pigeons are still very common, their numbers have been greatly reduced. The *passenger* pigeon is extinct, but other varieties are very frequently seen in cities and rural areas throughout the world.

Pigeons are about fifteen to eighteen inches long. DOVES are considered to be a smaller type of pigeon. Pigeon colors range from dull gray or brown to beautiful combinations of white, green, purple, orange, and magenta. Many have irridescent green and violet on their heads and necks.

It is believed that pigeons mate for life. Several times a year, a few white eggs are laid in a carelessly-made nest. Young pigeons, or *squabs,* are fed a secretion of regurgitated food from their parent's crop. This is called "pigeon milk." Mature pigeons eat small nuts, seeds, and grain. They can be easily trained to come for food, as is demonstrated by the flocks of pigeons that surround popcorn and peanut machines.

This bird is frequently raised as poultry and has long been used for racing and carrying messages. The *homing* pigeon is best suited for the latter activity. This is a type of pigeon developed through crossbreeding of several varieties to obtain a bird with speed and flight endurance.   J. A. D.

SEE ALSO: FOWL

WHAT HAPPENS WHEN TWO OR MORE PIGMENTS ARE MIXED TOGETHER?

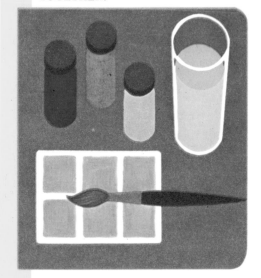

1 Water colors or oil paints may be used for this experiment. The object is to mix two different colors to determine the color of the resulting mixture.

2 Mix a small amount of yellow pigment to the same amount of blue pigment. What color is it now?

3 Try a combination of red and blue pigments, then red and yellow. Save each mixture.

4 Blend a small quantity of two of these together to obtain still another color. Record the results each time and draw conclusions.

5 Does there seem to be a pattern to pigment combinations? You will find that, unlike combining colored lights, pigment colors are subtracted by others. The color that is left is the one that is transmitted to your eyes.

Pigment Pigment is the substance which gives color to paint, to leaves, to skin, and to hair. Mineral pigment is used as a fine powder and can be mixed with liquids to form PAINT (the pigment does not dissolve in the liquid). Shellacs and varnishes show the surface beneath them because they do not contain pigment. Two common paint pigments are *white lead* and *zinc oxide*.

The pigment in the deeper epidermal layers of the SKIN that makes the difference in color in various races is called *melanin*. It is also the pigment of suntan.

Pigments gain their colors only by reflecting parts of the light shining on them. Transparent colors, however, gain their color by allowing the passage of only certain wavelengths of LIGHT.   E. M. N.
SEE ALSO: ALBINO, COLOR

Pika see Rabbit

Pike Pike is a blue or greenish-gray fish that lives in lakes and streams. It is called *jack pike* or *northern pike*. A pike usually weighs from two to ten pounds, but fishermen have caught some that weigh over forty-six pounds and are over four feet long. The walleyed pike is really a PERCH.

Pike eat other fish, catching them with sudden darts. They eat one-fifth of their weight each day. Pike are often used for food and they are delicious-tasting fish. They resemble pickerel but are larger and have scales only on the sides of their heads.

The pike breeds in spring, with the male and female swimming side by side, dropping and fertilizing over 100,000 eggs among weeds. Each egg is one-third inch long. Eggs hatch by themselves in two or three weeks. In five months the fish have grown to six inches long. In two years they are from fourteen to seventeen inches long. The adult fish have whitish or yellowish spots. P. G. B.
SEE ALSO: PISCES

Pile, atomic see Accelerators, Nuclear reactors, Nuclear science

Pilot see Aviation

Northern pike
Chicago Natural History Museum

American Forest Products Industries, Inc.

Some pines important for lumber: western white pine (left), lodgepole pine (center) and ponderosa pine (right)

Pilot fish Pilot fish follow ships and sharks in tropical and subtropical seas. These narrow, bluish fish, with dark-blue or purple bands across their backs grow to about 12 inches.

Pilot fish

Pine Pines are trees that always stay green. The pine family is easily recognized by its needle-like leaves and woody cones. The seeds are in the pine cones. When pine trees grow in great forests and are shaded, the trunks of the trees are usually clear of branches, except at the top where they can get sun. When pine trees are in the open, the branches may cover the whole trunk, almost to the ground. Sometimes the branches extend upward and outward and form flat or other shaped tops. Where pine trees are exposed to severe winds and cold, they grow in many strange shapes, with the branches and trunks twisted and bent. An example of this type is the *Torrey* pine, found along the southern California coast.

There are about ninety species of pines. They are widely distributed in Europe, Asia, and the Western Hemisphere. About one-third of all pines are native to North America. Pines are found mainly in temperate zones but extend well into the tropics and the Arctic. These hardy trees form great forests under conditions too severe for broadleaf trees to grow. They grow on steep mountains, in poor soil, in cold areas, and in swampy regions. Pine forests are storehouses for lumber and other wood products, such as paper pulp, fuel, and turpentine. They protect the soil from erosion,

The winged seeds of the white pine cone are scattered by the wind

Courtesy Society For Visual Education, Inc.

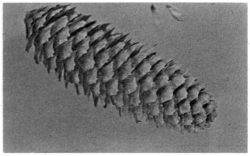

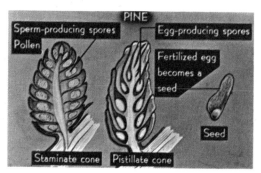

Courtesy Society For Visual Education, Inc.

Pine trees have male, or pollen-producing (staminate), cones, and female, or seed-producing (pistillate), cones

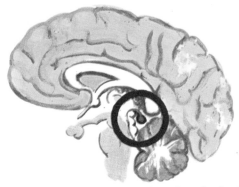

Location of the pineal gland within the brain

conserve rainfall and snowfall, and prevent serious flooding. Pine forests provide cover and feed for wild-life, and some species are among the most valuable of all lumber trees. Pines are highly prized by man and are praised in song, literature, and poetry. In addition they serve as the much loved Christmas tree.

Pines are classified by their wood, as white, or soft, hard or yellow. The wood of *white* pines is generally light in color and weight, and of soft, even texture. It is easily worked and does not splinter. It is used for interior trim and furniture, and where a smooth finish is needed and desirable. The wood of *yellow* pines contains a large amount of RESIN, which shows as yellow streaks when the wood is sawed across the grain. The resin makes the wood heavier and stronger that that of the white pine. It also makes it more difficult to work and to finish smoothly. Yellow pine is excellent for building heavy structures, such as bridges, and for other purposes where strength and durability are required.

The eastern and western white pines are both important lumber trees. These huge trees are used for furniture, doors and sashes, interior trim, patterns, boxes, and other purposes.

The *longleaf* pine of the southeastern United States is a huge tree of great commercial importance. It is the chief source of TURPENTINE and its strong, heavy wood is used for bridges, boxcars, and flooring. *Jackpine* is used almost exclusively for paper pulp and is usually second growth timber. The *loblolly* is found in the southern United States and is an important lumber tree. M. R. L.

SEE ALSO: FOREST PRODUCTS, LUMBER

Pineal gland The pineal gland is located in the lower central part of the BRAIN. It may be all that remains of a third eye that ancestors of VERTEBRATES (animals with backbones) once had. An ancient-type lizard in New Zealand (SPHENODON) has a light-sensitive place on its head above the pineal body. Scientists now know that the pineal is a light-sensitive gland that makes a hormone.

The pineal gland is rich in *serotonin,* a substance secreted by the nervous system. Recently a new hormone, *melatonin,* and an enzyme found only in the pineal were isolated. Research showed that the enzyme acted on serotonin to form melatonin, Melatonin acts on the sex glands to inhibit (stop) the sexual cycle.

Light controls the amount of hormone produced through the sympathetic nervous system. The concentration of melatonin shows a 24-hour rhythm, decreasing during the day and increasing at night. J. C. K.

SEE ALSO: NERVOUS SYSTEM

Pineapple The fruit of the pineapple looks like a giant pine cone. It is native to northern South America. It still grows wild in Brazil. Hawaii leads in the production of this fruit. The fruit may weigh from one to eighteen pounds. Its tough fruit wall is such a protection that it can be shipped to many countries without damage.

Pineapple plant and fruit

The pineapple is a tropical BIENNIAL in the monocotyledon group of flowering plants. The leaves, having very sharp points on the sides, form a rosette around a three-foot stem. The bloom is a bunch of small tightly packed flowers. This is topped by more leaves. The fruit that develops from this flower head is classified as *multiple,* having many ovaries and receptacles fused together. Since the fruit is usually seedless the plant must be propagated by other means. This is done by planting slips, suckers or the top cluster of leaves.

Besides using this plant's fruit, man also makes textile products from piña cloth woven from the white, strong, fibers found in the leaves.

Pineapple also refers to a plant family (*Bromeliaceae*) that includes SPANISH MOSS.
H. J. C.

Pinkeye see Conjunctivitis

Pinks Pinks are popular plants in the flower garden. There are many kinds of these charming garden plants. Some of the different kinds are the CARNA-TION, pink, baby's-breath, bouncing bet, and chickweed. Most pinks are hardy perennials. Members of the pink family have opposite leaves and swollen joints (nodes). The flowers are usually lovely and sometimes fragrant too. Pinks are easily raised in most garden soils.

Pinks properly belong to the genus *Dianthus,* but the name is used for many other plants such as helonias, PHLOX, spigelia, Limonium lobelia, and silene in genus *Lychnis*. Some of the pinks in genus *Dianthus* are the sweet William, which have dense, roundish flower clusters; the maiden pinks, which make turf-like mats and have small flowers; the grass pinks, which are low, fragrant, tufted plants.
M. R. L.

Pinna see Ear

Pinnate venation see Leaves

Sweet Williams, of the pink family

Pinworm Pinworms are parasitic organisms which live in the intestines of humans. They are widely distributed throughout the world in all age groups, but especially in children living in crowded conditions. The female pinworm is about one-fourth inch long and the male is smaller. The body has one pointed end.

The pregnant female lives in the lower intestine. It is either excreted or crawls out and lays eggs around the anus. Its movements produce intense itching. A coating on the eggs causes them to stick to undergarments, pajamas, skin or bedding. Eggs are transferred to the fingers when the infested area is scratched and on to food or directly into the mouth. The eggs hatch in the upper part of the intestine, the larvae travel down the intestine, attach there and mature.

The most effective prevention is to break the life cycle, by preventing scratching and keeping hands and clothing very clean. Physicians also administer drugs by mouth for five or six days to kill the worm. E. R. B.
SEE ALSO: NEMATHELMINTHES

Piranha see Tropical fish

Pinworm, enlarged several times

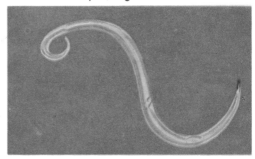

ALFRED B. NOBEL
1833–1896 •
Invented dynamite,
started Nobel Prizes

HIPPOCRATES
460–370? B.C •
"Father of Medicine"

MARIE CURIE
• 1867–1934
Discovered radium
and polonium

ENRICO FERMI
• 1901–1954
Produced first atomic pile and first
controlled nuclear chain reaction

THOMAS ALVA EDISON
1847–1931 •
Invented light bulb,
phonograph and mimeograph

NICOLAUS COPERNICUS
• 1473–1543
First astronomer to say that Earth
goes around the sun

LUTHER BURBANK
• 1849–1926
Invented new
varieties of plants

EDWARD JENNER
1749–1823 •
Discovered smallpox vaccine

CHARLES DARWIN
1809-1882 •
Conceived the Theory of Evolution
through Natural Selection

WILLIAM HARVEY
• 1578–1657
Discovered the circulation
of the blood

GEORGE WASHINGTON CARVER
1864–1943 •
Experimented with
practical botany

SAMUEL F. B. MORSE
• 1791–1872
Invented telegraph and Morse code

LOUIS PASTEUR
• 1822–1895
Invented pasteurization

BENJAMIN FRANKLIN
• 1706–1790
Invented lightning rod

GALILEO GALILEI
1564–1642 •
Discovered law of pendulum motion

CAROLUS LINNAEUS
• 1707–1778
Classified the plant
and animal kingdoms

SIGMUND FREUD
• 1856–1939
Started psychoanalysis

GREGOR JOHANN MENDEL
1822–1884 •
Discovered principles of heredity

BARON ERNEST RUTHERFORD
1871–1937 •
Contributed to knowledge of
radioactivity and atomic structure

GUGLIELMO MARCONI
• 1874–1937
Invented the wireless telegraph

LOUIS AGASSIZ
• 1807–1873
Investigated glacial motion
and marine life

MICHAEL FARADAY
1791–1867 •
Discovered electromagnetic induction

SIR ISAAC NEWTON
• 1642–1727
Discovered laws of light,
gravity, motion and color

ALBERT EINSTEIN
1879–1955 •
Conceived the Theory of Relativity

WILHELM KONRAD ROENTGEN
• 1845–1923
Discovered X-rays

ALEXANDER GRAHAM BELL
1847–1922 •
Invented
the telephone

JOSEPH LISTER
• 1827–1912
Started antiseptic surgery

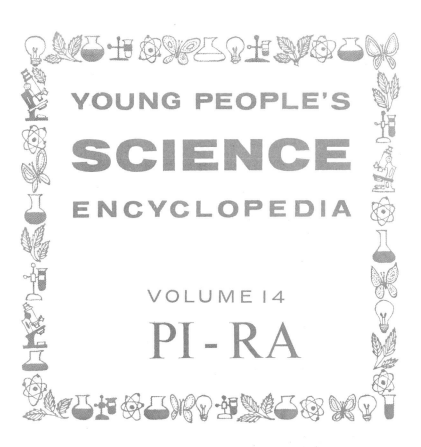

YOUNG PEOPLE'S

SCIENCE

ENCYCLOPEDIA

VOLUME 14

PI - RA

ALFRED B. NOBEL
1833–1896 •
Invented dynamite,
started Nobel Prizes

HIPPOCRATES
460–370? B.C
"Father of Medicine"

MARIE CURIE
• 1867–1934
Discovered radium
and polonium

ENRICO FERMI
• 1901–1954
Produced first atomic pile and first
controlled nuclear chain reaction

THOMAS ALVA EDISON
1847–1931 •
Invented light bulb,
phonograph and mimeograph

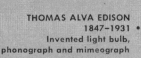

NICOLAUS COPERNICUS
• 1473–1543
First astronomer to say that Earth
goes around the sun

LUTHER BURBANK
• 1849–1926
Invented new
varieties of plants

EDWARD JENNER
1749–1823 •
Discovered smallpox vaccine

CHARLES DARWIN
1809-1882 •
Conceived the Theory of Evolution
through Natural Selection

WILLIAM HARVEY
• 1578–1657
Discovered the circulation
of the blood

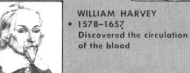

GEORGE WASHINGTON CARVER
1864–1943 •
Experimented with
practical botany

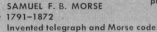

SAMUEL F. B. MORSE
• 1791–1872
Invented telegraph and Morse code

LOUIS PASTEUR
• 1822–1895
Invented pasteurization

BENJAMIN FRANKLIN
• 1706–1790
Invented lightning rod

GALILEO GALILEI
1564–1642 •
Discovered law of pendulum motion

CAROLUS LINNAEUS
• 1707–1778
Classified the plant
and animal kingdoms

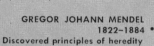

SIGMUND FREUD
• 1856–1939
Started psychoanalysis

GREGOR JOHANN MENDEL
1822–1884 •
Discovered principles of heredity

BARON ERNEST RUTHERFORD
1871–1937 •
Contributed to knowledge of
radioactivity and atomic structure

GUGLIELMO MARCONI
• 1874–1937
Invented the wireless telegraph

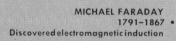

LOUIS AGASSIZ
• 1807–1873
Investigated glacial motion
and marine life

MICHAEL FARADAY
1791–1867 •
Discovered electromagnetic induction

SIR ISAAC NEWTON
• 1642–1727
Discovered laws of light,
gravity, motion and color

ALBERT EINSTEIN
1879–1955 •
Conceived the Theory of Relativity

WILHELM KONRAD ROENTGEN
• 1845–1923
Discovered X-rays

ALEXANDER GRAHAM BELL
1847–1922 •
Invented
the telephone

JOSEPH LISTER
• 1827–1912
Started antiseptic surgery

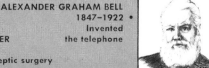

YOUNG PEOPLE'S
SCIENCE
ENCYCLOPEDIA

Edited by the Staff of
NATIONAL COLLEGE OF EDUCATION, Evanston, Ill.

ASSOCIATE EDITORS

HELEN J. CHALLAND, B.E., M.A., PH.D.
Chairman, Science Department, National
College of Education

DONALD A. BOYER, B.S., M.S., PH.D.
Science Education Consultant, Winnetka
Public Schools, Winnetka, Ill., Science,
National College of Education

W. RAY RUCKER, B.A., M.A., ED.D.
Former Dean of the College, National College of Education

EDITORIAL CONSULTANTS
ON THE STAFF OF NATIONAL COLLEGE OF EDUCATION

Elizabeth R. Brandt, B.A., M.Ed.

Eugene B. Cantelupe, B.A., M.F.A., Ph.D.

John H. Daugherty, B.S., M.A.

Irwin K. Feinstein, B.S., M.A., Ph.D.

Mary Gallagher, A.B., M.A., Ph.D.

Beatrice B. Garber, A.B., M.S., Ph.D.

Robert R. Kidder, A.B., M.A., Ph.D.

Jean C. Kraft, B.S., M.A., Ph.D.

Elise P. Lerman, B.A., B.F.A., M.F.A.

Mary-Louise Neumann, A.B., B.S. in L.S.

Lavon Rasco, B.A., M.A., Ph.D.

SPECIAL SUBJECT AREA CONSULTANTS

Krafft A. Ehricke, B.A.E., H.L.D.

Charles B. Johnson, B.S., M.A., M.S.

Raymond J. Johnson, B.B.A., Senior
Certificate in Industrial Engineering

Norma R. Rucker, B.S.

H. Kenneth Scatliff, M.D.

Ray C. Soliday, B.A., B.S., M.A.
(Deceased)

Fred R. Wilkin, Jr., B.S., M.Ed.

THE STAFF

PROJECT DIRECTOR	·	WALLACE B. BLACK
COORDINATING EDITOR	·	JEAN F. BLASHFIELD
ART DIRECTOR	·	BEN ROSEN
PHOTO AND ART EDITOR	·	MARTHA O'ROURKE
PRODUCTION EDITOR	·	ORLANDO T. CURCIO

YOUNG PEOPLE'S
SCIENCE
ENCYCLOPEDIA

Edited by the Staff of

NATIONAL COLLEGE OF EDUCATION
Evanston, Illinois

VOLUME 14
PI-RA

CHILDRENS PRESS, INC.
Chicago

8 9 10 11 12 13 14 15 16 17 18 19 20 21 22 23 24 25   R   75 74 73 72 71 70 69 68 67

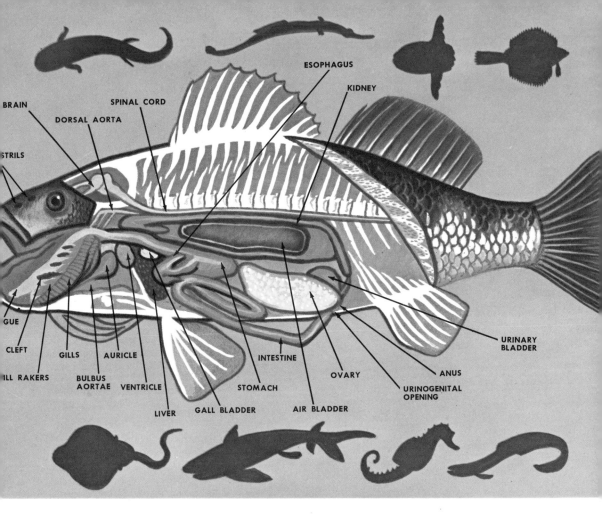

Labels on diagram:
ESOPHAGUS, KIDNEY, SPINAL CORD, DORSAL AORTA, BRAIN, STRILS, GUE, CLEFT, GILLS, AURICLE, ILL RAKERS, BULBUS AORTAE, VENTRICLE, LIVER, GALL BLADDER, STOMACH, INTESTINE, AIR BLADDER, OVARY, URINOGENITAL OPENING, ANUS, URINARY BLADDER

Pisces (Animal) (PIH-ceez) The scientific term for fish is *pisces*. Fish are found in almost every body of water. All fish are alike because they have backbones and need water in which to live. People use fish for food and find many ways to use the oils and skins. There are about 13,000 species. Not all animals people call "fish" belong to Phylum *Pisces*.

Fish appeared very early in the history of the earth. Scientists have found fossilized rock layers over four hundred million years old, from which it has been proved that fish first appeared in the Silurian Period and became numerous in the Age of Fishes, the Devonian Period that followed. Many millions of years passed before land animals appeared.

A true fish is cold-blooded, breathes through gills on each side, and depends almost entirely on water for life. It has a bony skeleton and a long-shaped body, narrowing at the tail. The fins at various parts of its body are used for steering, balancing, and moving it forward. An air bladder, often called *swim* bladder, helps it maintain balance to rise, descend, and adjust to water pressure. It has a heart which has two principal chambers: the *atrium* and *ventricle*. It reproduces by laying eggs.

Many variations, however, occur. LUNGFISH have limblike fins with air-breathing "lungs;" sharks bring forth their babies alive; the sturgeon has a cartilaginous skeleton. Other examples are the catfish which has no scales, the climbing perch which actually climbs trees, and the FLYING FISH which rises from the water in gliding flight.

Fish have many interesting characteristics. Some mature in a few weeks; others may take up to twenty years. They may range from one-half inch in size to forty feet. Though the maximum age for a fish is generally one year, some live fifty years.

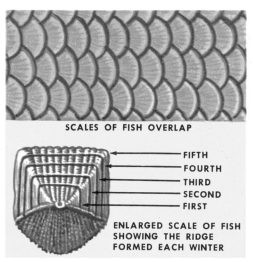

SCALES OF FISH OVERLAP

FIFTH
FOURTH
THIRD
SECOND
FIRST

ENLARGED SCALE OF FISH
SHOWING THE RIDGE
FORMED EACH WINTER

The age of scaly fish can be determined by the ridges on the scales

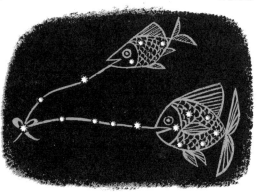

Pisces, the Fishes

Stinging rays, spines in the fins or on the head, speed of movement, armor coating, hardscales with tiny needlelike spines, and powerful electric shocks are typical of some of the varied protective measures EVOLUTION has given fish.

The most common food eaten by fish is plankton; a few eat large plants attached to rocks. Most of them devour worms, crabs, and shrimps, and some will attack oyster beds and shellfish. Many fish consume other smaller fish.

The fish have many enemies. Other fish and animals prey upon them. In fresh water the bladderwort traps and digests baby fish. Insect larvae seek them out as well as squids and jellyfish. Seals, whales, and porpoises eat fish, as do marine birds.

Fish are very useful. They provide an abundant food supply—nearly thirty billion pounds a year valued at seventy-five million dollars. The fishing industry is particuarly important in countries like Norway and Japan and on a smaller scale in the U.S.A. Fish also control the increase of harmful insects. Their oils provide man with vitamins A and D; the swim bladder is used for the production of isinglass, and the skin provides shagreen, a type of leather.

There are two main groups of fish, those with *cartilaginous* skeletons (sharks and rays) and those with *bony* skeletons (perch, gar pike, seahorse). The fish make up one of the large classes of vertebrates.   D. E. Z.

SEE ALSO: ANIMALS, CLASSIFICATION OF; FISH; PLANKTON; SHARK

Pisces (Constellation) (PIH-ceez)

Pisces is a group of stars that ancient people imagined to look like two fish in the sky. Pisces is an autumn constellation. Its stars are not very bright. The best time to look for Pisces is on a clear moonless night in autumn.

This constellation can be recognized by two streams of stars that come together in a V formation. The left side of the V ends in a small S shape. The right fish ends in a small circlet of faint stars. Ancient drawings of this zodiacal sign picture the two fish joined by ribbons on their tails.

According to the legend of Pisces, one day Venus and her son Cupid were walking on the banks of the Euphrates River. Typhon, a terrible giant, came along. Venus and Cupid jumped into the river and changed themselves into fish to escape Typhon. Minerva placed the fish in the sky in memory of their fortunate escape.

Pisces is the twelfth or last sign of the zodiac. The sun is in this sign at the time of the vernal equinox. On the first day of spring the sun's path crosses the celestial equator in Pisces.   C. L. K.

SEE ALSO: CONSTELLATION, ZODIAC

Pistachio see Nuts

Pistil (PISS-till)

The pistil is the part of a flower that produces seeds. When complete it has three parts. These parts are called the *ovary,* the *style,* and the *stigma.*

This most important part of the flower is located in the very center. Some flowers such as the buttercup and the raspberry have more than one pistil.

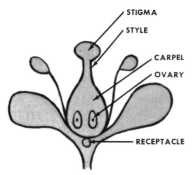

STIGMA

STYLE

CARPEL

OVARY

RECEPTACLE

The pistil (female part) of a flower

The typical pistil consists of an enlarged base, the ovary, within which the ovules are produced; a slender stalk (style) rising from the top of the ovary; and a somewhat enlarged tip (stigma) at the apex of the style. Without this pistil or female part of the flower, it would not be possible for the plant to reproduce. Pollen cells placed on the stigma eventually reach and fertilize the ovules in the ovary.   V. V. N.

SEE ALSO: POLLINATION

Piston see Automobile, Engine

Pitch see Resonance, Sound

Pitchblende Pitchblende is the mineral which is the chief commercial source of URANIUM and RADIUM. It is brown or black, streaked with green, and dull in appearance except for freshly broken surfaces which have a faint luster and a greasy look.

In its pure form pitchblende is an oxide of uranium, formula UO_2; but it usually contains lead and small amounts of other elements, including radium. There are many varieties of pitchblende, each made up of a different combination of ELEMENTS.

Pitchblende is found in Czechoslovakia, England, Norway, and many other European countries and in several parts of the United States. It is nonmagnetic, brittle, and has a specific gravity varying from 6.4 to 10.6.   E. R. B.

SEE ALSO: CURIE, MARIE AND PIERRE; RADIO-ACTIVE ELEMENTS

Pitchblende

Courtesy Society For Visual Education, Inc.

Insects fall down the tubes of pitcher plants and cannot escape

Pitcher plant The pitcher plant is an *insectivorous* flowering plant. This means that it is an insect-eating plant. There is a family of pitcher plants which are large and showy and grow in most marshy parts of the United States and Canada.

The pitcher plant has tubular, yellow-green leaves, brightly marked with deep red and purple veins which attract the insects. Fine hairs pointing downward grow at the mouth of the pitcher. The sweet smell of nectar at the rim of the leaf lures the insects into the leaves; then the hairs help to prevent the insect from crawling out where the walls are smooth and slippery. The insects fall to the bottom where there is water, and there they are trapped and digested by the plant. However, this plant still receives most of its food supply by PHOTOSYNTHESIS.

A single purplish flower grows at the end of a tall stem. While pitcher plants belong to several genera of two different families, those in genus *Sarracenia* are most widely distributed. The common name of the pitcher plant varies locally.   J. K. K.

SEE ALSO: PLANTS, INSECTIVOROUS

Pith Pith is the tissue found in the center of young stems. The cell's walls are thin. Pith functions primarily as a food storage tissue.

Certain plants have pith strong enough to put to a special use. The pith of rushes, for example, was used for wicks in candles and lamps.   M. R. L.

SEE ALSO: PLANT TISSUES

Pitot tube see Altimeter

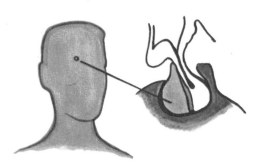

Location of the pituitary gland

Pituitary gland (pih-TOO-ih-tairy) The pituitary is a gland found in higher animals. It is an endocrine gland that pours its secretion directly into the blood stream. It is located on the underside of the BRAIN, where it is well protected. The pituitary gland controls growth and many other glands and organs of the body.

The pituitary, or *hypophysis,* is a very small egg-shaped gland of about one centimeter in diameter and about 0.6 gram in weight. It is frequently referred to as the "master gland," but this is not entirely accurate since among the ductless glands of the body there is great interdependence—that is, they influence one another. No one gland is the key to the total system. Nonetheless the pituitary is of great importance because it affects the functioning of several organs in the body. Experimentation by means of injections of individual hormones produced by the gland, as well as through removal of portions of the gland, has given much information about it.

The pituitary may be divided into three main areas, the front part called the anterior lobe, a narrow middle area, the intermediate lobe, and the rear portion or posterior lobe.

The *anterior lobe* produces a number of hormones. Oversecretion of one of these brings about a condition known as *gigantism.* This, occurring in young people, causes an overdevelopment and lengthening of bones. The absence of this hormone can also bring about underdevelopment or *dwarfism.* For this reason it is called a *growth hormone,* though there are hormones produced by other glands which also affect growth.

Other hormones of the anterior lobe control the development and functioning of sexual organs. Another brings about milk production. Still others stimulate the THYROID gland (affecting growth patterns) the adrenal cortex, and the parathyroid glands.

The *posterior lobe* of the pituitary produces a hormone called *pituitrin,* a hormone which can be divided into several fractions, each affecting certain processes of the body. Pituitrin plays an important role in childbirth, causing contractions of muscles of the uterus and assisting in bringing about the birth process. Inadequate secretion of pituitrin causes excessive urine formation, or *diabetes insipidus.*   D. J. I.

SEE ALSO: DIABETES, ENDOCRINE GLANDS, GIANT

Plain There are four great classes of land forms: plains, plateaus, hill country, and mountains. Plains—the broad, flat or rolling, usually treeless country —rank first in total area.

Vast portions of the world's plains are sparsely populated, largely because of insufficient rainfall or too cold a climate. However, favorable soil, drainage, and climate enable some large plain areas to support moderate to dense population.

Plains constitute the great agricultural lands of the world. An example is the great American corn belt, an area that extends from central Kansas to eastern Ohio. As much as 70 to 80 per cent of this land area is plowed and planted in crops.

Plains are characterized by gentle slopes. The local relief, or the difference in elevation between the lowest points to the highest points within a limited area, is generally less than 500 feet.   V. V. N.

SEE ALSO: RIVER

The great plains yield much wheat
Courtesy Society For Visual Education, Inc.

Planaria

Planaria (pluh-NAH-ree-uh) The planaria are fresh-water *flatworms*. One *planarian* is about one-half inch long, gray in color, and has a long, arrow-shaped body on which it slides over river-bed stones.

Planaria have two primitive sight organs or *eye-spots* and two touch-sensitive points at each side of the head. Strangely, the mouth and projectible tube-like pharynx are at the middle, *underside* of the body.

Flatworms are grouped in the phylum *Platyhelminthes*. They are in the most primitive phylum having true organ systems; these include a crude, network nervous system, a one-way digestive tract, and simple excretory tissue. The planarian's relatives include many species that are parasitic, such as the LIVER FLUKES and tapeworms. These have even more complex organ systems for reproduction.

The planarian's movements result from two devices: its body is covered with microscopic *cilia* which beat in whip-like fashion and help propel it along surfaces; also the *muscle cells* of its flat underside help it slide.

Planaria are famous among biologists for their ability to regrow new parts, a process called REGENERATION. If its head is cut off, a specimen will soon grow a new one; and the head piece may even regenerate a new tail. Also, if its head end is cut through vertically with a sharp knife, the split animal will, in a few days, grow into a two-headed worm. Cut-off head pieces can be grafted onto other body regions or onto another flatworm and these usually will grow where placed.

This whole regenerating ability is quite natural to planaria, for a fully-grown animal can, by itself, slowly pull itself into two halves which will soon grow into two complete animals.   D. A. B.

✳ THINGS TO DO

WILL A WORM GROW TWO HEADS?

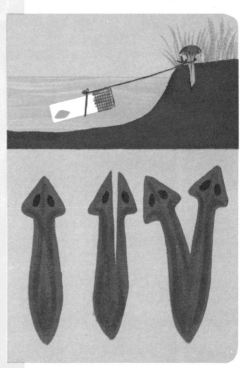

1   Planaria may be purchased from a supply company or may be found in quiet streams and collected in the following way. Put a piece of raw liver in a tall olive bottle. Cover the bottle's mouth with a wire screen to prevent larger animals from getting the food. Tie a cord around the bottle and lower it into the water. The other end may be fastened to a stake driven in the ground on the edge of the bank. It could take several hours before planaria find the liver. Check periodically for signs of a capture.

2   Transfer the planaria to a shallow dish of fresh water for its future home. To demonstrate its remarkable powers of regeneration place a planaria on a hard surface. With a sharp razor blade make a cut half way down its anterior end. Place the planaria back in the dish of water.

3   It will take about two weeks for each half to grow its other half. As soon as this is apparent feed it raw liver again. Leave the food in for an hour, then remove it to prevent spoilage.

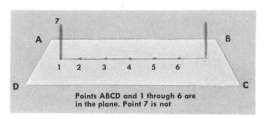

Points ABCD and 1 through 6 are in the plane. Point 7 is not

A plane surface

Plane A plane is a flat surface which has length and width but no thickness. On a plane surface every point on a straight line joining two points lies entirely within the surface.

SEE: GEOMETRY

Planet The name "planet" comes from a Greek word meaning "wanderer." One can easily see how a planet moves among the stars in a regular path if one watches the sky for a few nights.

The nine planets that revolve around the sun can be distinguished from stars by their changing positions among the stars. The stars, which appear fixed, give off their own light, while the planets do not. Like the earth and moon, planets shine by light reflected from the sun. When seen through a telescope, a planet looks like a ball; with the exception of the sun, stars look like pin points of light because they are so far away from Earth.

Planets travel in a path which is called an *orbit*. This ORBIT is around the sun, and is nearly a circle. Actually this orbit is a somewhat flattened circle, or *ellipse*. Although the planets move in the same direction, their orbits are different distances from the sun. Some of the planets, particularly the *terrestrial* or inside group, are made of heavy atoms of matter. The *Jovian* planets or outside group seem to be made of lighter atoms. All of them rotate on their axes, but at different rates. All the planets' orbits are about in the plane of the sun's equator, though Pluto's orbit is tipped.   V. V. N.

SEE ALSO: EARTH, SOLAR SYSTEM

A planetarium projector

Planetarium (plan-uh-TAIR-i-um) A planetarium is a machine inside of a dome-shaped building that can show the sun, the moon, the planets, and the stars. It portrays how all these heavenly bodies move. A planetarium is different from a telescope because a telescope can show a real but very small part of the sky. The planetarium actually makes a large artificial sky appear on its giant domed ceiling.

A planetarium can speed up, slow down, or stop its picture of the sky in action. It can show how the sky looked hundreds of years ago, how it looks now, or how it will look thousands of years in the future. It can show how the sky looks from any place on Earth. A person can sit in Adler Planetarium in Chicago, for instance, and look up at the domed ceiling and see a picture of how the sky looked in Egypt in 2000 B.C. He can see how the sky looks now from the South Pole, or he can see the sky that his great-great-grandchildren will be able to see.

A planetarium can depict the moon going rapidly through its phases. It can show a planet moving from one constellation to another, and the constellations rising and setting.

Modern planetariums can portray all of the heavenly bodies that are visible to the naked eye. The machine that projects the image of the sky is made up of many projectors, like slide projectors, usually over

✳ **THINGS TO DO**

CONSTRUCTING A PLANETARIUM

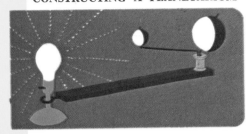

1   Secure a large rubber ball and a small one which is one-fourth its size. These will represent the earth and moon.

2   Insert a wire hanger through the center of both balls. Construct a wooden arm on to a table lamp by following the adjoining illustration. A large eye screw will permit the arm to revolve around the light which represents the sun. A spool nailed to the opposite end of the arm will hold the wires which are attached to the two balls.

3   The axis of the earth should always be tilted to the north as you revolve it around the sun. Observe the area on the earth which is directly illuminated by the light at each quarter turn. Can you figure out which season of the year it is? In what positions will the moon be when there are lunar and solar eclipses?

one hundred. Each projector's picture is a "still" picture. Some are spots of light that represent the sun, the moon, or the planets. Some of them are pictures of groups of stars. The pictures are fitted together to make a single, accurate picture of the night sky. Then, by means of electric motors, the projectors can all be moved to show the individual motions of the heavenly bodies. The complete machine is moved, too, to show the effects of the earth's rotation.

A typical modern planetarium can show over 9600 stars. It has over 100 separate images in each complete sky scene. The first modern planetarium was built in Munich, Germany, in 1923. Many major cities have them now for both public use and research. In New York City there is the Hayden Planetarium; Los Angeles has the Griffith Planetarium. Fels Planetarium is in Philadelphia.   C. L. K.

SEE ALSO: OBSERVATORY, TELESCOPE

Planetoid see Asteroid

Plankton Many living things in the sea belong to a group of plants and animals called plankton. This name refers to the countless marine plants and animals that live in surface water and are carried along by currents. Those organisms, especially animals, that actively swim at the surface of the water are called *nekton*.

There are a few fairly large types of plankton, such as the sargassum plants and the JELLYFISH. However, most of the organisms classed as plankton are very small. These range from the *copepods,* which are barely visible, to the microscopic forms called *diatoms* and BACTERIA.

The animal representatives of plankton are one-celled PROTOZOA and the larvae of such forms as oysters, snails, fish, and worms. These forms of plankton are a very necessary food supply to the fish of the sea. Small fish, as well as some very large whales, feed entirely on plankton. Larger fish feed upon the small fish. Eventually man uses some of the larger fish as a source of his food supply.

The terms *limnoplankton* and *haliplankton* are sometimes applied to fresh-water and marine organisms, respectively. There are also other subdivisions.   V. V. N.

SEE ALSO: DIATOM, MARINE BIOLOGY, OCEANOGRAPHY

Ocean phyto-plankton consists of many tiny organisms, including diatoms

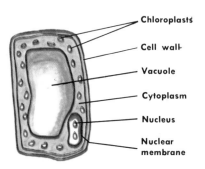

Chloroplasts

Cell wall

Vacuole

Cytoplasm

Nucleus

Nuclear membrane

Parts of a typical plant cell

Plant Plants were probably an early form of life that appeared on this earth millions of years ago. They may be so small one cannot see them without a microscope. It would take 5000 bacteria lined up in a row to measure one inch. The largest plants are the giant sequoia trees in California. Some of these are as tall as a twenty-four story building.

Plants are living things since they are made of cells, can grow and reproduce. They carry on most of the same life processes that animals do. They are different from animals in several ways. Most have chlorophyll and can make their own food. There is a wide range of size in plants of the same kind. The higher plants cannot move around from one place to another.

CELLULAR STRUCTURE

All plants are made of cells. The whole plant may be only one cell, such as unicellular ALGAE. Most plants though are made up of thousands of cells, with each cell designed to do a certain job for the entire group of cells. Plant cells may be microscopic in size or as long as twenty inches.

Most plant cells have a nonliving wall of *cellulose,* a complex carbohydrate. This material makes them more rigid than animal cells. The *cytoplasm* and *nucleus* surround a central *vacuole* of cell sap. A number of bodies are found in the cytoplasm which are lacking in most animals. *Plastids* help make food, store starch, and contain the colored pigments. The cytoplasm's primary purpose then is to make, store, and digest food.

The nucleus of a cell is the "team captain," controlling most activities carried on in each cell. It contains *chromosomes,* the bearers of hereditary characteristics. Plant cells may have from one to a thousand pairs depending on the species. They usually average from five to fifty pairs. The life span of plant cells varies. Some live only hours while others continue to function for hundreds of years.

METABOLISM

Plants must eat, drink, breathe, and burn up energy. They have one big advantage over animals since most plants make their own food. Plants cannot move and must depend upon the ATMOSPHERE to give them water and fresh air. They use less energy than animals because they do not move from place to place.

METABOLISM is the sum total of all the plant processes necessary to keep it alive. Those activities which build up cells by making complex material from simple materials are termed *anabolism.* Photosynthesis and assimilation are anabolic processes. By contrast, the tearing down of protoplasm, making simple materials from complex materials, is *catabolism.* Digestion and respiration are catabolic processes.

Unicellular plants carry on all life activities within a single cell. This would make this little mass of protoplasm much more generalized than any one cell found in the higher plant groups. Multicellular plants divide up the metabolic responsibilities among the cells. The roots of plants assume the task of anchoring the plant and absorbing the water and minerals from the soil. The stems support the leafy crown and conduct raw materials up to the leaves and, in turn, transport the manufactured food throughout the entire plant. Leaves carry on PHOTOSYNTHESIS, food making, and TRANSPIRATION, release of excess water. The gaseous exchange occurs through minute holes on the leaf.

Materials necessary for metabolism are received and transported in a number of ways. One-celled plants absorb and excrete through the cell wall. Simple multicellular plants pass the material from cell to cell. Higher plants have developed a *vascular* or conducting system. A variety of tubes and vessels are designed to permit a more rapid and continuous flow of raw materials and food products from one part of the plant to another. The *xylem* tissue in the root con-

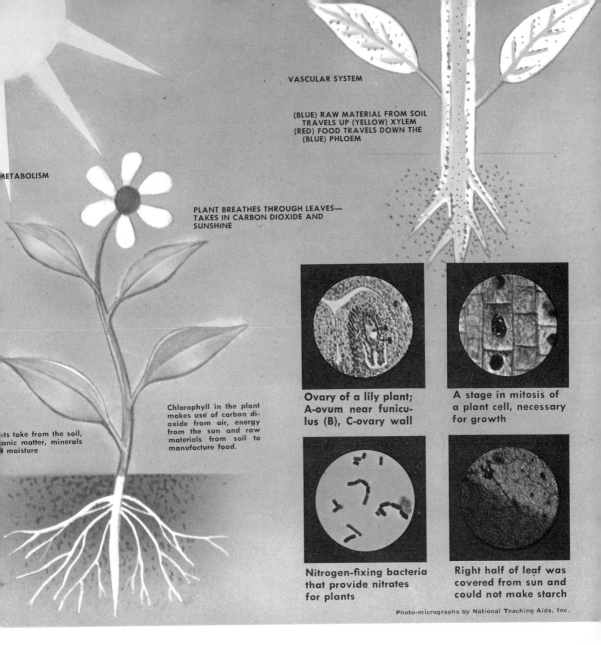

VASCULAR SYSTEM

(BLUE) RAW MATERIAL FROM SOIL
TRAVELS UP (YELLOW) XYLEM
(RED) FOOD TRAVELS DOWN THE
(BLUE) PHLOEM

METABOLISM

PLANT BREATHES THROUGH LEAVES—
TAKES IN CARBON DIOXIDE AND
SUNSHINE

Chlorophyll in the plant
makes use of carbon di-
oxide from air, energy
from the sun and raw
materials from soil to
manufacture food.

...ts take from the soil,
...anic matter, minerals
... moisture

Ovary of a lily plant;
A-ovum near funicu-
lus (B), C-ovary wall

A stage in mitosis of
a plant cell, necessary
for growth

Nitrogen-fixing bacteria
that provide nitrates
for plants

Right half of leaf was
covered from sun and
could not make starch

Photo-micrographs by National Teaching Aids, Inc.

tinues up the stem, out the *petiole* and through the leaf. *Phloem* tissues form a continuous pathway in the reverse direction, leaves to stems to roots.

Plants give off oxygen in the process of photosynthesis, and like animals, also release CO_2 in respiration and use O_2 for the oxidation of food. While photosynthesis is taking place during daylight hours, more oxygen than carbon dioxide is released.

GROWTH

Man and other animals do not grow to be tall giants if they eat and eat. Plants, however, do not stop growing if they are fed and watered more than usual. A geranium growing in Michigan may not get any taller than two feet. This same geranium living in a climate where there is a longer growing season, as in California, may grow taller than a human giant.

Plants will increase their size in only certain areas. *Meristematic* cells will divide to increase a plant in length and circumference. These four regions are the stem tip, ROOT tip, vascular cambium and cork CAMBIUM. Multiplication of cells occurs more often during the night, because the plant is busy making food during the daylight hours.

Two factors affect the growth in plants. *Genetically* they inherit qualities which affect their size. One can buy seeds to grow giant zinnias or dwarf phlox. Internal cellular activity is another genetic factor. The amount of plant-growth hormone, *auxin,* produced by the cells controls the extent of growth. Finally, the external environmental conditions play a part. Plants given the right amount of water, light, air, warmth and FERTILIZER will thrive better than those deprived of one or more of these.

Most plants will not live forever. There is a certain life span for each kind. ANNUALS will produce seed the first year they are planted. They have completed their life cycle and die. BIENNIALS grow and store food the first year, bloom and produce seeds the second year before they die. PERENNIALS will produce seeds year after year and have a rather indefinite life span. It is reported that some sequoias are 4000 years old.

REPRODUCTION

Plants must make more of their kind or they would soon disappear from the earth. The little one-celled plants just squeeze apart and make two of themselves. Many plants must make two kinds of cells, an egg and a sperm. When these two cells come together the resulting cell will begin to grow into a new plant. New plants usually look like the parent plants.

Plants reproduce asexually by fission, SPORE FORMATION, or by PROPAGATION. Fission is simple division of a cell as in bacteria. If environmental conditions are controlled, bacteria will divide every half hour. This does not appear phenomenal unless one counts the offspring produced in a day and a night. The 48 generations would number 256,000,000,000,000 bacteria.

Spores are cells produced by many plants, such as fungi and one generation of the mosses and ferns. When environmental conditions are adverse, some plants may form spores that have a rather thick wall. This is a protective device of the plant against extreme heat or drought. When conditions are more favorable the spore breaks from the shell and germinates.

Propagation of vegetative parts of a plant (root, stem, or leaves) may be done by the plant itself or by man. Many BULBS will form extra little bulblets. Drooping branches of weeping willows will take root if they come in contact with the ground. Strawberry plants and crab grass send out runners. New shoots and roots arise at the nodes. Man makes leaf, root, and stem cuttings (slips) to propagate the same species.

Plants reproduce sexually by production

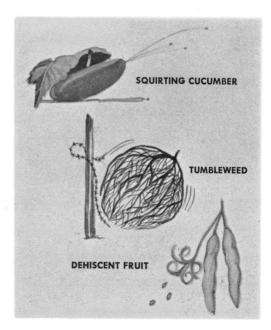

Some unusual types of seed dispersal

of either motile or non-motile sex cells or gametes—eggs and sperm. Conjugation is the union of two sex cells that look alike. Fertilization is the combining of sex cells which can be distinguished as male and female. Sometimes the sexes may be on the same plant as in the apple tree. The ash has male trees (*staminate*) and female trees (*pistillate*).

ADAPTATION

Plants cannot fly south when winter comes as birds do. They are not able to move into the caves or other shelters to hibernate as some animals do when food and warmth are scarce. Since plants cannot move they must adapt to all kinds of conditions. Plants that do not adjust to the environment soon die.

Plants go through seasonal adjustments according to their location. Floral life in California will grow mainly during the wet, cool winters. The hot, dry summers slow growth considerably, almost to inactivity. Many trees lose their leaves during this time. Plants in the frigid zones have adjusted their life activities to a very short growing season as the summers are short and the winters extremely long. In the equatorial rain forests, plants respond by growing almost continually. The forest is very dense and the undergrowth of small plants have adapted to surviving in dense shade.

Another adjustment by plants is the storage of food and water for future use. One

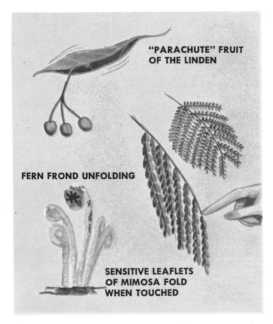

"PARACHUTE" FRUIT OF THE LINDEN

FERN FROND UNFOLDING

SENSITIVE LEAFLETS OF MIMOSA FOLD WHEN TOUCHED

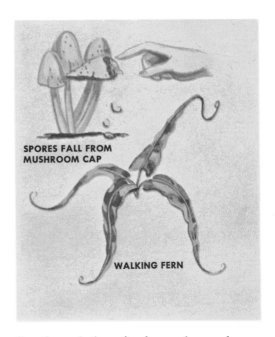

SPORES FALL FROM MUSHROOM CAP

WALKING FERN

could compare it to animals' preparation for the long winter months. Biennial plants die back to ground level with the roots storing enough material to start the plant on its second year of growth. Some perennials lose their aerial parts when winter arrives and store food in underground stems or roots. Other perennials, such as trees and shrubs, drop their leaves in fall. Roots are unable to absorb water from the frozen ground and must protect themselves from water loss in the leaves.

LOCOMOTION

Most plants do not move from place to place. This is one of the main ways one can tell a plant from an animal. A few of the simple one-celled plants are able to swim or crawl. Nevertheless they are still called plants. Plants are able to bend or turn in different directions. This helps the plant get the things it needs to live.

There are two kinds of movements that stationary plants exhibit. Some movements are due to unequal growth rates in cells and are called TROPISMS. Plants respond in the direction of growth to the direction of the stimulus. If the parts of the plant turn toward the stimulus this is a *positive* response, while moving away is a *negative* response. Stems and leaves turn toward the light but roots grow away from it. Roots grow with the pull of gravity while stems grow up and away from the earth.

Nastic movements are independent of the direction of the stimulus and are characteristically due to changes in *turgor pressure* (water content of the cells) rather than to growth. These are usually temporary or cyclical movements. Flowers open and close periodically. These are called *sleep movements*. If an object touches the leaves of the mimosa plant, they fold up in seconds. When an insect starts to crawl through the Venus' flytrap or sundew the trap folds up, catching the insect inside.

Time-lapse photography reveals the constant motion of plants. Tropic and nastic movements, not always visible to the naked eye, when recorded on film show the plant dancing in tune under the direction of nature's environmental factors.   H. J. C.

SEE ALSO: CELL; CELLULOSE; CHLOROPHYLL; HEREDITY; LEAVES; LIFE, CHARACTERISTICS OF; PLANT TISSUES; PLANTS, CLASSIFICATION OF

The roots on these seedlings are growing downward in response to gravity. The stems will grow toward the sun. These are tropisms

Apple cedar rust spreads from red cedar to apple trees

Plant diseases Plants have diseases just as animals and people do. These plant diseases come from bacteria, viruses, or fungi, infected seed, lack of room, light or moisture, frost, or poor soil. The records of the early Greeks and Romans show that plants had diseases found today, such as *rust* and *mildew* or *blight*.

There are times in history when people have starved to death because of serious outbreaks of disease. When the potato crops in Ireland failed in 1845 because of disease, there were many human deaths. Through the years, scientists have been working to learn more about plant diseases, and today many methods of control have been discovered to protect grains, fruits, and vegetables that are so important to animal and human life.

A plant is a delicate and complex machine. Young plants are more apt to get diseases because of poor soil and weather conditions than are older plants. The young cereal plants are more susceptible to smut than older plants. Wood rot fungi may enter a plant when there has been a wound or a mechanical injury to the plant. Plants that have been chilled by frost are subject to fungus infections. Root injuries and poisonous materials in the soil can contribute to diseases of plants. Burning or scalding of the leaves of plants will cause a diseased condition. This happens when there is a sudden change from cloudy, moist weather to clear, hot weather. Severe winter weather will cause frost-cracks and frost canker in plants and trees.

Sooty MOLDS on the surface of leaves and fruits will starve the plant. These black mold-like fungi cover the surface of the leaves so that the chloroplasts lose their green color, and the formation of starch and sugar is so greatly reduced that the plant cannot grow.

Bacterial diseases include the black rot of cabbage, pear or fire BLIGHT, and crown galls of the apple trees. The pear blight attacks the blossoms and young twigs, kills them, and turns them black. The tree looks as though it had been burned. The bacteria causing this blight may live for years in cankers on the limbs and trunk. The germs stay in a sticky gum that comes out of the cankers. Insects carry these germs from tree to tree. So far, no effective spray has been found to attack the pear or fire blight. It can be controlled by "operating" on the tree. Tools must be sterilized and the infected parts are cut out. Brown rot causes the most damage to peach trees. It makes the fruit rot and shrivel and become covered with olive-gray spores of the FUNGUS.

Stem rust, wheat smuts, and ergot are common diseases of cereals and grains. Rust is the most destructive disease of wheat. It causes small, rust-colored spots on the leaves, stems, and heads of wheat. There are two important kinds of rust—stem rust and leaf rust. There is little a grower can do to prevent these rusts except to destroy such plants as barberry which help grow the rust that later spreads to the wheat. Scientists have been successful in developing varieties of wheat that resist rust.

Apple trees and their fruit are attacked by many different diseases. The most important are the apple scab, cedar rust, and fire blight. The apple scab is a fungus which causes black spots on the leaves and blossoms and makes the apples spotted and poorly shaped. It can be controlled by spraying the tree with sulfur or copper. The cedar rust fungus, like the wheat rust, is grown on another plant and carried to the apple tree. In this case, the cedar rust spends part of its life on red cedar trees. Apple growers cut down all red cedars within three miles of their apple orchards to prevent the cedar rust disease.

Potato blight is one of the most destructive fungus diseases. The fungus grows on the leaves, and can be spread from plant to plant by wind or splashing of rain

Scale insects suck plant juices

VIRUS diseases cause various leaf mosaics and other infections in many of the most popular, edible fruits and vegetables.

Certain plant parasites, such as mistletoe, broomrapes, and dodders, rob the host plants of their food so that the hosts eventually become diseased.

There are almost as many plant diseases as there are plants. Some plants are attacked by one disease; some are victims of many. Botanists, farmers, growers, gardeners, and the United States Department of Agriculture are constantly seeking new methods of controlling plant disease. Some of the old methods which have been successful are the selection of disease-free seed, quarantine of diseased plants, development of resistant strains, rotation of crops, and the use of powders and sprays.　　　　J. K. K.
SEE ALSO: PARASITE, RUST

The boll weevil ruins cotton plant bolls

Plant hormones see Hormones, plant

Plant pests In addition to the many different kinds of plant diseases, there are a great number of plant pests that can destroy or stop the growth of plants. Insects, especially, carry many of the fungi and bacterial diseases from plant to plant. Bees carry the pear blight even though they do help in the pollination of the trees. The potato beetle carries the potato rot. Boring beetles spread ferment and woodrot fungi.

Insects injure plants when they feed on them. Biting insects such as certain grasshoppers can strip a plant of its foliage, thus killing it. Sucking insects and mites cause damage to plants by reducing their store of plant food, in which case the plant will stop

Courtesy Society For Visual Education, Inc.
Caterpillars damage plants by eating leaves

growing and eventually die. Scale insects, mealy bugs, plant lice, leaf hoppers, and "plant bugs" are the most destructive kinds because they suck the sap out of the plant tissues. Sometimes this only slows up the growth process, but other times it causes irritations by some material the insect may inject into the tissues of the plant. Then, the roots or leaves of the plant may develop gall-like swellings. Common injuries of this type are the *Phylloxera* (grape lice) on the leaves and roots of grapes, woolly apple louse on the roots of the apple, and cockscomb gall on the elm.

The growths known as GALLS are also caused by insect larvae developing from eggs

Corn borer

laid in young tissues of a plant. Thousands of plants are attacked by nematode worms which go after the roots and cause gall-like swellings. These worms invade field and truck crops.

Borers injure their host by cutting off the flow of food between the root and leaves of a tree or plant when they bore rings around the trunk or stem. The corn borer is blamed for a great loss of corn corps each year, and this is true; but actually, corn is a favorite food of over 350 other insects. Some of them are the corn-ear worms, chinch bugs, grasshoppers, and the white grubs. The boll weevil does great damage to the cotton crop in the United States each year. It feeds on the silky fiber inside the seed pods or bolls of the cotton plant.

Most birds are friends to the farmers and gardeners because they eat insect pests that are harmful to the crops, but there are some birds which are harmful and are considered plant pests. The crow goes after the farmer's corn crop, and other birds eat or damage fruit in orchards and vineyards. Small animals, mainly in the rodent family, eat grain in the fields and vegetables in the truck gardens.   J. K. K.

SEE ALSO: PLANT DISEASES

Plant tissues Most plants are made of many cells. These cells are usually organized into groups called tissues. If a group of cells is basically alike, it is called simple tissue. Complex tissues are made of different kinds of cells which do the same job.

Some tissues appear in all organs of a plant; the stem, root, leaf, fruit, and flower. Other cell groups are so specialized they occur in selected parts of a mature plant. Each kind of tissue has the cellular composition to do a particular function for the life of a plant.

The adjoining table outlines the kinds of cells found in complex plants, their life span, location, and appearance.   H. J. C.

SEE ALSO: PLANT

Plants, aquarium see Aquarium, Tropical fish

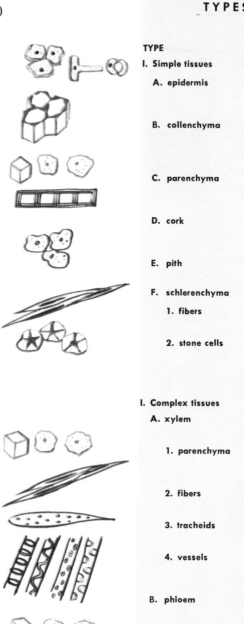

TYPES

TYPE

I. Simple tissues
   A. epidermis

   B. collenchyma

   C. parenchyma

   D. cork

   E. pith

   F. schlerenchyma
     1. fibers

     2. stone cells

I. Complex tissues
   A. xylem

     1. parenchyma

     2. fibers

     3. tracheids

     4. vessels

   B. phloem

     1. parenchyma

     2. fibers

     3. sieve tubes

     4. companion cells

III. Meristematic tissue

OF TISSUES IN PLANTS

LOCATION	FUNCTION	LIFETIME	APPEARANCE
outer layer of young plants, fruits, leaves of older plants	protective and absorptive	living when functional	irregular shapes may have cutin on outside
many parts of entire plant beneath epidermis of herbaceous stems, petioles, midribs of leaves	strengthening	living at maturity	prism-shaped, elongated, more cellulose in angles of cells
all organs, most common	conduction and storage	usually living	isodiametric, spherical, cubical, many-sided
outer layer of woody plants	water proofing protective	most functional after death	rectangular or box-shaped thick walls of suberin
center core of young plants	food storage	living when functional dies as plant matures	large, thin-walled cells
	strengthening		
many parts of entire plant		cell contents die at maturity	long, slender, thick-walled
many parts, especially fruit walls		cell contents die at maturity	short, irregular shapes
extend through all parts			
	food storage	usually living	isodiametric
	strengthening	usually dead at maturity	long, slender, thick-walled
	conduction	usually dead at maturity	long, tapering, pitted walls
	conduction	usually dead at maturity	chain of long cells, lack end walls
			annular, spiral, sclariform, pitted
extend through all parts			
	food storage and conduction	usually living	isodiametric
	strengthening	cell contents die at maturity	long, slender, thick-walled
	conduction	living at maturity	rows of long cells, ends perforated to form a sieve
	helps sieve tubes	living at maturity	long, tapering cells, dense cytoplasm, prominent nucleus
root tip increase length stem tip cork cambium increase vascular cambium circumference	increases plant growth in length and circumference— cell multiplication	living when functional	rectangular cells

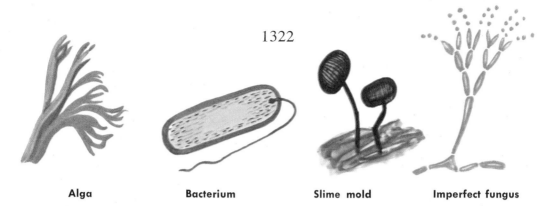

Alga   Bacterium   Slime mold   Imperfect fungus

Plants, classification of While hiking through the United States, one would have difficulty finding a plant that has not been discovered and given a name. The unexplored tropics, though, would prove good hunting grounds for new plants. Every plant that man finds is given two names in Latin or Greek. For example, in France, Australia, or Brazil, *Rosa alba* is a white rose. Over 350,000 plants have been named so far. There are many more to be discovered.

Today plants are classified according to their basic structure and life history. Theophrastus, called *"father of botany,"* was the first scientist to start a classification system, and some of the names he gave plants are still used today. During the Middle Ages man grouped plants according to their uses: medicinal plants, food plants, or harmful plants. This is considered artificial classification. In 1753 CAROLUS LINNAEUS formed a natural classification system based on the number of floral organs. Plants were grouped according to basic similarity of structure.

Plants of relatively like structure and function are classified in the same *species,* related species into a *genus,* genera grouped into *families,* and these into *orders.* Similar orders are placed into *classes,* which are finally classified into divisions called *phyla.*

Taxonomy is a variable science and always is changing because scientists disagree as new plants are discovered.

The earliest FOSSIL plants date back 500 million years to the Cambrian period. *Corallines,* which are algae, were uncovered. This plant life evidently was well established before the first marine animals. It is believed that land plants made their appearance about 350 million years ago. It has been difficult to trace the ancestral progression of existing plants since the soft tissue of many have not left fossil prints. Therefore, there are gaps in the chain of evolution. However, as plants are studied from simple to complex forms, some pattern or thread is found that runs throughout.

ALGAE

The green scum on ponds and the green film that appears in an aquarium is probably some form of algae. They are among the simplest plants that can make food. The entire body of many algae is only one cell. Some cells tend to hang together and form a string or filament. Even when the algae are made of many cells, each cell looks and acts very much like all the others. They do not have roots, stems or leaves.

Algae are put into groups or classified by their color (pigmentation), by the kinds of food they store, and by the kind of cell movement. Algae have one-celled sex organs, or if the organs are multicellular, each cell forms a sex cell. They reproduce asexually by *fission* and by *fragmentation.*

The *blue-green* algae lack an organized *nucleus* and *plastids.* They appear to be the simplest plants within the algae group. The *flagellates* move about and for this reason they are also claimed to be animals by zoologist. The *diatoms* have secreted walls of *silica.* Many move with flagella or an ameboid action. They leave fossil remains. Brown algae are multicellular. The giant KELP of the Northern Hemisphere may reach a length of 150 feet. The Sargasso Sea gets its name from a brown alga called *Sargassum.* Red algae are multicellular organisms found at greater depths in the ocean than any other plant. Irish moss is a type of red algae.

BACTERIA

Bacteria are often called "microbes" or "germs." They are the smallest living thing

KINGDOM, PLANT

SUBKINGDOM, THALLOPHYTA

Division, Cyanophyta (blue-green algae)

Division, Euglenophyta (euglenoids)

Division, Chlorophyta (green algae)

Division, Chrysophyta (diatoms, yellow-green and golden-brown algae)

Division, Phaeophyta (brown algae)

Division, Rhodophyta (red algae)

Division, Schizomycophyta (bacteria)

Division, Myxomycophyta (slime mold)

Division, Eumycophyta (true fungi)

SUBKINGDOM, EMBRYOPHYTA

Division, Bryophyta (moss, liverworts)

Division, Tracheophyta

Subdivision, Psilopsida (fossil forms, two living genera)

Subdivision, Lycopsida (club moss)

Subdivision, Sphenopsida (horsetails)

Subdivision, Pteropsida

Class, Filicinae (ferns)

Class, Gymnospermae (conifer, ginkgo, cycad)

Class, Angiospermae (flowering plants)

Subclass, Monocotyledoneae

Subclass, Dicotyledoneae

in the world. Only a few have CHLOROPHYLL. They grow in three shapes, round, rod-like, or spiral.

Bacteria usually exist as single cells though some form filaments or colonies. They lack a true nucleus and cellulose in their cell walls. Some are able to move by means of projections called *flagella* or *cilia*. Most of these plants are parasitic or saprophytic. A few bacteria can make food and get energy by a process called *chemosyn-*

thesis. It is believed that bacteria are related to the blue-green algae.

SLIME MOLD

This plant creeps along much like the movement of an ameba. It is a slippery, colorless mass of protoplasm. Slime mold is difficult to classify. The reproductive stage is plant-like, while the vegetative stage is animal-like. Therefore, it has received the description of a *fungus-like animal*.

ALGAE

MOSS

LICHEN

DICOT

MONOCO

GYMNOSPERMS

ANGIOSPERMS

FUNGI

BACTERIA

FERN

| Lichen | Fungus | Moss and liverwort | Club moss |

FUNGI IMPERFECTI

The plants in this group are not perfect. They lack the sexual stage in their life cycle. Members of the group include *Penicillium* and other blue-green molds, apple blotch, and a fungus that causes fever and a lung disease in man.

LICHEN

This plant is a combination of plants that could be compared to a happy marriage. Just as the man brings home the bacon and the woman cooks it, so the fungus, one of the pair, gathers the water and minerals so the algae can make the food. This living together of two different plants, where one helps the other, is called *symbiosis*.

Lichen grows slowly and in such bleak areas it does not have to compete with more vigorous plants.

FUNGI

Some people train their pigs or dogs to find a fungus plant that is good to eat. These plants are called *truffles*. The entire lives of these plants are spent under the ground. They give off strong odors.

The true fungi are the largest group of plants without flowers. They do not have chlorophyll. Many fungi are single-celled, but a *puffball* was found that was one foot high and four feet wide.

Fungi, with the exception of YEAST, are generally classified according to form and life history instead of function. They lack roots, stems, leaves, and conducting tissue. Usually the plants have two parts: the *vegetative,* consisting of filaments which anchor and absorb; and the *fruiting body,* which does the reproducing.

Fungi usually reproduce by spores. A mushroom will produce as many as two thousand million spores. Some fungi propagate by making a massive ball of *hyphae* (threadlike elements). This ball forms a tough outer coat. Some are as large as footballs and are eaten by Australians who call them "blackfellows' bread".

Many fungi go from one host to another to finish their life cycle; this is called *alternation of hosts*. Wheat rust needs the barberry bush and wheat. The white pine and gooseberry exchange a . fungus growth, as do the cedar apple and juniper. The most efficient way to control this alternating fungi pest is to eliminate one of the hosts and halt the cycle.

True fungi include mushrooms, toadstools, tree brackets, smuts, morels, mildews, stinkhorns, ergot, and the beautiful little earthstar.

MOSSES AND LIVERWORTS

These little green plants have parts that begin to look and act like leaves, roots, and stems. Some of the cells in this group are now doing different jobs for the whole plant.

MOSS reproduces by two alternating stages. One shoot of the plant forms eggs while another one makes sperms. Water is needed to carry the sperm to the egg. This fertilized egg germinates, forming a stalk with a capsule on the end. This plant (*sporophyte*) must live on the female plant (*gametophyte*). When the spores are released they will form the male and female plants, thus continuing the cycle.

Different species of moss are grouped according to the position and arrangement of leaves and the shape of the capsule.

CLUB MOSS

Club moss in general appearance resembles true moss but has cones or clubs of spore-bearing leaves. Their life history is similar to ferns but differs in several ways. The spores may not germinate for five years and then do so underground. The *prothallus* grows very slowly, with the sex organs appearing sometimes a dozen years later. After fertilization of the sex cells, a sporophyte germinates. This is the familiar CLUB MOSS.

HORSETAILS

Horsetails are closely related to the ferns, with much the same life cycle. They have underground RHIZOMES as do the ferns.

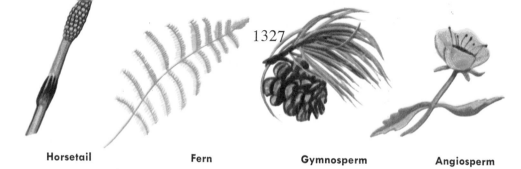

| Horsetail | Fern | Gymnosperm | Angiosperm |

They have an erect, jointed shoot instead of compound leaves. There are whorls of little branches around each joint. Cone-like structures produce the spores. Some kinds in tropical America are thirty feet tall.

FERNS

These plants have true roots, stems, leaves, and conducting tubes. The LEAVES are compound, meaning many little leaflets on a stem. This makes them more like the flowering plants. Many FERNS have stems underground, with only the leaves (*fronds*) above the soil. A few fern stems have reached a height of sixty feet and a width of two feet. This is unusual, however.

There are two plants in a fern's life cycle. The spore germinates into a tiny, heart-shaped *prothallus*. It produces sex cells. Ferns, as mosses, are still dependent upon water for fertilization, to carry the sperm to the egg. The fertilized egg develops into a spore-forming plant (the conspicuous fern plant), which is independent. This is an advance over the *moss cycle*.

GYMNOSPERMS

These plants are woody trees, shrubs, and vines. They are missing the flowers and FRUITS. This is the first group to have seeds. The seeds are not enclosed in a pod, nut, or other organ. Most of them are "evergreen," which means they do not lose their needles or leaves every year. The larches and bald cypresses are exceptions.

Cycads are one of the most primitive seed plants dating back to the Mesozoic Era. They usually have large fern-like leaves, an erect stem, and a tap root. They develop cones in the reproductive cycle.

Ginkgo's have thin, fan-shaped leaves that resemble the maiden-hair fern. The sexes are on separate trees. The male tree has drooping *strobili* (cones). The female tree develops a fleshy covering over the seeds which looks like a yellow mottled plum. This is not classified as a true fruit.

The conifers (cone-bearers) include the pine, hemlock, spruce, fir, juniper, and many others. Most of them bear both sexes on the same tree but in different catkins. They produce two kinds of spores. The pollen grain is the male gametophyte, while the ovule is the female. The union causes the embryo development which, when mature, is the seed.

ANGIOSPERMS

Any plant with a flower belongs in this group. Man has discovered and named more ANGIOSPERMS than all the lower plants put together. They are the most complex and most recent plants in the world. They are adapted to living in a wider range of places than any other single group.

Flowers may be large and conspicuous or small and less striking. Most angiosperms have the STAMEN and PISTIL on the same plant and frequently in the same flower. A flower is *complete* when it has all floral parts, *incomplete* when one or more is missing. A perfect flower has both stamen and pistil, while an imperfect has only one, as in the willow, poplar, and mulberry trees. Only in the flowering plants is there double fertilization. One sperm in the POLLEN grain unites with the ovum in the ovary to form the embryo. The other sperm joins the polar nuclei to form the *endosperm*. This feeds the embryo.

Angiosperms are separated into two groups. *Monocotyledons* have one *cotyledon*, leaves with parallel venation, flower parts in multiples of three, vascular bundles in the stem, no cambium, and include such plants as grasses, lilies, and orchids.

Dicotyledons have two cotyledons, leaves with netted venation, flower parts in multiples of four or five, vascular bundles in a ring, a cambium for secondary growth, and include such plants as legumes, roses, mint, and most forest and fruit trees.   H. J. C.

SEE ALSO: ALTERNATION OF GENERATIONS; EMBRYOPHYTA; EVOLUTION; GEOLOGIC TIME TABLE; PLANT; PLANT TISSUES; REPRODUCTION, ASEXUAL; REPRODUCTION, SEXUAL; THALLOPHYTA

Courtesy Society For Visual Education, Inc.
Leaves of Venus' flytrap close on insects

Some plants used to obtain medicines: (from left) coffee, cinchona, poppy

Plants, insectivorous (in-seck-TIHV-uh-ruhs) Some plants have the ability to trap insects and digest them. Most of these plants are small. They are found in swamps or bogs, or in dry, rocky places.

There are over five hundred different kinds of insectivorous plants. Although these plants are green and capable of manufacturing their own food, they have leaves that can trap insects and small animals. These insectivorous plants even secrete a juice that digests and absorbs the animal remains.

Most of the insectivorous plants are found in five families of dicot angiosperms. The bladderwort family includes common aquatic and amphibious plants, such as the bladderwort and butterwort. There are three families of PITCHER PLANTS; the common pitcher plant of the swamps and bogs of the United States and Guiana, a single species of pitcher plant found in the Australian bogs, and in the tropics a family of pitcher plants with elaborate and brightly colored pitchers for catching animal food. The most highly developed of all the insectivorous plants are found in the sundew family, among whose members are many clever devices for trapping small insects. Members of the sundew family include the sundew, the flycatcher, and the very remarkable VENUS' FLYTRAP.   M. R. L.

Plants, medicinal Since ancient times when man first gathered the seeds, stems, leaves, and roots of plants, he has tried to use them to cure illnesses. Early man would boil, dry, or powder the plants to make herb medicines.

In modern times, medical scientists have found that some of these plants proved useful, while others either needed much refining or were useless, or perhaps even harmful.

One of the old plant medicines scientifically proved valuable is QUININE. When the Spanish explorers came to Peru in the sixteenth century, South American Indians were using cinchona tree bark with its quinine to treat "swamp fever." Quinine is still one of the best drugs for malaria.

Two long known beverage plants, coffee and tea, provide the useful drug CAFFEINE ($C_8H_{10}N_4O_2$). Caffeine is extracted from the beans of the coffee plant. Its pure white crystals are prescribed by doctors as a stimulant to nerve activity. Often caffeine is mixed with aspirin and sedatives used for colds because it offsets their depressing action on heart and brain.

Certain plants of the nightshade-potato family (*Solanaceae*) give man two medicines: *atropine* and *belladonna*. These will slow the secretion of certain glands and will relax over-tense intestinal muscles. Atropine will enlarge the eye pupils so that the doctor can examine one's eyes.

People of old China, as in other old cultures, used many herbs now shown to be useless. But the ancient Chinese did use plants of the *Ephedra* group which act like the modern animal gland extract ADRENALIN. The plant they called *ma huang* (*Ephedra equisetina*) has the chemical *ephedrine* which helps people who have asthma.

The shiny-leaved, tiny wintergreen of the north woods has a medical use in addition to its value in flavoring. Wintergreen oil is prescribed as a liniment rub for sore muscles. A cheap grade of liniment is now made from camphor (tree) extract.

Several medicines for heart diseases come from long known herbs. *Digitalis purpurea,* the common garden FOXGLOVE, was used by early peoples of Africa and the East Indies. Careful doses of digitalis extract speed up a weak, slow heart. By contrast, the drug *aconite* from leaves of monkshood will slow down the heart when it beats too fast, as during high fever.

All parts of castor oil plants, grown as garden oddities, contain both the poison *ricin* and also (in the castor beans) the skin lubricant and laxative, castor oil.

The two most widely grown narcotic-yielding plants are the Asian OPIUM poppy and the South American coca tree. The coca tree (*Erythroxylon coca*) is not to be confused with cacao trees (chocolate, cocoa) nor with cola trees (cola beverage). Poppy seed pods yield crude *opium* and *morphine;* coca leaves give *cocaine*. All NARCOTICS are dangerously habit-forming but are valuable in small, brief doses for severe pain.

Many other plants contain chemicals used in medicines. These include: juice of grapes, sugar cane, and beets (fermented to make medicinal alcohol); *henbane* and Jimson weed (drugs similar to belladonna); *cascara* leaves (laxatives); tanbark oak (tannic acid for skin burns); and several mint family plants (menthol, peppermint, etc. for tonics).   D. A. B.

SEE ALSO: DRUGS, PHARMACOLOGY

Plants, succulent

There are two main types of succulent plants. One kind is able to store water, like the *cactus* and *sedum* plants. The other kind is able to get along without water for a very long time, like the agave and yucca plants. Succulent plants get their name from the Latin word *succus,* meaning juice. Succulent plants can live in places too dry for other plants. They have many ways of protecting themselves from dry weather.

Succulent plants that store water have very fleshy leaves and stems, where they store water for use in dry periods. Succulents nearly all grow in regions of intense

Many desert plants are succulents

summer heat and dry weather. They are usually grown in desert gardens of the Southwest, in rock gardens, in garden areas lacking moisture, and in desert terrariums. They are more often grown for their interesting shapes than for their beauty. But some succulent plants have gorgeous flowers. The CENTURY PLANT flowers are prized because they are rare. Other unusual succulents are the stone plants, which look like living rocks. Lithrops are known as "window plants," because they have translucent leaves that lie flat on the ground. The leaves of haworthias are so close together that they form a solid column.

Drought-resistant succulents have been known to survive for years without a single rainfall.   M. R. L.

SEE ALSO: CACTUS, SEDUM, YUCCA

Plants, tropical

Plants that grew originally in the regions near the equator are called *tropical* plants. They grow in deserts, on mountains, in jungles, grasslands, swamps, and forests. Tropical plants are common in the East and West Indies, Central and South America, Malaya, parts of Africa and Australia, and India. Tropical countries have a wet season and a dry season. Because there is no winter season, tropical plants grow during the entire year and grow large, dense, and in great variety. Many tropical plants are evergreen; others shed their leaves during the dry season, but new growth starts immediately.

EXPORT PLANT PRODUCTS

Man depends on tropical plants for many food products, medicines, clothing, and

Buchsbaum

The passion flower of tropical America

building materials. Pineapples, bananas, dates, coffee, bamboo, cocoa, tea, sugar, nuts, hemp, quinine, avocados, citrus fruits, cotton, coconuts, melons, beans, and hardwoods come from tropical plants.

Some tropical plants such as dieffenbachia, poinsettias, begonias, and cacti are raised as house plants in cold climates. Palms, rhododendrons, orchids, and ferns are often found in greenhouses and conservatories.

TROPICAL PLANTS IN THE GARDEN

Many common garden plants which originated in the tropics have been adapted to temperate climates. *Cleome,* or SPIDER PLANT, has claw-like pink and white clusters of flowers that give the plant a spidery appearance. *Bleeding-heart* has red and white tubelike flowers that resemble small hearts. *Clematis* is a tropical vine that likes rich, moist soil and has many pink, purple, blue, white or yellow blossoms. *Lantana* shrubs are tropical plants with dense clusters of tiny flowers. The *oleander* has large clusters of red, pink, white, or purple flowers. The *canna* has bright, showy leaves and flowers. *Water lilies* and *lotus* plants have thick, fleshy stems, with air pockets that enable leaves and flowers to float. Most bloom during the day, but the Egyptian white lotus is an exotic night-blooming plant. The beautiful blue *Nymphaea* lotus was revered by ancient Egyptians. The Hindus consider the Indian lotus a sacred plant. The largest water lilies, *Victoria Cruzianas,* are sturdy enough to support a small child.

TROPICAL FOOD PLANTS

There are many tropical food plants that are so perishable, difficult to transport, or costly to market that they are seldom seen outside of the tropics. These foods are often mentioned in stories, poems, and songs. The tropical MANGO tree is well known for its delicious fruit. Its leathery leaves on wide spreading branches make mangoes valuable as shade trees as well as fruit trees. Mango fruit is rich, sweet and spicy tasting. The oval, large, red-orange fruit is rich in vitamin A and C. *Breadfruit, jackfruit,* and *durian* are tropical fruits with rough spiny outer coverings. Breadfruit resembles a muskmelon. When cooked, it tastes something like a sweet potato. Jackfruit is a giant fruit that is sometimes two feet long, and weighs up to forty pounds. Durian is a fruit with a characteristic strong odor. PAPAYA is a juicy melon-like fruit. This yellow fruit grows directly out of the tree trunk. The *soursop* is an evergreen tree bearing oval-shaped, green fruit. The tart, juicy flesh of the fruit is used in beverages and sherbets. The *sweetsop* is a deciduous tree. Its cone-shaped, eight-inch-long fruit tastes like sweet custard. The *passion* fruit grows on a vine called *passiflora.* The *passion flower* of tropical America is purple and white and about three inches wide. The markings of the flower resemble the cross used in the Crucifixion. This gives the plant its name. Natives of the tropics chew the *Betel* palm fruit. Their teeth are stained by the red fruit, but it is considered an aid to digestion. Roots of the *cassava* are eaten as starchy vegetables or ground into flour. *Tapioca* comes from cassava. *Yams* are *tubers* from a vine. Sometimes these tubers weigh more than forty pounds. YAMS are prepared like potatoes.

SOME ORNAMENTAL PLANTS

A beautiful tropical flower is the *bird of paradise.* The tall thin stalk and orange and blue flower head resemble a bird's neck and head. Stiff leaves, three to four feet long, are at the base of the plant. *Bougainvilleas* are vines belonging to the four-o-clock family. Their colorful modified leaves enclose small flowers. This adds to the size and beauty of the blossoms. Flowers are shades of purple, red, or gold, and bloom in long, waving sprays. The *wooden rose* vine grows like a morning-glory. The dried

1—UMBRELLA PALM   5—BREADFRUIT
2—BOUGANVILLEA   6—ACACIA TREE
3—BANANA (FLOWER)   7—TREE FERN
4—HIBISCUS

Phyllis Neulist

Buchsbaum

Phyllis Neulist

Buchsbaum

seed pods it produces look like a rose carved from wood. These seed pods are used in dried flower arrangements. The *climbing pothos* vine is raised for its beautiful shiny leaves, that are sometimes two feet long. Air slots appear in the sides of the larger leaves, allowing wind to pass through the vine without damage. This vine grows on palm trees for support. Its weight often kills the tree. *Frangipani* or *temple* tree is a deciduous tree about thirty-five feet tall. The tree flowers before the leaves appear and continuously thereafter. Fragrant yellow, white, or red clusters of flowers are at the ends of the stiff, blunt branches. Frangipani flowers are used in making Hawaiian leis. In Ceylon and India these trees are planted in temple gardens. The *African tulip* tree or *Spathodea,* is a fifty-foot, evergreen tree Throughout the year red flowers, shaped like cups, bloom on the ends of the high branches. The *traveler's-tree* has leaves that resemble banana tree leaves. They are arranged like parts of a giant fan, up to forty feet tall. Rain water collects at the base of the leaf stalks, and water can be obtained by cutting into these stalks. The EUCALYPTUS is sometimes called the *stringy-bark* or *gum* tree. These evergreen trees grow rapidly up to three hundred feet tall. *Acacias* are shrubs or trees. Their flowers are yellow or white and grow in fluffy clusters. The national flower of Australia is the *wattle,* an acacia.

OTHER UNUSUAL PLANTS

Giant flowers are found among *Rafflesia* plants. The tubers of this plant weigh over one hundred pounds. The plant is a PARASITE which attaches itself to ground vines. The flowers may be three feet wide and as tall as a man. They give off an unpleasant odor to attract carrion flies. *Krubi* is a giant flower that grows up to eight feet tall and has a disagreeable odor. *Mangrove* trees grow in salt water swamps and support themselves with prop roots. These roots grow down from the trunk and branches. Many of the wild FIG and EBONY trees produce fruit and flowers on their trunks and branches.

The tree fern is a true fern which grows to 60 feet tall. It is similar to coal age ferns and thus is termed a "living fossil." M. R. L.
SEE ALSO: GEOLOGIC TIME TABLE

Plasma see Blood

Plasma membrane see Cell

Plaster Plaster is a hard material that is coated on walls and ceilings inside buildings. Plaster comes as a powder of cementing chemicals and fine sand.

Different plaster powders contain various amounts of unslaked lime, GYPSUM, and Portland cement. Hair or fibers are also included in the powder mix in order to give strength to the finished plaster coat.

When a plastering job is started the dry plaster powder and sand are mixed with water. The thick, creamy mixture is quickly applied to the *lath* or other plaster base. Plaster bases are the rough surfaces of walls and ceilings. They may be made of concrete blocks, hollow tile, brick, gypsum board or lath. Lath consists of strips of wood or steel having air spaces between strips. The soft, fresh plaster works into such spaces and thus helps keep the dried plaster clinging to the surface.

When mixes of plaster are used for outdoor wall coatings, they are called *stucco*. For smoothly finished, indoor surfaces, a second coat of fine, sandless lime plaster is put onto the first, or rough, undercoat.

Plasterboard is machine-made wall covering. It consists of pairs of sheets of heavy paper or fiberboard containing a sandwich-like filling of gypsum plaster.   D. A. B.
SEE ALSO: CEMENT

Plaster of Paris When gypsum is heated to 120° C, it loses water and becomes the white powder, plaster of Paris ($CaSO_4$) $2H_2O$. When water is added to the powder, it hardens into a solid mass; so plaster of Paris is used for plasters, models, and molds.
SEE: GYPSUM

Plastic surgery Plastic surgery is the branch of surgical medicine concerned with building up external tissues damaged as a result of burns or wounds, with restoring lost parts, or with repairing defects. It is done to improve both the appearance and functioning of the body.
SEE: SURGERY

Rohm and Haas photo
High impact plastic toys resist breakage

Plastics Plastics are organic materials made by man which can be shaped by heat or pressure, or both. Plastics are used for brush handles and bristles, toys, transparent wrappings, fountain pens, insulators, costume jewelry, dishes, and many other items. Some day they may be used in place of metals in the building of houses, automobiles, and airplanes.

Plastics are either *thermoplastic* or *thermosetting*. Celluloid, which was discovered about 1869 by John W. Hyatt, is thermoplastic—it can be softened again and again by high temperatures and remolded. Bakelite, discovered by Leo H. Baekeland about 1910, is thermosetting—once formed, it becomes insoluble and cannot be remelted. These two properties are caused by the fact that the molding operation does not change the atomic order or chemical structure of thermoplastic materials, whereas the heating operation does change the molecular weight and chemical structure of thermosetting resins. (The vulcanization of rubber is similar to the thermosetting of a plastic.)

Plasticizers, high-boiling-point liquids, are used in paints and in thermoplastics. These materials make the plastic pliable at lower temperatures and improve such properties as water resistance, firmness, and flexibility in the final product.

POLYMERIZATION

Many plastics are formed through polymerizing simpler chemicals. *Polymerization* means the joining together of small molecules into larger ones under the influence of

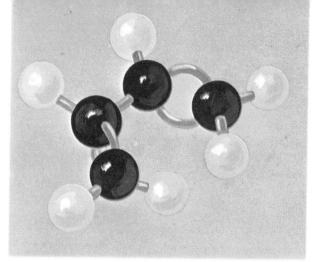

Structure and uses of one basic plastic chemical, butadiene with formula C_4H_6

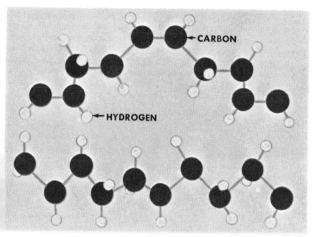

← CARBON

← HYDROGEN

Polybutadienes, or butadiene plastic polymers: the molecules can join together, or polymerize, in different ways. The plastic in the upper figure is rubbery; the lower one is fibrous

In this example of polymerization (right), the original molecule is ethylene, a gas. The linear chain is a polyethylene plastic

Rohm and Haas photo

The Climatron at the Missouri Botanical Garden has a roof, or protective "skin," of acrylic plastic

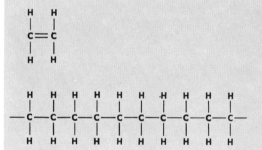

heat and a catalyst. The high polymers are of particular importance. High polymers include textile fibers, rubber, protein, starch, wood, hormones, and, of course, plastics and resins.

The most important polymers fall into two basic groups: *long-chain* and *cross-linked*. Two familiar chain polymers are STARCH and CELLULOSE. The building blocks of these chains are units of sugar molecules, *glucose*. They differ only in the way the sugar links are joined. The effect is that man can digest starch but not cellulose. Cattle and goats can digest both. Thus, there is available food in potatoes, but not in the bark of a tree. By vulcanizing rubber (reacting raw rubber with sulfur at high temperatures), one gets a

cross-linked polymer. The cross links serve to strengthen the rubber.

When *ethylene,* as a liquid, is heated under a very high pressure with small amounts of oxygen, many molecules combine to form the product *polyethylene*. Polyethylene is of great commercial importance. It is a tough solid which has valuable insulating properties and is little affected by most chemical reagents and solvents. It is used as a protective coating and for making containers.

Similar molecules, called *vinyls,* polymerize to become useful as insulating materials, garden hoses, and packaging as in the transparent trade product, *Saran.*

PHENOLIC OR FORMALDEHYDE RESINS

Resins, organic substances from certain

1333

SOME PLASTICS AND THEIR USES

THERMOSETTING (hardened by heat)
Method of obtaining: Condensation polymers (adjacent molecules join by splitting off water)

COMPOSITION	RAW MATERIALS	SOME USES AND CHARACTERISTICS
Phenol-formaldehyde (Bakelite, Textolite)	air, coal, water, oat hulls, fillers	utensil handles, bottle caps, small boxes, plywood adhesives
Urea-formaldehyde	air, coal, water, limestone, fillers	small cases, buttons (plastic has extreme toughness; also can be made in bright colors)
Melamine-formaldehyde (Melmac)	coal, water, limestone, fillers	dishes, electric appliance covers, adhesives, fabric surface (can be made in bright colors)

THERMOPLASTIC (soften when heated)
Method of obtaining: Additional polymers (as in illustration on page 1333)

COMPOSITION	SOME USES AND CHARACTERISTICS
Alkyd resins	protective coatings (paints, etc.)
Casein	costume jewelry, buttons, adhesives
Cellulose nitrates, Cellulose acetates	plastic rods, wrappings, film
Ethyl cellulose	auto hardware, moldings, electrical insulation
Polystyrene	toys, boxes, novelties (water resistant)
Methacrylate	dental plates, optical lenses, rods and tubes (has optical properties)
Polyvinyl acetates, Chlorides	shower curtains, drapes, garden hose
Super-polyamides (Nylon, etc.)	bearings, gears, bristles, fabrics
Tri-chloro-fluoro-ethylene	tubing, electrical insulation
Polyethylene	film, insulation, freezer bags
Polyvinylidene chloride (Saran)	sheets, tubes, molded products (resists solvents)

plants, are among the earliest synthetic plastics. Their commercial development was a realization of the efforts of the American chemist, Leo H. Baekeland, who studied the properties of these plastics around 1910. These resins were known as *Bakelite*. The terms "resin" and "plastic" are often used interchangeably. In more careful use, resin refers to the polymer and plastic to the product obtained from the resin by incorporating plasticizers, fillers and, if desired, dyes.

Continuous heating of a phenolic resin creates larger and larger chains. The polymerized product becomes firmer and firmer.

Wood pulp and other fillers with coloring matter are added to this powder and further heated in molds to give the final product. Some of these resins are water soluble. They are mixed with textiles, and with further heating, the polymerization continues, resulting in water repellent fabrics such as the popular "drip-dry" materials.

A polymerization reaction does not continue indefinitely. Actually, as the molecular weight increases the activity decreases so that there is a practical limit to the size of a polymer molecule.

GLYPTALS

Polymers prepared from *glycerol* and *phthalic* acid are known as *glyptals*. They have cross-linking which makes them useful in the synthetic enamels for finishes on automobiles and household appliances.

FOAMED PLASTICS

These materials, which are porous and of low density, are valuable for insulation, for cushioning, and for structural materials. They can be made by dispersing a gas evenly throughout a resin before it is set. When the resin is set, the gas expands and is entrapped in pores, or escapes leaving pores. Two important foamed plastics are *styrofoam* and *urethane*.

ION EXCHANGE RESINS

When special chemical groups are attached to phenol-formaldehyde resins, they are useful as water softeners. The ions which cause the water to be "hard" are exchanged for sodium ions. The resin is regenerated by treatment with sodium chloride.　　　　　　　　　　　　J. R. S.

SEE ALSO: ORGANIC COMPOUNDS, RESIN, SYNTHETIC FABRICS

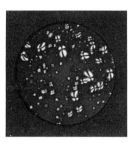

Cell of potato tuber. Leucoplasts enclose the developing starch

Photo-micrographs by National Teaching Aids, Inc.

Spirogyra, a green alga. ''A'' is the chloroplast

Photo-micrographs by National Teaching Aids, Inc.

Plastid (PLASS-tidd) There are small bodies in plant cells that are made of colored material. They are named *plastids*. The CHLOROPHYLL in plastids makes the leaves green. A carrot has orange plastids, and a beet has red ones. The plastids in a white potato have no color. The plastids help a plant to make food or to store it for use later.

Plastids are formed from the cytoplasm in the cell or from the division of other plastids. Usually plastids have a definite shape and are the center of a special chemical action. *Chloroplastids* (*chloros*—green) make carbohydrates from carbon dioxide, water, and light—the process of PHOTOSYNTHESIS. Chlorophyll is always contained in plastids, except in blue-green algae and photosynthetic bacteria. *Chromoplastids* (*chromos*—color) may contain two chemicals—XANTHOPHYLL and carotenes—which give the yellow color to many fruits, vegetables, and autumn leaves. *Leucoplastids* are colorless and contain starch.   H. J. C.

Plateau (platt-TOH) A plateau is an elevated flat area. Plateaus may be a few hundred feet high or thousands of feet high. In most cases they are distinctly above the surrounding lands, but some are flat lands surrounded by mountains.

Some plateaus are small, but most are hundreds of square miles in area.

Plateaus developed from upheavals of the earth's surface when mountains were being formed from lava flows and from settling of the surface which left one portion higher. Most plateaus are worn and gullied away, giving the appearance of being a mountain region. A dramatic example of EROSION at work on a plateau is the Grand Canyon, formed in the Colorado Plateau of the West. The greatest plateau, however, is found in Tibet.   D. J. I.

SEE ALSO: GEOLOGY, MESA, NORTH AMERICA

Platelets see Blood, Circulatory system

Platinum (PLATT-ih-nuhm) Platinum is a grayish-white metallic element. It is more precious than gold. Platinum was discovered in the 15th century by an Italian chemist. It is usually found in ores with other related elements, but some pure platinum occurs. Pure and compound ores are found mainly in the Ural Mountains of Russia; Colombia, South America; Canada; and the Pacific Coast of the United States.

Platinum is heavy and malleable. It can be drawn into a fine wire and hammered into thin sheets. It does not oxidize in air, which means that it will not tarnish. It is resistant to heat and most chemical reagents but will dissolve in aqua regia. It is corroded by chlorine, sulfur and caustic alkalies. It combines readily with most metals. Platinum melts at 1770° Centigrade, making it useful in high-melting-point alloys.

Platinum is easily welded and therefore is valuable in the manufacture of delicate laboratory and surgical instruments and various electrical apparatus.

Containers made of platinum are resistant to heat and reactions. Jewelers use it for settings for valuable gems and surfaces to be delicately and finely engraved. The finest fountain pen points are made of platinum. Some platinum compounds are used to make fluorescent screens for X-rays.

Platinum (symbol Pt) has atomic number 78. Its atomic weight is 195.09 (unchanged for carbon as standard).   W. J. K.

SEE ALSO: ATOM, ELEMENTS

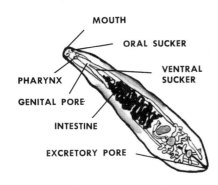

MOUTH

ORAL SUCKER

VENTRAL SUCKER

PHARYNX

GENITAL PORE

INTESTINE

EXCRETORY PORE

Liver fluke, a typical flatworm

Platyhelminthes (platt-ee-hell-MINN-theez) Platyhelminthes are animals better known as *flatworms*. With their wide, thin bodies, they look like pieces of ribbon. Some of the ocean flatworms are shaped like tree leaves. They have beautiful, striped bodies with ruffled edges.

The smallest flatworm cannot be seen except under a microscope. Some live under stones on the damp forest floor. Others cling to plants and rocks in ponds and oceans. Most of the largest, like the fluke and tapeworm, live hidden in the bodies of animals where they cause disease.

Movement from place to place is slow. Most flatworms propel themselves by beating rows of tiny *cilia,* which cover their bodies. Many secrete a carpet of *mucus,* over which they glide. Muscles help them to wriggle and squirm, and to change position. Obtaining food is difficult for a slow-moving worm. Since food is plentiful in the body of other animals, many flatworms have adopted a parasitic way of life.

The free-living flatworms are a busy, active group, found in water and on land. Most of them are *carnivores* which feed upon tiny animals. They often work slowly upon a dead animal or upon an oyster or barnacle, which cannot run away. While a few members have no DIGESTIVE SYSTEM, others have a simple digestive cavity, shaped like a glove, with three or more branching pockets. Since there is only one opening to the digestive cavity, food enters and waste is eliminated through the mouth.

The fresh-water *planaria* is perhaps the best known member of this group. The mouth is located on the bottom of the body at the end of a muscular pharynx. The animal feeds by pushing the *pharynx* or muscular, tongue-like organ outside the body cavity. Food, taken directly into the pharynx, is crushed into smaller pieces. The PLANARIA has a well-developed head with two clusters of eyes and two sensory areas on either side of the head. Planarias have great powers of regeneration. Almost any medium-sized piece will grow into a complete worm. If the head is cut down the middle, the planaria will grow two new heads.

Just as all animals must adapt to a new environment, the body of the parasitic flatworm is modified, in order that it may live inside another animal. The adult attaches itself tenaciously to the body of its host by means of suckers or sharp hooks. Since the adult no longer needs to move in search of food, it loses its outer covering of cilia. which is replaced by a thin protective cuticle. The TAPEWORM which absorbs its food directly through the body wall from its host, has neither a mouth nor a digestive system.

A few of the PARASITES spend their lives in the body of only one animal. Some *flukes* are external parasites, which live on the skin or gills of fish. Other one-host flukes are internal parasites which enter the host through openings like the mouth, anus, or excretory pore. Many are found living inside fish, amphibians, and aquatic reptiles.

Most parasitic flatworms have a complicated life history. In order to develop from egg to larva, and finally to adult form, they need to find two or more hosts in whose bodies they may pass through various stages. This is called *alternation of hosts.*

Adults of both the fluke and tapeworm usually develop in the bodies of vertebrates such as man, fish, cow, or mouse. The fluke LARVA, which passes through four larval stages, generally develops in the body of a small invertebrate animal, like the snail or copepod. The Chinese LIVER FLUKE, for example, passes through four larval stages in the body of a particular species of snail. The larva swims to the body of a fish and finally enters a human host, when raw fish is eaten by man. The tapeworm usually needs two vertebrate hosts. The larva of the beef tapeworm develops in the cow.

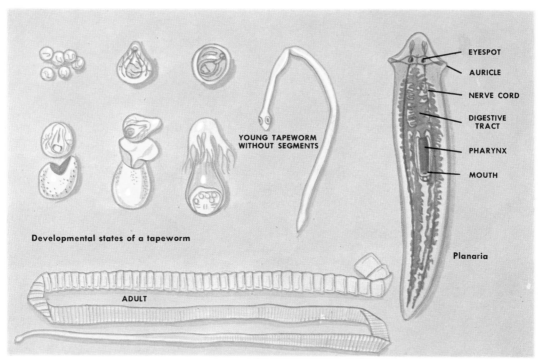

EYESPOT

AURICLE

NERVE CORD

DIGESTIVE TRACT

PHARYNX

MOUTH

YOUNG TAPEWORM WITHOUT SEGMENTS

Developmental states of a tapeworm

Planaria

ADULT

Adapted from Turtox Key card 5.5, courtesy General Biological Supply House, Chicago

Representative animals in the phylum Platyhelminthes

When undercooked diseased beef is eaten by man, the tapeworm matures in the human intestine.

While flatworms are primitive animals, they are the first phylum in the history of life to show "two-sided" or *bilateral symmetry*. Flatworms have three body layers. The outer layer of adult parasites is often only a thick cuticle, but the free-living flatworms have a ciliated epidermis. The middle layer, or *mesoderm,* is a solid layer, containing muscles, as well as excretory and reproductive organs. While some of the free-living flatworms have well-developed nervous systems, many parasites, like the tapeworm, have only a few sensory cells around the suckers. No special circulatory or breathing systems are present.

Most flatworms produce both eggs and sperm. Flukes and tapeworms are very specialized for the business of reproduction. Their reproductive systems are more complex than those of any higher animal. To insure reproduction of the species, these worms produce thousands of eggs, because many eggs do not find a suitable host and so die. E. P. L.

SEE ALSO: ANIMALS, CLASSIFICATION OF

Platypus see Duckbill

Pleiades see Taurus

Pleistocene see Cenozoic Era, Geologic time table

Pleurisy (PLOOR-uh-see) Pleurisy is an inflammatory disease of the *pleura*. The pleura is the serous membrane that lines the chest cavity, and each lung has a separate pleura. Pleurisy is generally caused by a cold, or by another disease such as cancer, pneumonia, or tuberculosis.

The symptoms of pleurisy are a dry cough and sharp pain. Rasping sounds may be heard in the chest. Breathing becomes difficult, resulting in short gasps. There is weakness, headache, a rapid pulse, and loss of appetite. Pus in the pleural cavity is very dangerous and is indicated by chills; fever, and a changing temperature. Rest and inactivity are required for relief. Antibiotics may be prescribed as medication. M. R. L.

Plexus see Nervous system

Pliocene see Cenozoic Era, Geologic time table

Plover

Plover Plovers are a family of birds. There are many different species, or kinds, of plovers. All of the plovers are shore-birds. They live near water and are generally wading birds.

Plovers usually have short bodies and short, thick necks. Their legs are rather long so they can wade in shallow water. Most types of plovers have three toes.

Plovers make their nests on the ground. Almost always the females lay four spotted eggs that look like pebbles.

Plovers migrate great distances. Some plovers spend the summer on the Arctic shores and fly to the Hawaiian islands or Central or South America during the cold winter weather. The *lapwing* is a beautiful European plover.   C. L. K.

Plum A plum tree has smooth-skinned, juicy, tart fruit. The plum is often dried to make prunes. In the United States, plums for prunes are grown in the Pacific states, where drying conditions are most favorable.

Plums are shrubs, or small trees, with white flowers, and large, smooth, clustered fruits. When dried for prunes they must be fully ripe.

Plum trees are usually bought as one-year-old trees and are planted in the fall, or early spring, in the colder climates. Plums need heavy, well-drained soil. The young

Plum tree with ripe fruit

Courtesy Society For Visual Education, Inc.

trees must be pruned to shape and to develop better quality fruit.

The European plum is the most important type in the United States. The Japanese plum includes most of the varieties produced on the west coast for the fresh fruit market. Native American varieties are quite desirable in their own areas and are good in home orchards.   M. R. L.

Plumeria

Plumeria (ploom-AIR-ee-uh) The plumeria is also called the *frangipani* or *temple* tree. It is a small tree or shrub that grows only in tropical areas. It is well known for its beautiful and fragrant flowers. The large waxy flowers are funnel-shaped and can be white, pink, red, or purple. This flower is frequently used in making Hawaiian wreaths or leis. It is also used in making perfume.

Plumeria belongs to the *dogbane* family, and so is related to the oleander and periwinkle. The most common plant is the *Plumeria rubra,* which attains the height of fifteen feet. The fruit of the plumeria consists of leathery pods. Leaves are oblong, about four inches wide, and can be twelve to sixteen inches long.   J. A. D.

Plumule The plumule is the terminal bud at the end of the *hypocotyl* (embryonic stem) above the cotyledons in the seed of a plant. It is a shoot having two distinct leaves.

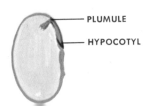

PLUMULE

HYPOCOTYL

NEPTUNE

PLUTO

Pluto has an eccentric orbit, part of which lies within the orbit of Neptune

Pluto Pluto is the ninth planet away from the sun. It was discovered in 1930. No planets beyond Pluto are known to exist. Pluto is thought to be one of the smallest planets. It is probably very dense. It does not seem to have a thick atmosphere as the gas giants do. Its path is not on the same level as the other planets. The orbit of Pluto is a long and drawn out ellipse (oval). The sun is not exactly at the center of Pluto's orbit.

Pluto does not seem to be very much like any of the other planets. The four inner planets are called *terrestrial* or "earth-like" planets. The next four are the *gas giants*. Because it is small and dense, Pluto is put in the group of terrestrial planets.

After Uranus and Neptune were discovered, astronomers thought that they had solved the mystery of the changes in Uranus' motion. They found, though, that Uranus was still not moving according to predictions. They wondered if perhaps there might be still another planet beyond Neptune. Early in the 1900's, an American astronomer Percival Lowell worked out by mathematics some approximate figures for "Planet X." Lowell's description of the planet that no one had ever seen turned out to be remarkably close to what was later discovered to be true. Although Percival Lowell looked for Planet X for several years, he never found it. He died in 1916. Other astronomers took on the search. In 1930 Clyde W. Tombaugh found the mystery planet. He used Lowell's figures and took pictures of the area of the sky that supposedly would show the planet. Pictures taken on different nights showed an object that looked like a faint star. But this "star" was in a different position on different nights. It was moving. It was the new planet.

Even through very powerful telescopes, Pluto only shows itself as a tiny point of light. It is difficult for astronomers to get much accurate information about this tiny speck of light. What is more, astronomers are not at all sure that Pluto is even what it seems to be. The point of light that they are studying could be only a small reflecting patch on the surface of a much larger planet.

There is very little reliable information about Pluto. It seems to be a planet that is smaller than Earth. Its diameter is estimated to be about 3600 miles, but it could be as small as the moon or it could be about the size of Mercury. Because it influences the motion of other planets, astronomers think that Pluto must be very dense. Its average distance from the sun is over 3½ billion miles. Its temperature is probably nearly 400 degrees below zero Fahrenheit. From Pluto the sun would look like a very faint star.

It takes Pluto about 248 years to make a trip around the sun. Pluto's orbit is not circular; it is elliptical. The sun is not at the focus of the ellipse. When Pluto is at its closest point to the sun, Pluto is actually inside of Neptune's orbit. Then Pluto is nearer to Earth and the sun than Neptune is. From 1968 to 2009 Pluto will be nearer to Earth than Neptune. Then astronomers will be able to get a closer look, and they may find out more about Pluto.

All of the other planets revolve around the sun in about the same plane or level. Some of the other orbits are slightly tilted, but Pluto's orbit is inclined at a sharp angle of 17 degrees. This means that sometimes Pluto is high above the other planets in their journey around the sun and sometimes Pluto is rather far below the others.

Because it is difficult to see Pluto's disk, astronomers find it difficult to determine Pluto's period of rotation. It is thought that Pluto rotates in about 6½ days. Astronomers have not been able to discover any satellites of Pluto.

Some theories have suggested that Pluto

is not a planet at all. It could be a burned-out star that used to make the sun a double star. Or Pluto could have been a moon that used to revolve around one of the large planets but went astray and was trapped in an orbit around the sun by the sun's gravity. The difference between Pluto and the other planets lead some astronomers to suppose that Pluto's origin was different from the origin of the other planets.   C. L. K.

SEE ALSO: NEPTUNE, URANUS, SOLAR SYSTEM

Plutonium (ploo-TOH-nee-um) Plutonium is the 94th element. It was discovered in 1940 by GLENN SEABORG. In its pure form it is a silvery-white metal and has chemical properties like those of TUNGSTEN.

Plutonium is found in the uranium ore PITCHBLENDE in extremely small amounts. Man-made plutonium was first produced, however, by bombardment of the element URANIUM by atomic particles known as *deuterons*. Actually the element neptunium is formed first (93rd element), and a radioactive decay takes place to form plutonium. Plutonium is important in atomic energy because fission can occur when a neutron enters the plutonium nucleus.

The plutonium isotope having mass number 239 (Pu^{239}) is a very important source of atomic energy. Uranium with a mass number of 238 (U^{238}) is found in large amounts but can be made to fission or split only by absorbing neutrons of high energy ("fast" neutrons). Pu^{239} will fission when it absorbs either high energy or low energy ("slow") neutrons. On this basis, plutonium is a more efficient material than natural uranium. In a NUCLEAR REACTOR, plutonium is formed when U^{238} absorbs neutrons resulting from the fission of U^{235}. An isotope of neptunium, Np^{239} occurs as an intermediate in the reaction. The reactions are:

$$_{92}U^{238} + \text{neutron} \rightarrow {}_{92}U^{239}$$
$$_{92}U^{239} \rightarrow {}_{93}Np^{239} + \beta^-$$
$$_{93}Np^{239} \rightarrow {}_{94}Pu^{239} + \beta^-$$

A reactor producing one nuclear fuel (Pu^{239}) as it uses up another nuclear fuel (U^{235}) is called a *breeder* reactor. The plutonium produced can be separated from uranium by chemical methods. But the separation of the rare U^{235} from the abundant U^{238} is more difficult because these materials are chemically identical.

As with other metals, salts of plutonium are known and have been produced in the laboratory. Among these compounds are the oxides, halides (chlorides, bromides and iodides), and carbides. The mass number of its most stable isotope is 242.   M. S.

SEE ALSO: ELEMENTS, NUCLEAR ENERGY

Lamination of plywood

Plywood Plywood is made by gluing wide thin slices, or layers, of wood together in order to make a strong wide board.

Each layer, or *ply,* is peeled from a log and so arranged that the grain will run at right angles to that of the layer above and below it. This keeps the wood from warping and splitting. The plies are glued together under pressure, either in a wet or dry state. Dry plies make a better plywood as the tendency toward shrinkage is reduced.

Varieties of plywood called *laminated* and *batten* are made by having the veneers lie perpendicular to the outside layer. Plywood is always made with an odd number of veneers, as 3 ply, 5 ply, etc.

Plywood is used where large, lightweight, strong panels are desired as in walls, doors, furniture, railroad cars, boats and boxes.

If properly glued, plywood is very weatherproof.   J. M. C.

Pneumatics (new-MAT-iks) Pneumatics is the branch of physics which deals with the mechanical properties (such as density, elasticity, pressure) of air and other gases.

Pneumonia bacteria, magnified about 2000 times

Photo-micrographs by
National Teaching Aids, Inc.

Pneumonia (nyoo-MOH-nee-uh) Pneumonia is a disease that affects the lungs and causes hard coughing, high fever, chest pain, and difficult breathing. There are several kinds of pneumonia and many causes for it.

With *lobar* pneumonia an entire lobe of the lung is inflamed. In *lobular* pneumonia only parts of the lobe are involved. With *bronchial* pneumonia the bronchi are infected.

Pneumonia may be caused by a VIRUS, or by various types of BACTERIA, the most common of which is the *Pneumococcus*. The breathing in of gases and chemicals can cause forms of the disease. Oil in the lungs causes *lipoid* pneumonia. Such diseases as *tuberculosis, bubonic plague,* or *tularemia* may involve varieties of pneumonia.

The first signs of the disease are weakness, chills, repeated coughing, often with a rising fever. The person may cough up blood-tinged mucous. Fever and other symptoms may continue for a week or more. The *crisis* or period of highest temperature may, under proper treatment, be followed abruptly by a fall in fever, eased breathing, and gradual recovery of strength. Severely weakened people and very old people may die of pneumonia despite the best treatment.

The best protection against pneumonia is a healthy body to ward off INFECTION. Proper care during and following illness includes bed rest, prompt administration of antibiotics, and care during convalescence. Poorly-ventilated, overheated rooms and crowds in raw, wet seasons may foster pneumonias as they do the common cold.

Treatment depends upon the type of pneumonia. *Penicillin, streptomycin,* and *sulfa* drugs combat bacterial types but do not affect the viral types.

In pneumonias caused by TUBERCULOSIS, rheumatic fever and other systemic diseases, the offending disease should first be treated. Likewise, treatment of noninfective pneumonias with chemical, allergic, or physical causes should begin with removal of the causative factor. In pneumonias, oxygen is frequently administered to aid respiration.

Infective varieties may be contagious and, therefore, quarantine measures are prescribed. All animals seem to be susceptible to pneumonia.　　　　　　　J. M. C.

SEE ALSO: LUNGS, RESPIRATORY SYSTEM

Poi see Taro

Poinciana (poyn-see-AN-uh) Poinciana trees are small, broad-topped trees with large, brightly colored flowers. They grow in the tropical areas of the world. They belong to the pea family.

The *royal poinciana* is one of the most striking tropical trees. It grows 20 to 40 feet tall, spreading wide at its top. Its leaves are one to two feet long, each divided into many small leaflets. The five petals of the flower are orange or scarlet and have uneven edges. Ten stamens stand up from the petals. The seeds are contained in pods which are flat and from six inches to two feet long. This species is native to Madagascar but is cultivated in southern Florida and other warm areas where the colorful plant blooms mostly in the summer.

The *dwarf poinciana* is a ten-foot shrub with prickly branches. It has delicate leaves and orange or yellow flowers, each two inches across. It is widely distributed throughout the tropics.　　　　　　　E. R. B.

Poinciana tree and scarlet flowers

F. A. Blashfield

White poinsettias

Poinsettia (poyn-SETT-ee-uh) In the northern parts of the United States, the poinsettia is a Christmas-time plant. It is grown in greenhouses and used as decorations in homes and churches. In the southern states poinsettias grow in gardens. Originally, the poinsettia came from Central America and Mexico and was brought to the United States by Dr. Poinsett of Charleston, South Carolina, for whom it was named.

Poinsettias grow from two to six feet high and have clusters of tiny yellow flowers surrounded by a brilliant red rosette of *bracts*. Recently, white and pale pink poinsettias have been developed. The green leaves grow rather sparsely on slender, smooth, sometimes crooked stems. Growing outdoors, or inside in a pot, the poinsettia likes shade and moisture.   J. K. K.

Poison Any substance which, when taken into the body, affects health or causes death is a poison. Poisons are very common. Every household contains poisonous items such as ammonia, medicines, and kerosene. Chemical warfare utilizes poisonous gases. Many classical stories and dramas refer to one or another poison.

Poisons are classified according to the bodily part affected. Most poisons, if used in proper quantities or for the original purpose, are of great help to mankind.

A large group of poisons are called *nerve*

poisons because of the effect on the nervous system of the body. Among nerve poisons are *strychnine, chloroform, alcohol,* and *belladonna.* These poisons cause delirium, convulsions, and stupors.

Irritant poisons are caustic poisons caused by *acids, alkalies,* and mercuric and phosphorus compounds. The irritant poison taken into the body burns the throat, the passage to the stomach, and the intestine.

Poison gases are used in wartime or are sometimes released in an industrial accident. These gases can stop the action of the heart or eliminate the oxygen supply to the body.

Numerous poisons are found around the house. Many household cleaners such as ammonia, lye, turpentine, and kerosene, if taken by mouth, are poisonous. Extremely dangerous are the very common INSECTICIDES. If food is neither prepared nor refrigerated properly, food poisoning may occur. Medicines are often taken in too large dosages or by mistake. Most medicines, if not taken as directed, will cause serious illness or death. The type of deadly mushroom called the *death cup* may be eaten by unsuspecting people. Most poisons have a known *antidote* which, if given promptly, will offset the effects of the poison.

The American Red Cross, the National Safety Council, Scout organizations, as well as many other medical and civic organizations, sustain a continuous campaign to prevent accidental poisoning.

Fundamentally important to remember is the prevention of accidental poisoning. Several safety rules are: (1) keep all household cleaners, insecticides, and medicines out of the reach of small children; (2) poisonous medicine and drugs, labeled with a skull and crossbones, should be locked up; (3) older children should be trained as to the dangers of poisons; (4) all unnecessary poisonous items should be thrown away; (5) the family should know the first-aid treatment for poisons.   P. F. D.

SEE ALSO: ANTIDOTE, ARSENIC, CHEMICAL WARFARE, FIRST AID

UNIVERSAL ANTIDOTE

Two parts—Burned toast, powdered
One part —Milk of magnesia
One part —Strong brewed tea

The burned toast supplies absorbent carbon; the milk of magnesia is mildly alkaline buffer against acids; the tea has tannic acid that neutralizes alkalies.
For emergency only

The water moccasin has poison glands which lead into the fangs

Poison glands of a bee (left) and a scorpion (right)

Poison gland A poison gland is a specialized gland found in some animals. This gland produces *venom.* Poison glands are used for protection or as a means of getting food. Venom may cause pain, dizziness, swelling, paralysis, or even death of the victim.

Among animals that have poison glands are some SNAKES. Their fangs contain saliva that can poison other animals when it is injected into the blood stream. Scorpions kill their prey with a poison stinger at the end of their tail. Toads have small poison glands in their skins. The GILA MONSTER bites, and venom flows from glands in its lower jaw into the wound. BEES, wasps, and hornets are well-known for their effective stingers. The sting ray lies on the ocean or river bottom and with its tail drives a sharp spine and poison into its enemy. The Portuguese man-of-war floats like a balloon and has tentacles with stinging cells, reaching down underneath. Some tropical catfish have poison glands in their spines. M. R. L.

Poison ivy Everyone should know what poison ivy looks like in order to avoid it. The tissues of this plant contain a poisonous oil which causes fever and itching, burning and blistering of the skin.

Poison ivy belongs to the cashew family. Although it may be a low shrub, it is often a vine climbing upon tree trunks or other supports. It does not twine like many vines. Some vines cling to supports with *tendrils.* These are modified stems, leaves or parts of leaves. Poison ivy clings with roots growing out from the stem. Its leaf is compound, made up of three shiny green leaflets that change to bright red in autumn. The small flowers are followed by fruits that are *drupes* but look like whitish berries.   J. C. K.

SEE ALSO: POISON OAK

Poison ivy
Courtesy Society For
Visual Education, Inc.

Poison oak   Poison sumac

Poison oak The leaves of the poison oak plant looks much like those of the poison ivy except they are wavy on the edges. They come in groups of three leaflets, are light green above but lighter underneath, and are thickly covered with fine hairs.

One form of poison oak that grows on the Pacific Coast of North America is a shrub about eight feet tall. There is another variety found in the southern states.

Contact with poison oak will cause the same itching and blistering of the skin as poison ivy, and requires the same treatment. The skin should be scrubbed with hot water and alkaline soap immediately.   J. K. K.

Poison sumac see Sumac

Pokeweed see Wild flowers

Polar bear see Bear

Polar climate see Climate

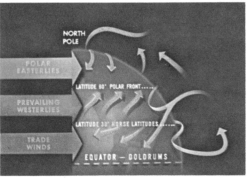

Civil Air Patrol

The polar easterlies meet the prevailing westerly winds at approximately latitude 60°

Polar easterlies The heating and cooling of the earth's surface, plus the rotating movement of the earth upon its axis, causes massive movements of air. Scientists have observed and recorded information about the air movements, and classified them into what is called the *planetary wind system.* The *polar easterlies* are part of that system of winds which are characteristic of the polar regions near the North and South poles.

Weather in the middle latitudes, where most people live, is greatly affected by the polar winds. Their extreme force and cold cause many hardships for men attempting to explore the polar regions. When the pressure is sufficient, great air waves break out of the polar zones and reach far into the middle latitudes. As they travel toward the equator, they are deflected to the west in the Northern Hemisphere. At some point they interact with the *prevailing westerlies* on their way east. This impact is sufficient to cause *cyclonic* storms. When large bodies of polar air are caught in the westerlies and carried eastward, they become traveling *anticyclones,* or highs.   E. M. N.

SEE ALSO: WEATHER, WESTERLIES

Polar regions see Antarctica; Arctic; Earth; Poles, North and South

Polaris (poh-LAIR-iss) Polaris is the star that is always almost directly above the North Pole. It is also called the *Pole Star.* For many years sailors and explorers in the Northern Hemisphere have used this star to find directions. When a person faces Polaris,

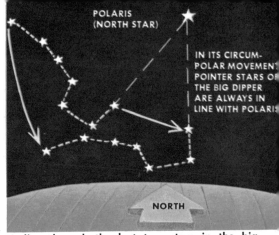

A line through the last two stars in the big dipper will point directly at Polaris

he is facing true north. Polaris is sometimes called the North Star.

Polaris is not one of the brightest stars in the sky. It can be found easily, however, with the help of the "pointer stars." The pointers are two stars in the Big Dipper that point to Polaris. They are the two stars that form the side of the dipper which is farthest from the handle. A line through these two stars leads to Polaris. Polaris is the last star in the handle of the Little Dipper. The dippers are parts of the constellation *Ursa Major* and *Ursa Minor.*

Polaris cannot be seen at all in the Southern Hemisphere. In the Northern Hemisphere it is visible the year round. Polaris is not exactly above the North Pole. If it were, it would not seem to move at all. As the earth rotates, however, Polaris traces a very small circle around the celestial North Pole. The constellations near Polaris are called *circumpolar* constellations. They seem to move in a circle around Polaris.

Besides helping to find directions, Polaris can tell a person in the Northern Hemisphere what latitude he is in. The degree of the angle from the horizon to Polaris is about the same degree of latitude that the observer is from the equator. At the equator this angle is zero for Polaris is on the horizon. At the North Pole, the angle is 90 degrees. Polaris is directly overhead.

Polaris has not always been the pole star. Many years ago, *Thuban* was the star used to find the north direction. The earth's axis changes its direction very slowly. It is moving away from Polaris now. In about 12,000 years *Vega,* a very bright star, will be the north star.   C. L. K.

SEE ALSO: BIG AND LITTLE DIPPERS, CONSTELLATION, URSA MAJOR AND MINOR

Polaris see Missile, Submarine

Polarization (poh-ler-uh-ZAY-shun)
When the *electrodes* in a *voltaic cell*
or any other cell become surrounded
by atoms of nonconducting gases, the
internal resistance of the cell increases. The result of the increased
internal resistance is a drop in the
emf (electromotive force) of the cell.
This decreased emf is due to *polarization* of the electrodes.

The process of polarization in a voltaic
cell is somewhat as follows: The electrodes
of the cell, in which the CATHODE is copper
and the ANODE is zinc, are placed in a weak
solution of sulfuric acid. Inside the cell some
positive hydrogen ions flow toward the copper, where they combine with free electrons
to form neutral atoms of hydrogen. These
neutral hydrogen atoms cling to the copper
as a gas and coat it entirely, thus causing
the copper electrode to act like an electrode
of hydrogen. However, the potential difference between zinc and hydrogen is less than
it is between zinc and copper and the emf
of the cell is reduced. Due to the decreased
emf the cell cannot supply as much current to an external circuit as before; hence,
it is polarized.   A. E. L.

Polaroid see Land, Edwin

Pole (general) A pole is either end of
an *axis*. For instance, in physics either
end of a MAGNET is its pole. In electricity the pole is one of the two
terminals of the current source. In
biology, the pole is one of the opposite
ends of the organism or cell which
are physiologically different.

Pole, magnetic see Magnet, Electricity

Poles, North and South The earth
turns, or rotates, on an axis which is
pictured as an imaginary slanted line
running through its center. The end
point of the imaginary line in the
Northern Hemisphere, or northern
half of the world, is the North Pole.

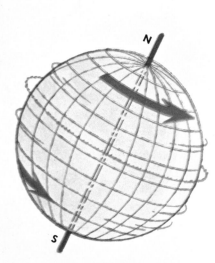

A POLE IS THE END OF THE
AXIS AROUND WHICH THE EARTH
APPEARS TO ROTATE

The end point of the line in the Southern Hemisphere is the South Pole.
Many times when people speak of the
North Pole or the South Pole, they
mean the general regions around the
end points of the earth's axis.

For years these two regions have been
the goal of many explorers. Only in this
century, did men actually stand at the ends
of the earth. On April 6, 1909, the American explorer ROBERT E. PEARY, his assistant
Matthew Henson, and four Eskimos reached
the North Pole. These men were the first to
see the sun and stars go around the sky in
horizontal circles. Peary had 32 observations
to substantiate his claim.

On December 16, 1911, the Norwegian
ROALD AMUNDSEN and four companions
crossed the South Pole. On May 9, 1926,
RICHARD BYRD (U.S.) led an air expedition
which successfully crossed the North Pole.
Especially since the INTERNATIONAL GEO-
PHYSICAL YEAR (1957-58) many more expeditions have penetrated the polar regions
by land and undersea. The first undersea
exploration was made by the atomic-pow-
ered submarine *Nautilus*.   E. M. N.

Polecat see Weasel

Poliomyelitis (pole-ih-oh-MI-eh-LIE-tis) Poliomyelitis is an infectious disease of the *central nervous system*. People all over the world get the disease. Scientists do not know exactly how the disease-producing *virus* gets into the body to make a person sick.

The VIRUS probably enters the body through the mucous membranes of the mouth. It travels in the blood stream and lodges in the intestinal tract and brain and spinal cord. It is excreted from the intestinal tract during the illness and for weeks after recovery, and may be spread by flies to food. In underdeveloped areas of the world where sanitation is poor, mild cases of poliomyelitis are common, and most children over four have acquired immunity to it.

The virus causes inflammation and partial or complete destruction of the *motor neurons* of the spinal cord. In 99 per cent of the cases, the illness is mild and flu-like; the symptoms last three to four days, and there is no PARALYSIS. Symptoms of more severe but nonparalytic poliomyelitis include pain and stiffness in the back and neck due to muscular spasm. In the severe paralytic type, there is pain and weakness in the muscles and sometimes complete paralysis of arms, legs, respiratory, and other muscles, depending on the area of the central nervous system attacked by the virus. Massage and exercise help restore paralyzed limbs if the spinal cord cells are not completely destroyed. If respiratory muscles are affected, a *respirator* or IRON LUNG is used to help the patient breathe.

The *Salk vaccine* for poliomyelitis was introduced in 1954. It is prepared from three strains of *formalin-killed viruses*. This vaccine needs a series of injections. The *Sabin vaccines,* also covering all three types of polio viruses, can be taken by mouth. The polio vaccines are now being distributed all over the world.   E. R. B.

SEE ALSO: MEDULLA OBLONGATA; NERVOUS SYSTEM; SALK, JONAS; VACCINE

Pollen (PAHL-enn) If a lily or a dandelion flower is dusted across one's hand, a yellow powder can be seen. That powder is made of tiny grains of pollen.

DO ALL POLLEN GRAINS LOOK ALIKE?

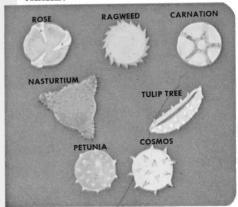

ROSE   RAGWEED   CARNATION
NASTURTIUM   TULIP TREE
PETUNIA   COSMOS

1   Collect flowers from as many plants as you can find.
2   Spread a thin film of glue in the center of several glass microscope slides. Shake a different flower over each slide. The pollen will adhere to the glue. Carefully place a cover glass over each.
3   Observe them under a microscope. How many shapes and sizes did you find?

Pollen forms in the *anthers* at the ends of the male part of the flower called the *stamen*. If the flower develops properly, some of the pollen grains are dusted onto the head of the female part of the flower called the PISTIL. From each pollen grain a slender hair-like tube grows down through the pistil. A pollen nucleus travels through the tube and unites with the little seed-to-be, the *ovule,* in the ovary (the seed case).

      V. V. N.

SEE ALSO: ALLERGY; PLANT; REPRODUCTION, SEXUAL

Pollination (PAHL-ih-nay-shun) Seeds develop after flowering only if pollen is transferred from the male part of the flower (*stamen*) to the female part of the flower (*pistil*) of the same kind of plant. This transfer of pollen to the ovule (*future seed*) in gymnosperms, or to the receptive structure of the ovary (*the stigma*) in flowering

Pollen forms in sacs in the anther. A—pollen tetrad; B—pollen mother cells; C and D outer layers of cells which dry and crack open to release pollen

Photo-micrographs by National Teaching Aids, Inc.

plants, is called *pollination*. Without pollination, there would be no new seed for a new plant.

There are two basic types of pollination. They are called *self-pollination* and *cross-pollination*. Self-pollination is the transfer of pollen from the STAMEN to the PISTIL in the same flower or to the pistil of another flower on the same plant. If pollen from the stamen of one plant is transferred to the pistil of another plant, it is cross-pollination.

When pollen is transferred from one plant to another in cross-pollination, an outside agent or help is needed. The chief agents of pollination are insects, other animals, wind, and water.

BEES are the chief insect pollinators. Moths, butterflies, and certain kinds of flies also visit flowers regularly and in so doing bring about cross-pollination.

Insects visit the flowers to obtain sweet *nectar,* which is secreted deep in the flower from special glands at the base of the petals. The plump, hairy body of the bee is ideal for this process. When the bee tries to reach the nectar glands, located at the base of the flower, it must rub its hairy body against the male anthers of the stamen. These are in most cases located near the entrance of the flower. Then as the insect visits the next flower, some of the pollen is rubbed against the sticky stigma of the female pistil. At the same time a new supply of pollen is brushed off from the stamen onto the bee.

Flowers have brightly-colored petals and sweet odors which attract insects. Nectar guides in some flowers may be ´brightly colored strips located on the petals. Also flowers arranged in showy clusters make them more noticeable to traveling insects passing by.

There is one type of bird that assists in pollination. The little HUMMINGBIRD feeds on the nectar of certain types of flowers. It has a long bill and a long tongue to reach

HOW DOES THE POLLEN GET TO THE EGG TO FERTILIZE IT?

1   Make a thin sugar solution. This will serve as a medium in which the pollen grains can grow.

2   Locate a freshly-opened flower. Place the solution in a shallow dish and shake the stamens (the stalk usually with yellow knobs) over the solution. Cover the dish and permit it to stand for an hour.

3   Using a hand lens observe the long extension which has sprouted from each grain. This is the pollen tube which grows down the pistil until its nucleus joins the nucleus of the egg.

down into the nectar glands while it hovers with its delicate wings overhead.

Flowers of wind-pollinated plants are much less striking in beauty than those pollinated by insects. They are usually in dense clusters at the ends of branches. Petals are lacking, and the flowers seldom have any nectar. The stamens are long and produce a large amount of pollen light in weight. The pistils are also long and the stigma large and often sticky, so that they are able to catch wind-blown pollen grains. Pines, cottonwoods, willows, walnuts, corn, oats, and other wind-pollinated plants fill the air with pollen when their stamens are ripe. Some people are allergic to the pollen.   V. V. N.

SEE ALSO: FLOWERS

Pollution   see Purification

The colorful flowers attract bees, (below) who spread pollen by carrying it between stiff hairs on their legs (right)

Photo-micrographs by National Teaching Aids, Inc.

Courtesy Society For Visual Education, Inc.

Polonium (puh-LOH-nee-um) Polonium is a chemical element. It is radioactive, like uranium and radium. Its symbol is Po and its atomic number is 84. The mass number of its most stable isotope is 210.

Polonium was discovered by Madame Curie in 1898. She named it after her native land, Poland. Madame Curie discovered polonium in some samples of uranium she had obtained from pitchblende.

Polonium is mainly used to produce neutron sources. It is also used in spark plugs and in devices to eliminate static.

Polonium is not found in a natural, simple state. It is found in all uranium minerals, and can be obtained by separating it from uranium residues. It can be produced by bombarding bismuth with neutrons. C. L. K.
SEE ALSO: ELEMENTS

Polycotyledon (pohl-ih-cot-uh-LEE-dun) *Cotyledons* are seed leaves. The food supply of the seed is usually in the form of one, two, or many cotyledons. The term "polycotyledon" refers to seeds that have more than two seed leaves. Pines, spruces, hemlocks, and other cone-bearing trees are polycotyledons.
SEE: COTYLEDON, GYMNOSPERMS

Polygon see Geometry

Polymer Molecules of the same kind can be chemically joined together to form a single larger molecule. The new, heavier molecule is made up of the same elements in the same proportions. Its molecular weight is a multiple of the original molecule. This new molecule is called a "polymer."
SEE: CHEMISTRY, PLASTICS

Polymorphism Polymorphism is the occurrence of a plant or animal in different forms or colors. A chemical substance like sulfur is polymorphous when it exists in several crystalline forms.

Polyps Polyps are *coelenterates* of the class *Anthozoa*. They are also the attached forms of some coelenterates which have two forms. They are cylindrical, attached at one end, and have a mouth at the other end.
SEE: COELENTERATA

Pomegranate

Pomegranate The pomegranate tree has been known to man for thousands of years. It is a tree or tall shrub that grows only in tropical or semitropical lands. In the United States it grows best in southern areas.

Small clusters of reddish-orange flowers bloom in the spring and are followed by a reddish or deep yellow fruit called pomegranate. This fruit is the size of a large orange. The outside covering, or rind, of the pomegranate is hard, but inside this sectioned fruit are many seeds surrounded by juicy pulp. J. A. D.

Pomes Pomes are a type of fruit. They are often good to eat and provide one with vitamins and minerals needed for good nutrition. The apple, pear, quince and hawthorne are pomes.

The fleshy part which surrounds a core is the part of pomes that is eaten. The core is a compound of several carpels that have grown together. The *carpel* is the place where seeds develop. These FRUITS usually have many seeds. The seeds of pomes are sometimes called *pips*. M. R. L.

Cross section of a typical pome, the apple

FLESHY
RECEPTACLE

SEEDS
EXOCARP
MESOCARP

Pompano

Lombardy poplars
have a tall graceful
shape

Pompano Pompano is the name given to a group of fish found mainly along the Atlantic coastline and in the West Indies. They include the common pompano, sometimes called the *butterfish,* the round pompano and a larger variety, the jack pompano. The butterfish is popular as a food fish.

Pond lily see Water lily

Pons see Brain, Nervous system

Pontoon bridge see Bridges

Popcorn Unlike other CORN, popcorn kernels have an almost moisture-tight coating. When the kernel is heated the steam from the germ inside expands and explodes the starch into fluffy white bits. If regular corn is heated, the steam leaks out slowly at the base and along the soft channel of the kernel.

Poplar (PAHP-ler) Poplars are fast growing but short-lived trees. They form great forests in low lands and on the slopes of mountains. They have broad, heart-shaped, leathery leaves that are pale green above and silvery beneath. The leaves are on long stems. Their flowers are long, and a tiny seed is attached to a cotton-like material by which it is carried through the air.

The wood of the poplar tree is light, soft, and brittle. It is used for making packing cases and paper pulp. Poplars love the sun. They are often planted as WINDBREAKS or between farms to mark boundaries.

The *cottonwood* grows on the western plains where few other trees can grow. The *aspen,* with a smooth, gray bark, and leaves that ripple in the wind, is the prettiest tree of the poplars. The *balm of Gilead* secretes a wax that the Indians used for sealing up the seams of their birch-bark canoes. The *Lombardy* poplar has upward pointing branches and a long, narrow shape. M. R. L.
SEE ALSO: DECIDUOUS

Poppy The poppy family contains about 200 kinds of flowers in shades of red, orange, and white. Poppy seeds are used to flavor rolls and bread, and are sold as bird food.

The white poppy raised in the Orient produces *latex,* a milky juice found in the unripe fruit. OPIUM, a dangerous drug, comes from this juice. *Morphine* and *codeine,* pain-relieving drugs, are also refined from it.

The red poppy grows wild throughout Europe. Oriental poppies, native to Mediterranean regions, grow to four feet in height. The California poppy was found in 1815 growing in masses where the city of San Francisco now stands. It is the state flower of California. P. G. B.
SEE ALSO: PLANTS, MEDICINAL

California poppies

Poppy seed Poppy seeds are tiny, deep blue or black seeds used in cooking. Hundreds of tiny seeds are found in each seed pod of the poppy.

Although used by the Egyptians before 1500, it was the Dutch people who developed one species of the poppy plant which gives the walnut-flavored seed used today. The seeds do not contain narcotics.

Poppy seeds are used in baking and flavoring vegetable dishes, salads, and sauces. A gray poppy seed called *maw* is found in commercial birdseed mixtures.

J. K. K.

Courtesy Society For Visual Education, Inc.

North American porcupine (above) and prehensile-tailed South American (below)

Porcelain (PORS-uh-luhn) Porcelain is the finest and most expensive type of pottery. It is usually white and *translucent,* meaning that light will shine through it.

Porcelain is made of a mixture of *kaolin* and *feldspar*. These materials are finely-ground and washed and then mixed into a clay. The clay is then worked and kneaded. When the clay reaches the proper consistency, it is shaped into the desired piece either on a potter's wheel or in a mold. If the piece is to have a handle and spout, these are separately molded and attached to the piece with the clay. Then it is set aside to dry, after which it is baked in a kiln or oven at a comparatively low temperature. The baked piece is known as a *biscuit*. The biscuit is then dipped in *glaze* and again fired at a very high temperature.

The secret of making porcelain was discovered in China. The earliest pieces date to about 900 A.D. Porcelain was introduced to Europe in the 15th century. Various Europeans tried unsuccessfully to duplicate this highly-prized chinaware. It wasn't until 1709 that Boettger, a chemist to the Elector of Saxony, succeeded in discovering the materials that compose porcelain. W. J. K.

Porcupine (PAWR-kyuh-pyne) Often called *quill pigs,* porcupines are rodents, animals that gnaw. Unlike other rodents, porcupines have coarse hair mixed with long, stiff quills. The sharp tips of the quills are pointed backward like the end of a fishhook. These slow-moving animals have short legs, broad tails, and thick-set bodies. Although found in many kinds of forests, they prefer evergreen forests.

The barbed quills, which are controlled by muscles in the skin, are loosely attached to the porcupine and easily catch on anything which touches them. Porcupines cannot throw their quills as is commonly believed. The porcupine often slaps at its enemy with its powerful tail, causing many of the long quills to become imbedded in the enemy's skin. Once imbedded, they are very difficult and painful to remove because of their barbs. Some enemies of the porcupine, such as the fox, lynx, coyote, and mountain lion, attempt to turn the porcupine over on its back; however, this is difficult to do because the porcupine is able to roll itself up into a compact spiny ball.

Porcupines are gnawing mammals (rodents), feeding mainly on the leaves, buds, and bark of trees and the roots and stems of tender plants. They are especially fond of salt. They are excellent climbers and frequently climb trees searching for food.

Porcupines have one to three babies each year in early summer. They are usually born under a rock ledge, in a crevice or cave. The babies are large and well-developed at birth, having fur, spines, and teeth. They can live alone in just one week.

There are several species of porcupines. The Canadian porcupine and the yellow-haired or European porcupine are two. The Canadian porcupine, found throughout North America, grows to be about three feet long, weighing up to forty pounds. The European species is smaller. D. J. A.

SEE ALSO: RODENTIA

Pore see Skin, Sweat gland

Tan sponge

Buchsbaum

Porifera (poh-RIFF-er-uh) Most people use a cloth for scrubbing cars or for washing windows. But some people use an animal, better known as a *sponge*. Although there are many different kinds of sponges, all sponges are covered with thousands of tiny holes or pores. The name *porifera* means "pore-bearer."

People who have used the bath sponge know that it is light in weight. It also remains tough, even when it is wet. The bath sponge has a soft, elastic skeleton of *spongin*. All sponges are held up by stiff, outside skeletons. However, most sponges have a scratchy skeleton of sharp chalk or glass needles.

All sponges live in water. Most of them live in the ocean. Many of those in the warm, shallow oceans have beautiful colors —pinks, scarlets, and greens. Sponges which live either in fresh water or many thousand feet under the ocean are usually colored brown or gray.

The members of this phylum used to be called "plants" or "plant-animals." Adult sponges do not move from place to place. Like plants, they attach themselves to solid surfaces, such as rocks, ground, wharfs, and even the backs of crabs. While many are shaped like branching plants, others look like vases, tubes or cups. Since most sponges live in colonies, they spread out over large areas like thick, flat cushions of moss.

A sponge is like a small, filtering plant. Water enters continually through small pores on the sides of the body. Inside the sponge, it passes into a large, hollow cavity or through an elaborate system of canals. As oxygen and small organisms are removed, wastes and carbon dioxide are passed into the water. From one or more large holes at the top of the body, water leaves in a steady jet stream.

A sponge may also be thought of as a small community of cells, working together in groups. Each group is specialized for

carrying out a particular duty. The flat outer cells, which fit closely together like floor tiles, are the protective cells. *Collar* cells line the internal cavity. At the free end, this unusual cell has a long whip-like *flagellum,* protruding from a delicate collar of *protoplasm.* As the flagella beat, they drive water through the inner channels and pull food particles into the collar.

Between the inner and outer cells, there is a jelly-like, non-living substance. Embedded in this are the *mesenchyme* cells, which move like the AMEBA. Some of them receive the partly-digested food from the collar cells, digest it further, and transport it throughout the body. They probably also pass waste materials to the surface. Specialized mesenchyme cells, shaped like hollow rings, are called *pore cells.* These form the openings of pores which lead to the internal cavity.

Perhaps the most important duty of the mesenchyme cells is to secrete the skeleton which supports this great mass of cells. Sponges are classified according to the shape and composition of the needles and fibers of the skeleton. *Chalk,* or *calcareous,* sponges have needles, or *spicules,* of *calcium carbonate.* Since the needles are com-

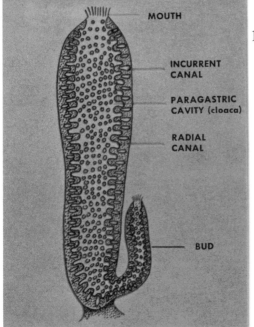

Longitudinal section of a sponge

Porpoise

monly shaped like a "T" or a "Y", they interlock and overlap. Most chalk sponges are small marine animals with drab color. Found in the deepest ocean water, the true *glass* sponges have beautiful six-rayed spicules of silica.

Four-fifths of all sponges belong to the class of *horn* sponges. Included are all glass sponges without six-rayed spicules, as well as sponges with horny, elastic skeletons, made of a protein secretion, called *spongin*. A few members have skeletons of both silica and spongin. Apart from the bath sponge, the horny sponges have little commercial value since the skeleton collects foreign matter, such as bits of rock.

Any portion of the sponge is able to produce an entire new animal. Some sponges reproduce asexually by budding and branching. However, all sponges are able to reproduce sexually. Eggs and sperms may be produced within the same individual, or within separate individuals. Since the free-swimming larva moves about before it settles down to become an adult, sponges are distributed over a wide area.   E. P. L.

SEE ALSO: AMEBA; ANIMALS, CLASSIFICATION OF; SILICON

Porosity Porosity is the characteristic of being *porous,* or filled with tiny holes through which water, air, or the like pass. Sponges and sandstone are porous. VIRUSES can pass through pores in porcelain filters.

Porpoise (PAWR-puss) The porpoise is a sea animal with a rounded head and blunt snout. Its name means *pig fish*. It is a small, toothed whale that lives in warm, shallow coastal waters. Porpoises are related to the large whales and DOLPHINS and belong in the same group of animals called the *cetaceans,* meaning *large sea animals*. These hairless, fish-like animals are sea mammals that bear their young alive and suckle them.

Porpoises swim near the surface of the water, traveling in large schools or herds. Sometimes these schools include several hundred porpoises. They are air-breathing animals. Warm air is exhaled through a single breathing hole (*blow-hole*) on the porpoise's head. This warm air vaporizes into a hissing jet of steam when it is expelled into the colder outside air.

The common porpoise is about six feet long, weighing from 100 to 120 pounds. Its smooth whalelike body is black above and white below. It has a triangular dorsal fin in the middle of its back. This porpoise has twenty-five pairs of short, sharp teeth in each jaw. It eats salmon, mackerel, herring, cuttlefish, and crustaceans. Schools of these porpoises often travel great distances in their search for food. Baby porpoises, about three feet long, are born in the spring. They, like other mammals, are nursed by their mothers.   D. J. A.

SEE ALSO: CETACEA, MAMMALIA, WHALE

Portuguese man-of-war see Man-of-War, Portuguese

Portulaca (pohr-tchuh-LACK-uh) Portulaca is a small herb or flower that deserves respect. A native of Brazil, this little flower grows where nothing else will. It thrives in hot, dry, almost impossible places. Portu-

Portulaca thrives in dry soil

laca is also called *rose moss* for its low showy flowers.

Portulaca grows close to the ground, seldom reaching over one foot in height. It has narrow, fleshy leaves and brightly colored flowers. They may be white, red, pink, yellow, or purple.

There is a kitchen-garden variety of portulaca that is used as a cooking herb. It grows to one and one-half feet tall, has bright yellow flowers and leaves one-half inch wide. J. K. K.

Positron (PAHZ-uh-trahn) The positron is a particle smaller than an atom. It is identical to the *electron* in size and weight, but has a positive rather than negative charge. It was discovered by C. D. Anderson at the California Institute of Technology in 1932. He discovered positrons while studying cosmic radiation with a CLOUD CHAMBER. He named the positron for its *posi*tive charge and its similarity to the elec*tron*.

Positrons can be formed through the change of a PROTON into a neutron inside the nucleus of an atom. Such a change occurs spontaneously in many radioactive elements. The positron can combine with a free ELECTRON and the two disappear by forming two gamma rays. This is called *annihilation radiation* because the electron and positron disappear. In the absence of electrons (in vacuum) the positron is stable and can live forever. In the presence of matter, such as most solids, the positron lives a very short time (one-billionth of a second).

Positrons were predicated theoretically, before their experimental discovery, by the English physicist P. A. M. Dirac. In Dirac's theory, negative energies for electrons exist as well as the ordinary positive energies. A positron comes into existence when an electron is removed from the region of filled negative energy states. The "hole" left by the electron is the positron. To form such a hole, energy must be put into the region. When a PHOTON is absorbed in the vicinity of a charged particle, one negative electron and one positive positron are created. This process is called *pair production*. J. K. L.

Posterior Posterior means at, or toward, the hind end of an animal. It also means *caudal* on some animals. SEE: ANIMALS, CLASSIFICATION OF

Posture To have good posture should be one of the most important health goals. With head held high and shoulders level, a person will feel better. Standing correctly helps the blood move freely to the brain and circulate better throughout the body. The organs with which people breathe, digest food, and get rid of waste materials do their best work when in their proper position.

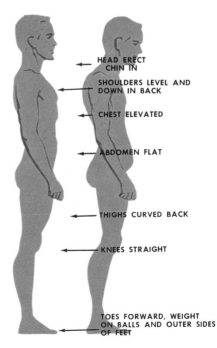

HEAD ERECT
CHIN IN

SHOULDERS LEVEL AND DOWN IN BACK

CHEST ELEVATED

ABDOMEN FLAT

THIGHS CURVED BACK

KNEES STRAIGHT

TOES FORWARD, WEIGHT ON BALLS AND OUTER SIDES OF FEET

GOOD POSTURE   BAD POSTURE

Potash Potash is a name often used for a chemical known as *potassium carbonate*. This chemical was originally obtained from wood ashes and thereby received its name. Potash is used in the manufacture of soaps and glass.

Potassium carbonate is very soluble in water, and the solution that results is alkaline. In its dry or *anhydrous* form, it takes up water very readily even from the air itself. For this reason it is used to remove water from organic liquids when the water is not wanted.

In its pure dry form, potash is a white, odorless, granular powder. Its chemical formula is K_2CO_3. Its molecular weight is 138.2.   M. S.

Potassium (puh-TASS-ee-um) Potassium is one of the alkali metals and the 19th element. It was first prepared in the pure form by SIR HUMPHRY DAVY in 1808. It appears as a soft silvery-white metal when pure. In the form of various minerals and salts, it makes up 2.4% of the earth's crust.

Potassium is one of the most active metals known. It reacts with the oxygen in the air and very vigorously with water. In order to keep potassium from reacting in storage, it must be immersed in a liquid that does not contain oxygen, such as petroleum or other liquid hydrocarbons.

Its main uses are in chemical reactions to make other compounds or salts containing potassium. Some of the more familiar compounds and their uses are as follows: potassium *bicarbonate* in baking powders; potassium *bromide* as a sedative; potassium *carbonate* (potash) in soap manufacturing; potassium *chlorate* in fireworks and EXPLOSIVES; potassium *chloride* in medicine; potassium *dichromate* in leather tanning; potassium *ferrocyanide* in dyeing wool and silk; potassium *hydroxide* in soap manufacturing; potassium *iodide* in analytical chemistry; potassium *nitrate* in gunpowder; potassium *oleate,* a soap; potassium *permanganate,* an antiseptic; potassium *persulfate* for bleaching fabrics; potassium *sulfite* in photographic developers.

Potassium (symbol K from Latin *Kalium*) has atomic weight 39.102 (39.100, O = 16).

Recently, potassium has become important in dating materials that are older than the carbon-14 method can date. A very active ISOTOPE of potassium, K^{40}, slowly but steadily changes into argon-40. For example, it would take 1 3/10 billion years for half of 18 K^{40} atoms to decay to argon-40. The time is long but it can be calculated from the number of K^{40} atoms remaining. The discovery that man may be one million years older than previously thought is the result of such calculation.   M. S.
SEE ALSO: ELEMENTS, ELEMENTS IN THE HUMAN BODY, NUCLEAR SCIENCE

Potato In France the potato is called "apple of the earth" for the potato grows under the earth. Just as the apple is the most popular fruit grown, the potato is the most popular vegetable grown.

The potato plant looks like its relative, the TOMATO plant, with spreading stalks and dark green leaves. The flowers are small and white, bluish or yellow. Underground, the plant grows stems called *stolons*. The end of the stems develop into *tubers* which are called potatoes. *Buds,* or *eyes,* grow on the potato. New potato plants can be started by planting a piece of potato that has an eye.

Great Britain, Germany, Maine, Montana and Idaho grow many potatoes. Spanish explorers discovered the potato in South America and brought it to Europe in the sixteenth century. It has become an important food, being easy to digest and nutritious and cheap.   P. G. B.

Potato plant; underground are stolons and tubers

Potential Potential is a measure of the amount of a stored quantity available for possible use. Potential ENERGY is energy of position. It is the work which has been done to put something in a potential where it is ready to move due to the presence of some force. This force may be gravitational, mechanical, electrical, magnetic, etc.

Potentilla

Potentilla (poh-tuhn-TILL-uh) Potentilla is the name of certain plants that grow wild on lawns and prairies in the eastern part of the United States. They are sometimes called *five-finger* plants because each leaf is divided into five parts. Since some are creeping vines that resemble strawberry plants, they are also called *false strawberry*. The flowers are bright yellow, and grow in small clusters.

Potentilla plants grow in poor soil. If many plants grow in an area, it may be a sign that the soil is acid or sour and trees should not be planted.   P. G. B.

Poultry see Chicken, Fowl

Pound see Foot-pound, Measurement

Power Power depends upon how fast work is done. WORK is done whenever a push or pull moves something. The work may be done slowly or quickly. If work is done quickly, greater power is expended than when it is done slowly.

The push or pull needed to move something is called *force* and the work done is the force times the distance the object is moved. Power $= \dfrac{\text{work}}{\text{time}}$. If a boy weighing

80 pounds climbs 20 feet up a ladder, 1600 ft-lbs. of work is done against gravity. The force the boy needs to climb the ladder equals his own weight. If the boy climbs the ladder in 4 seconds, the power $=$ $\dfrac{1600 \text{ ft-lbs.}}{4}$ or 400 ft-lbs. per sec. If he takes 8 seconds to climb, the power is less. Power $= \dfrac{1600}{8}$ or 200 ft-lbs. per sec. Thus power is the time rate of doing work.

Power may be expressed in many different units such as *horsepower* and *watts* (*joules* per second). When the time rate of working is 550 ft-lbs. per second (or 33,000 per minute) the power is one horsepower. The watt rating on an electric light bulb gives the rate at which electrical energy (work) will be consumed when the bulb is used. The 100 watts means 100 joules per second. This is a unit of power MEASUREMENT in the metric system.   J. H. D.
SEE ALSO: ENERGY; MACHINES, SIMPLE

Prairie A prairie is a broad stretch of grassland. The name was given to the large area of the Mississippi Valley by early French explorers. The prairie is the region located in the central part of the United States. It is bordered by heavy forests on the east and the mountains on the west. It is from 300 to 1400 feet above sea level.

The prairies are considered treeless, but the streams running through them are lined with many varieties of trees. The open country is covered with coarse grasses and other kinds of vegetation. The soil is dark and fertile, and covered with a layer of fine dust. The climate of the prairies is severe since it is unprotected from the winds in winter and the intense heat in the summer. It has an annual rainfall of about 30 inches, occurring mostly in the spring and summer.   W. J. K.
SEE ALSO: GEOGRAPHY, NORTH AMERICA

Prairie chicken see Grouse

Prairies are vast open areas with few trees
Courtesy Society For Visual Education, Inc.

Prairie dogs above their burrow

Prairie dog The prairie dog is a small, wild rodent with very short ears and a short, flat tail with a black tip. This stout, sturdy little animal is about fifteen inches long, and has coarse brownish fur with some gray and black hairs. Prairie dogs like the high dry prairies of the west. They are found from Texas and Kansas to the Rocky mountains, and north to Montana.

Prairie dogs live in large colonies. Their underground burrows are very cleverly constructed and may cover many miles. Each opening into the burrows has a mound of earth around it to prevent rain water from running in. The prairie dog will sit in the opening like a guard and watch for danger. In case of danger, it sounds a shrill alarm and quickly ducks into the burrow. Just inside the burrow entrance are rooms where it goes to listen for the danger to pass. Farther down in the burrow are many passages and rooms. Some are lined with grass for care of the young. Prairie dogs live on grasses, weeds, and some insects.   M. R. L.
SEE ALSO: RODENTIA

Prairie wolf see Coyote

Praseodymium (pray-see-oh-DIMM-ee-uhm) Praseodymium is a scarce metallic element of the *rare-earth* group. It occurs in *cerite* and other rare minerals. Its symbol is Pr. Its atomic number is 59 and atomic weight is 140.907 (or 140.92 with oxygen as the standard). It is naturally silvery white but its salts are green.

Its common oxide (Pr_6O_{11}) is a black powder. The salts of praseodymium are produced by dissolving the black oxide in an acid. These salts are used in the ceramic industry for glazes and coloring glass.

Von Welsbach discovered the element in 1885 when he separated the salts of didymium into praseodymium and NEODYMIUM.
                                        E. R. B.
SEE ALSO: ELEMENTS, OXIDATION

Courtesy Society For Visual Education, Inc.
A mantis searching for prey

Praying mantis The mantis or *mantid* is an insect that has long, folding front legs. It usually sits on a plant with these legs poised ready to snatch another passing insect for its prey. This posture reminded early naturalists of a human attitude of prayer, and thus suggested the name. The mantis is actually harmless to large animals and is valuable because it eats grasshoppers and other insect pests. Most species live in the tropics, but the American and common European species live well north. The European species is becoming common as an imported species in the United States.

The mantis is a cannibal, for it eats other mantises as well as other insects. The female often eats its own mate.

Related to the grasshoppers, crickets, and cockroaches, the mantis is slender with long, locust-like legs, oval wings, a long neck or *prothora,* and an angular movable head with large, protruding eyes. The front legs are stout, spiny, and fitted for seizing their prey like a spring trap. Mantises measure two to five inches long. They resemble the leaves of plants.   J. K. K.
SEE ALSO: INSECTA

Pre-Cambrian see Geologic time table

Precious stones see Gem

✳ THINGS TO DO

HOW TO MAKE A PRECIPITATE WITH LIMEWATER TABLETS

Materials: Limewater tablets (from drugstore), 2 tumblers or test tubes, funnel, filter paper, soda water, straw

1   Dissolve 1 or 2 small limewater tablets in a tumbler of cold water. Keep weak lime solution off of skin.

2   Filter the milky solution with a funnel lined with filter paper. Do this within ½ hour, since carbon dioxide of the air will recloud the clear liquid coming through filter.

3   Divide the resulting clear limewater into two portions. To one, add a little fresh carbonated water. The white precipitate formed is calcium carbonate.

4   Show that your breath also contains carbon dioxide that will make lime carbonate precipitate. Simply blow with a soda straw into the weak, clear limewater.

Note: If you breathe too long, the white carbonate will redissolve. This is because it forms soluble, non-precipitated calcium hydrogen (bi-) carbonate.   **D. A. B.**

Precipitation (chemical) (pruh-SIPP-ih-tay-shunn) When some specific chemical is added to a solution, a solid mass of new chemical is often formed. This solid material is the result of a reaction between the solution and the chemical which has been added to it. The new, insoluble substance is a *precipitate;* and the process by which it forms is called *precipitation.*

Two common examples of precipitation are: (1) the formation of a white, finely-divided cloudy mass (*calcium carbonate*) when a person blows his breath (with *carbon dioxide* in it) into clear *limewater*; (2) the formation of a white scum (which in most hard waters is *lime-* and *magnesium-soap salts*) when soap is mixed with hard water.

Four conditions or factors affect precipitation: (1) the solubility of both original and newly formed chemicals in a given reaction; (2) the particular concentration of chemicals—including *ions,* if any—in the mixture being studied; (3) the temperature of the mixture; (4) the chemical nature (*chemical equation*) of the mixture being studied. Other factors important in some complex precipitations include (a) the effect of *super-saturation,* and (b) the law of *mass action,* which is a mathematical rule concerning the strength of each type of *molecule,* or ion, in the reacting solution.

Certain changes in complex *colloidal* solutions seem to be precipitations but actually are not. For example, when clear egg white is cooked to a white solid or when milk curdles, the change is a molecule-clumping one, called *coagulation*—not true precipitation. Again, when a solution is merely heated to remove water and obtain a solid residue, that process is *separation by evaporation.*

Precipitation is widely used in chemistry. It finds its two most important uses, first, in the identification of chemicals in mixtures of unknown composition, and, second, in the separation of certain chemicals into a pure, solidified form from their natural or processed mixtures.   **D. A. B.**

SEE ALSO: CHEMISTRY

WHERE DOES RAIN COME FROM?

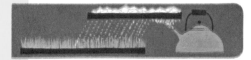

1 Place a wooden flat of grass on a table near a kettle of boiling water. Hold a pan of ice cubes or crushed ice over the spout. As the steam hits the cold bottom of the pan droplets of water will form. As the drops increase in size they will fall on the grass as rain.
2 The warm air coming from the teakettle is laden with water vapor. As it hits the cold surface it must condense some to liquid water. Cool air cannot hold as much moisture as warm air.

Precipitation (weather) (pruh-SIPP-ih-tay-shunn) To the weather student, the word "precipitation" means "rain," "snow," "hail," "dew," or "frost." Except for dew and frost, all these forms of precipitation fall from the sky onto the earth's surface.

Weather scientists (*meteorologists*) constantly try to increase the knowledge about how precipitation occurs. Weather experts, besides observing and predicting daily movements and changes of winds and temperature, must understand the basic physics of precipitation.

Four factors determine whether or not "tomorrow it will rain"—first, the HUMIDITY of an approaching low-pressure air mass; next, the air-mass temperature; then the nearness of another approaching, cold-air mass; finally, the kind of dust particles (called *nuclei*) in the air masses. Recent research has revealed still another factor—the position and motion of high-altitude jet streams of air.

Under ideal conditions, some form of precipitation will occur when a warm, moist (*humid*) air mass meets a cold, dry and dense mass. The meeting boundary of these two masses is a *front*. The cold air will usually push along the earth's surface underneath the warm mass. Thus the humid, warm

mass starts to rise; in so doing it expands and starts to cool. This rising and cooling (*adiabatic expansion*) makes the warm, humid mass unstable; it can no longer hold its contained water vapor as a gas. Instead, this vapor must condense either into *rain drops* or into *ice crystals*. This condensation appears as precipitation (nimbus or cumulonimbus) clouds. Still rain has not fallen.

The resulting rain droplets (or ice crystals) are so dense that they begin at once to fall through the up-drifting currents of the cloud. If, in their downward course, they meet air at or below freezing, the condensed particles reach earth as snowflakes or ice pellets called *sleet*. If, however, the lower air is above freezing, the falling particles reach the earth as raindrops.

Sometimes, right after the first droplets are condensed in a rain cloud, a stronger up-draft sweeps them upward several thousand feet and into the cold anvil-head of the nimbus. There they freeze quickly, not into crystals, but into *hailstones*. Their gravitational force finally gains over the up-draft; and these small hailstones start downward, often meeting other freezing droplets that add more layers to their icy globes and finally reach the earth.

Dust particles of certain types (sea salt and clay dust) are important in starting precipitation; for a rising, warm-humid cloud often will not start condensing into drops or snowflakes when in pure, dust-free air. Scientists say that the cloud's vapor is super-cooled. The nimbus cloud may move away without rain or snow ever forming and falling from it in that region. If dust particles are present, however, they form precipitation nuclei that enable the cloud's vapor to condense upon them, acting as "starters" for droplets.

In 1946, scientists first used the idea of providing artificial precipitation nuclei to cause rainfall. Powdered *silver iodide* and *dry ice* were used for the nuclei, or *cloud-seeding,* chemicals. To distribute the chemicals, they flew airplanes which carried the powder in spraying machines. The planes flew over nimbus clouds, and also above warm-air masses, and thus "seeded" them. Results of these and later rain-making experiments have been considered promising, but not always clearly successful.   J. R. S.
SEE ALSO: CLOUDS, RAIN-MAKING, WEATHER

Predator see Balance of nature

A four-toed prehistoric horse (left) and a prehistoric bear (right)

Pregnancy Pregnancy is the period during which a baby is contained in its mother's uterus, or womb, before it is born. Human pregnancy lasts about nine months; during this time the baby grows from a tiny fertilized egg to a baby of about seven pounds.

First signs of pregnancy are cessation of MENSTRUATION, enlargement of the breast, and other bodily changes, and sometimes a kind of *nausea* called "morning sickness."

Pregnancy begins at *conception* when the *sperm* fertilizes the *ovum*. The fertilized ovum sends out little threadlike *villi* which attach themselves to the wall of the *uterus* and grow to become the fetal portion of the *placenta*. The placenta is a special structure of glands and blood vessels through which the baby receives nourishment.

By the end of the fourth month, the mother feels "signs of life," the restless movements of the baby, or *fetus,* and the doctor can distinguish the fetal heartbeat.

Pregnancy ends with *labor,* the process by which the baby is expelled from the uterus and given BIRTH to or *born.*   J. M. C.
SEE ALSO: GESTATION PERIOD; REPRODUCTION, SEXUAL

Prehensile Prehensile means able to seize or grasp by coiling around and clinging to an object. It is illustrated by the folding of the fingers around an object in the palm, or by the action of a MONKEY'S tail.

Prehistoric mammals Mammals first appeared on Earth during the Mesozoic Era (the Era of Reptiles). They were small, warm-blooded animals with hair, that looked very much like the reptiles from which they descended. Toward the end of the MESOZOIC ERA, the earth and its climate gradually began to change. The climate became colder and the swamplands, covered with thick green vegetation, began to disappear.

Over a period of thousands of years, mammals gradually developed which were able to survive in these new surroundings. Their warm blood and hair protected them from the cold. Their larger brains and ability to move quickly made it possible for them to escape from enemies and to catch food. They developed special teeth and more efficient digestive systems. Instead of laying their eggs on the ground and forgetting about them as the dinosaurs did, they were live-bearing animals which carried their fertilized eggs inside of their bodies until they had developed into baby animals. After their babies were born, they fed and cared for them until the young animals were able to take care of themselves. These changes made it possible for more mammals to survive.

During the end of the Mesozoic Era and the beginning of the CENOZOIC ERA, the period in which man now lives, the ancestors of modern mammals, such as the HORSE, CAMEL, and BEAR, appeared on Earth. The first camel, the *Protylopus,* looked like a baby goat. The first flesh-eating (carnivorous) mammals, called *Creodonts,* looked like weasels. The *Miacis* was one of these early carnivores. The *Barylambda,* an ancient animal eight feet long, ate both plants and small animals.

The Cenozoic Era (Era of Mammals) followed the Mesozoic Era (Era of Rep-

Chicago Natural History Museum

Moropus, a prehistoric relative of the horse

tiles). During the middle of the Cenozoic Era, there appeared dog- and cat-like animals. The *Hyaenodon,* a hyena-like animal, lived during this time. Later in the era the ancestors of the ELEPHANT developed. During the Ice Age, less than one million years ago, *wooly* MAMMOTHS and MASTODONS roamed the ice-covered lands. Early camels, *llamas,* one-toed horses, and *giant ground sloths* wandered over the plains.

Some present-day mammals, such as the *opossum* and *rhinoceros,* look very much like their prehistoric ancestors. Others, such as the horse and elephant, look very different.

Ancestors of modern man were prehistoric mammals. Fossil remains of these primates have been found in Asia, Africa, China and Java. Fragments of skeletons plus artifacts show the gradual change which was taking place in his form and structure. The body was erect but posture poor; the brain was larger than in lower mammals; the teeth were more even. The chin developed and the nose became smaller. As each year passes, the prehistoric story becomes more complete.

The horse family began with a small horse the size of a fox. It was called the *dawn horse (Eohippus* or *Hyracotherium).* It had a few stiff hairs (instead of a mane), a small tail, and short neck. It had four toes on its front feet and three on its hind feet. After thousands of years the dawn horse developed into a three-toed horse known as the *middle horse (Mesohippus.)* About the same time, there lived a similar animal called a *Moropus* that developed claws instead of hoofs. Over the years, horses grew larger and larger. Their three toes gradually evolved into one toe which became a hoof.

The elephant family began with a small piglike animal with two large front teeth. It was called a *Moeritherium.* As its descendants grew bigger, they developed longer legs, and necks, tusks, and a trunk. The *Palaeomastodon* stood three feet tall and had a short trunk and short tusks. The elephant family continued to change for

millions of years.

Other Ice Age mammals included the *giant ground sloth (Megatherium),* a plant-eating beast with a heavy body, a large thick tail, strong legs and huge curved claws; the *Glyptodon,* a huge armadillo-like animal with a spiked tail and a suit of armor; the *Irish elk,* which had antlers seven to eight feet wide; and shaggy-coated *ancient bison.* Many of these large mammals died out as the earth changed. Others developed into the mammals known today.   D. J. A.

SEE ALSO: EVOLUTION, PALEONTOLOGY

Prehistoric man see Evolution of man, Stone Age

Presbyopia see Optometry

Prescription see Drugs

Preserves In an effort to preserve some of man's NATURAL RESOURCES (which include plant and animal life) from public and private misuse, preserves or reserves have been established by Federal, state and local governments and by individuals.

Large tracts of land have been set aside by agencies for the protection of those species of wild animals and birds commonly hunted as game. The killing and disturbing of wild life on these reservations usually is prohibited at all times.

The game preserve of today usually is established for the sake of the game and is, in essence, a wildlife sanctuary.

In this nation's early days, the timber supply was considered inexhaustible and no measures were taken to perpetuate the forest areas. With the rapid development of the lumber industry, timber depletion became so acute that steps were taken to protect and reestablish the forests.

A project which teaches conservations and the importance of guarding wildlife and wild flowers is the Bowman Hill State Wild Flower Preserve in·Pennsylvania. Here is a collection of wild flowers and shrubs established for their certain preservation.

Mountain Lake Sanctuary in Florida is a "miscellaneous" nature preserve. It was given to the American people by Edward Bok in 1929 to provide a retreat for man and refuge for Florida's birds.   D. L. D.

80 LB. BOY ON BARE FEET (ABOUT 1¾ LBS. PER SQ. IN.)

120 LB. WOMAN IN SPIKE HEELS (ABOUT 2000 LBS. PER SQ. IN.)

80 LB. BOY ON ICE SKATES (ABOUT 200 LBS. PER SQ. IN.) (ON ONE SKATE)

80 LB. BOY ON SKIS (ABOUT .5 LBS. PER SQ. IN.) (ON ONE SKI)

The pressure exerted by an object on a surface depends in part on the size of the object

Pressure Pressure is the force (or push) on some area of an object. Pressure is often measured in pounds per square inch. For example, pressure of the air at SEA LEVEL is about 15 pounds per square inch. Pressure may be produced by solids, liquids, and gases. When a person dives under water, the pressure on the body is greater than AIR PRESSURE because the weight of the water above exerts pressure too. When a boy or girl skates on ice, the pressure under the runner of the skates is very great because of the weight of the body on the small area of the runner.

Pressure in a LIQUID depends upon the height (depth) and the density of the liquid. The pressure (p) at any depth (h) for a liquid of density (d) is given by $p = d \times h$. When a submarine dives to a depth of 400 feet, the pressure due to the weight of the sea water is about 26,000 pounds per square foot. Sea water has a density of about 65 pounds per cubic foot, and the pressure equals 400 ft. $\times$ 65 lbs. per cubic foot or 26,000 lbs. per square foot. The total force on the hull of the submarine is much greater because of the large amount of surface exposed to the water. A submarine is limited in how far it may descend because the pressure increases with an increase in depth.

In the metric system, pressure may be expressed in many different units such as grams per square centimeter, dynes per square centimeter, and bars or millibars. A bar is 1,000,000 dynes per square centimeter. The United States Weather Bureau uses millibars to report air pressure on the daily weather maps. Newscasters report air pressure in terms of inches.   J. H. D.
SEE ALSO: BAROMETER, GAS, HYDRAULICS, MEASUREMENT, WEATHER

Pressure gauge A pressure gauge measures PRESSURE, the force which acts evenly upon a unit area. Usually a pressure gauge consists of a metal tube or diaphragm which bends as the pressure varies. An attached hand acts as a pointer against a scale.
SEE: BAROMETER, MANOMETER

Prickly heat Prickly heat, or *miliaria,* is a rash which is usually located in, or near, the sweat glands. The rash itches and burns. It is caused by extreme heat. It may provide an opening for a skin infection.

Prickly pear see Cactus

Priestley, Joseph (1733-1804) Though Joseph Priestley is primarily known as the English clergyman who discovered oxygen, he was a man with many talents. Priestley was awarded a doctor of law degree from the University of Edinburgh for an essay on education and for writing biographies of important men through the ages. While collecting materials for his biographies, Priestley traveled to London where he met Benjamin Franklin. At Franklin's request, Priestley wrote a *History of Electricity* which was so successful that Priestley was invited to become a member of the Royal Society. He was thirty-three years of age at the time.

In 1767, after disagreeing with the trustees of the school in Warrington, Priestley resigned his teaching post and became the pastor of a small chapel near Leeds. Living next door to a brewery, he became interested in the "fixed air" (carbon dioxide) which

Joseph Priestley

hung above the liquid in the large fermentation vats. Soon he moved to another location, and there he was successful in making carbon dioxide by pouring acid on chalk. Then he dissolved the gas in water and obtained carbonated water.

In 1774, Priestley obtained a new gas from mercuric oxide that he called a new kind of air. He suggested that it might be used to aid breathing in certain instances, and this suggestion proved to be the forerunner of oxygen tents.

This discovery of a new gas brought Priestley even more fame and led to a meeting with ANTOINE LAVOISIER and other important scientists in Paris. Lavoisier immediately repeated Priestley's experiments with the new gas, and then named the gas *oxygen* because of its acid-forming properties.

By 1780 Joseph Priestley had alienated his patron Lord Shelburne, whom he had been serving as librarian and literary companion since the time he had received the Copley Medal. In searching for a place to go, he found a small, liberal, outcast group in Birmingham that wanted a minister. For ten years he lived happily in Birmingham. There he wrote the last two volumes of the six-volume treatise *On Different Kinds of Air*. However, he made many enemies by writing sympathetically about the cause of the American Revolution, and later about the French Revolution. His *History of the Corruptions of Christianity* also aroused many people. On the second anniversary of the French Revolution (July 14, 1791), a mob descended on Birmingham and destroyed Priestley's home, his church, and his laboratory. The siege lasted three days. Fortunately Joseph Priestley escaped to London in disguise, where he lived for three years. He was so unhappy there that he decided to go to America. Upon arrival, he was offered a post as minister and another as teacher, but he declined both. Instead, he settled in Northumberland, Pennsylvania, where he built a house and laboratory. There he lived for the last ten years of his life. D. H. J.

Primary color see Color

Primates (PRY-mahts) Primates are the group of mammals of which man is a member. Many primates walk uprightly or semi-uprightly. They live in warm regions. The primates include the monkey and similar animals. They often live as families within groups.

Primates are generally distinguished from other mammals in several respects. The nervous systems tend to be more highly developed. The brain case is larger. Primates have "hand-like" parts and flat walking feet. Nails, at least on some digits, instead of claws are typical. The two eyes surrounded by a bony ring, are aimed frontward, and focus on the same object. This ability promotes distance perception, a valuable adaptation to tree-swinging animals.

There are eight families among the primates. Animals representative of each are as follows, with the scientific family name in parentheses:

Aye-Aye (Chiranyidae): This cat-sized animal has a long bushy tail and claws on its back feet except the flat-nailed big toe. Aye-Ayes live in Madagascar.

Lemur (Lemuridae): This squirrel-sized animal is quite unlike other primates except for the feet. There are many kinds of lemurs, some very peculiar looking, especially the loris. *Lemur* means "ghost." They are found principally in Madagascar.

Tarsier (Tarsiidae): These are among the most primitive primates. They have big staring eyes, long ankles, and jump like frogs. They are rat-sized, living in the East Indies.

Marmoset (Hapalidae): These small primates have prehensile tails and resemble monkeys. They are natives of Central and South America.

Baboon (Cercopithecidae): This is one of the Old World monkeys. They typically have nostrils close together, directed downwards. They have heavy-skinned sitting areas. The face is dog-like.

Capuchin monkey (Cebidae): Of many New World monkeys, the Capuchin is popularized as the organ grinder's monkey. Animals of this group are smallish with opposable thumbs and great toes. They have long prehensile tails and widely-spaced, side opening nostrils.

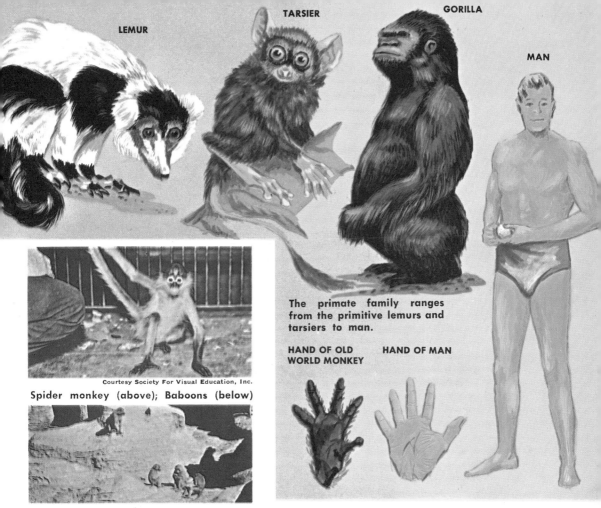

LEMUR TARSIER GORILLA MAN

The primate family ranges from the primitive lemurs and tarsiers to man.

Courtesy Society For Visual Education, Inc.

Spider monkey (above); Baboons (below)

HAND OF OLD WORLD MONKEY   HAND OF MAN

Manlike apes (Simiidae): These are the anthropoid apes, or manlike apes, man's closest animal kin. All probably had a common ancestor as, similarly, would dogs, cats, lions, and wolves. The *anthropoids* (manlike) are larger than monkeys, possessing larger brains.

Four main anthropoid types are the long-armed *gibbon;* the reddish-haired *orangutan;* appealing *chimpanzee* (easiest to train to amusing human ways); and the powerful *gorilla,* mentally less acute than the chimpanzees, and most ferocious. Gorillas are short-lived in captivity.

Anthropoids are skeletally like man. Ears are round and flat; unlike man's they are not lobed. They aren't completely upright creatures and cannot talk or use fire. They are more manlike than the monkeys.

Man (Hominidae): Man, *Homo sapiens,* has a brain twice that of the highest ape. He is a completely upright, two-footed walker. He is less hairy than other primates. His mental development has become his chief adaptation to living anywhere he desires; he is indeed "king of beasts." This advanced mentality has replaced physical adaptations and developments by which lower animals live successfully. D. J. I.

SEE ALSO: APE, CHIMPANZEE, EVOLUTION, EVOLUTION OF MAN, GIBBON, GORILLA, LEMUR, MAMMALIA, MONKEY, ORANGUTAN

Prime meridian see Time zones

Primrose The stem of the garden primrose is underground. A leafless flower stalk grows up from a circle of leaves. Flowers come in most colors and are tube or bell shaped. The fruit is a dry pod containing seeds.

There is also a family of plants called primrose (*Primulaceae*) that includes cyclamen. Many are native to England and Asia and are found in temperate regions of the United States. H. J. C.

Primroses

Helen Challand

Printed circuit A printed circuit is an electrical circuit which is made without the use of wires. It is usually made by imprinting a thin sheet of a non-conductor (such as plastic) with the circuit in a conducting material (such as silver).

Since printed circuits have no joints or other parts which can become loosened, they are very reliable; since they can be printed on flat sheets, they can be made very small. For these reasons they are used both commercially (as in TV sets) and in scientific instruments, as in space vehicles.   D. A. B.

SEE ALSO: ELECTRONICS, TELEVISION

PRINT IS MADE FROM WOOD BLOCK

IMAGE CHISELED IN WOOD IN REVERSE

PRINTERS INK

The basic process in printing is pressing one object against another

Printing Most people have watched a grocer stamp prices on cans of food. He first presses a small rubber stamp against a pad of wet ink. Then he presses the stamp against the can and it leaves an ink mark. The stamp is a special tool for making a print. It may be used for making thousands of identical marks. Printing is done by pressing one object against another so that it leaves a mark.

Almost any object will make a mark on another object. Some objects make deep prints in soft materials. Fingers leave prints in cookie dough.

But a hand pressed against the hard surface of a table will not leave a mark. The hand, like the grocer's stamp, must be dampened with ink.

People have learned how to make tools and machines which print. The typewriter is a machine for printing words. The letters are raised on metal blocks. As they strike hard against the inked ribbon, they press a mark into the paper. But small typewriters could not print the millions of books needed. Newspapers and books are printed on *presses* (large machines run by electricity). These presses are able to print thousands of pages an hour.

There are so many newspapers and magazines printed today that millions of pounds of used paper are turned over to scrap collectors each week.

Used paperback books lie dusty on shelves. And yet, the earliest printed books and pamphlets are preserved in museums. People are so accustomed to reading printed matter that it is hard to realize a method for printing was developed only about fifty years before Columbus discovered America.

HOW PRINTING BEGAN

In all civilizations, people have wanted to record their ideas. Early man scratched and painted on rock pictures of men or of animals he hunted. Like stories in a printed book, these rough sketches are records which tell of the events of man 200,000 years ago. In later civilizations, man learned to make symbols which represented particular words. It was not until 25,000 years ago, however, that the Phoenicians finally worked out a system for writing individual sounds. From this discovery, they were able to produce the first alphabet. Later other alphabets came into existence. With an alphabet, spoken words could be accurately recorded.

The next problem was that of reproducing identical copies of words and pictures. The ancient Egyptians and Babylonians were the first to develop tools for printing. By carving symbols into wood or stone, they made small hand stamps. These were used for making prints in soft metal coins or clay pots. In fact, the Babylonians invented a tool for printing a complete paragraph. Letters were scratched around the surface of a wooden cylinder. An entire paragraph could

Pages and sample letters from the Gutenberg press with movable type

be rolled onto a soft clay tablet with one turn of the cylinder.

People had not as yet learned how to make ink marks on paper. It was not until the 5th century A.D. that the Chinese began to use similar wooden stamps for making ink marks on paper. These small stamps were gradually replaced by blocks large enough to print a complete picture. After the block was carved, a damp sheet of paper, placed over the inked surface, was rubbed by hand until a print was made. So successful were the Chinese with wood blocks that they produced millions of copies of paper money.

THE INVENTION OF MOVABLE TYPE

When letters are formed separately, they may be grouped into words, sentences, and paragraphs. They may be taken apart and reassembled to form new words. Typewriters have movable type. The individual letters may be used in any combination.

Block printing was an important step to the invention of movable type. Although the individual letters could not be reused, the blocks produced identical ink prints. In the 11th century, the Chinese were again the first to print from movable type. They made individual letters out of baked clay, which were then assembled in a frame.

THE FIRST PRINTING PRESS

It is interesting to think that people wrote for almost 2000 years before they learned how to print by machine. In the middle of the 15th century, a goldsmith from Germany, Johannes Gutenberg put together the first workable press. Used originally for making wine, the press operated with a screw which brought together two flat surfaces. Each page of movable type, set by hand, was locked into a wooden frame, inked, and placed on the lower surface, or *press-bed*. After a sheet of paper was placed over the type, the upper surface was lowered by means of the screw. As the two surfaces came together, a print was made.

The press, which later became known as the *platen* or *flat bed press,* could produce about 300 pages a day. Although today this

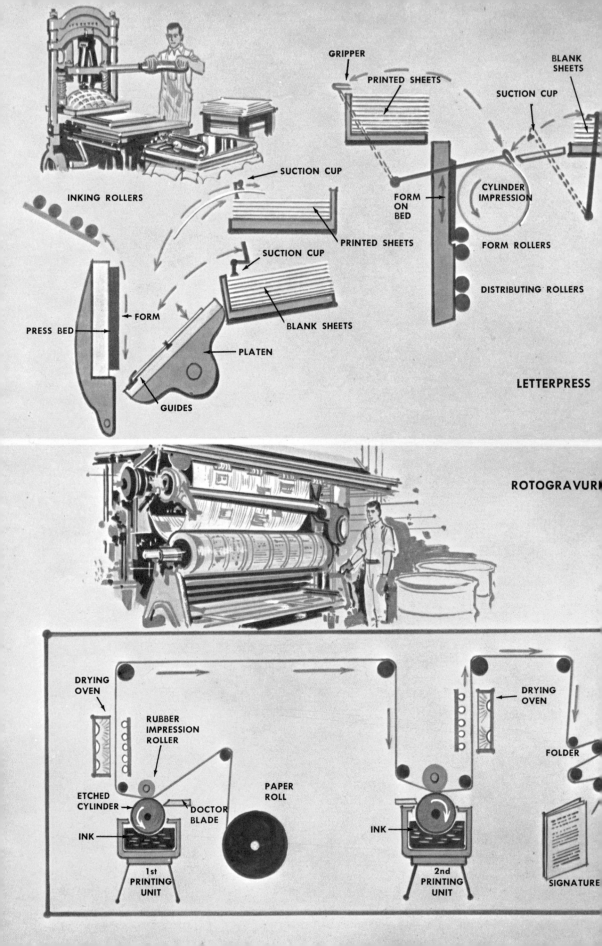

GRIPPER

PRINTED SHEETS

BLANK SHEETS

SUCTION CUP

SUCTION CUP

INKING ROLLERS

PRINTED SHEETS

FORM ON BED

CYLINDER IMPRESSION

SUCTION CUP

BLANK SHEETS

FORM ROLLERS

DISTRIBUTING ROLLERS

FORM

PRESS BED

PLATEN

GUIDES

LETTERPRESS

ROTOGRAVURE

DRYING OVEN

RUBBER IMPRESSION ROLLER

DRYING OVEN

FOLDER

ETCHED CYLINDER

PAPER ROLL

DOCTOR BLADE

INK

INK

1st PRINTING UNIT

2nd PRINTING UNIT

SIGNATURE

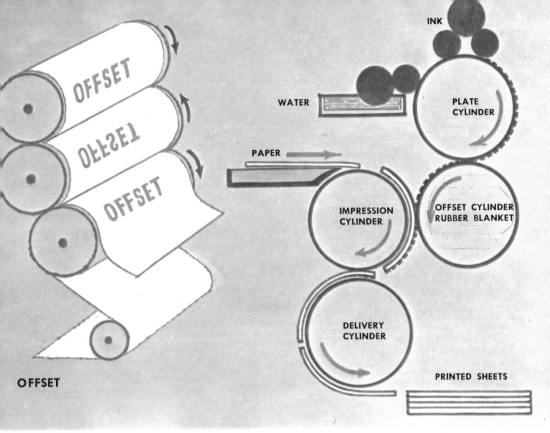

OFFSET

INK

WATER

PLATE CYLINDER

PAPER

IMPRESSION CYLINDER

OFFSET CYLINDER RUBBER BLANKET

DELIVERY CYLINDER

PRINTED SHEETS

OFFSET

A large four-color offset lithography press as used in modern printing plants

Miehle Printing Press and Manufacturing Co.

MIEHLE

would amount to about three or four copies of one magazine, the speed output was superior to either handwriting or hand printing.

With the advent of the industrial revolution, steam was used to drive the press. However, the press itself did not change for about 300 years. Not until 1813 did the first *cylinder press* appear. While the type remained on a flat bed, the paper was placed on a revolving cylinder, which moved from one end to the other, much as a rolling pin moves across dough.

The next problem facing the printers was how to place the type over the cylinder. Finally, the *stereotype,* a light-weight metal copy, or mold, of the type was invented. It was made by placing a sheet of moist cardboard over the type which was already set in the wooden frame. As great pressure was applied, the cardboard, forced against the type, made an impression, or mold, of the whole page. In shape, the cardboard mold was to the type what jelly mold is to jelly. By pouring a thin layer of hot lead alloy over the cardboard mold, a second stronger metal copy was made.

The sheets of type could now be bent to fit the curve of the cylinder. The *rotary press,* in which both type and paper moved over cylinders, was the next development.

Many improvements continued to be made. A machine called the *linotype,* which set and cast each line of type ready for printing, was patented in 1885. Finally the *camera* was used in printing. Pictures were transferred by chemical means, from photographic film to a metal printing plate.

Today, much printing is still done by hand. For mass production, commercial printing must be done on high-speed presses. In spite of the new and interesting techniques, there are still only three major methods of transferring ink to paper.

RELIEF PRINTING

Since block printing is a type of relief printing, this is the oldest process. The principle is simple. Like letters on a typewriter, those parts of the plate which print are raised. Those which do not print are below the surface. The largest volume of printed material is produced by this method, since it is used for printing newspapers, books, and magazines. Commercially it is known as *letterpress printing.*

When a black and white picture is to be printed, it is first photographed onto a glass plate and printed on a treated zinc plate, just as a picture is photographed on film and printed on paper. After being treated with chemicals, the parts which will not print are eaten away with acid, leaving those parts which will print raised.

But most pictures have light and dark shadows. In order to print accurately shaded areas, the *half-tone* process is used. One who examines newspaper photographs, finds that they are made of tiny dots, smaller in light areas and larger in dark areas. The picture is photographed through a half-tone screen onto a treated metal plate. The screen consists of two sheets of glass, having parallel diagonal lines, filled with black pigment. These are placed face-to-face so that the lines are at right angles to one another, giving the effect of a window screen. The size of the dot varies with the amount of light striking the metal plate.

The most inexpensive color printing is the three-color process. Since any number of colors may be printed, the term is misleading. By making a separate plate for each color, the plates may be printed like the regular black and white plates. However, the colors are flat and less subtle than they are in other color processes.

The most expensive but most accurate color printing, the *four-color process,* is similar to the half-tone process. The picture to be printed is photographed through color filters and half-tone screens to produce four separate colors—red, yellow, blue, and black. Thus, the printer has four dotted plates. By printing these on top of one another, practically any color may be made.

In letterpress printing, after copy and pictures are assembled, a stereotype, or copy, of the entire page is made. The giant *rotary presses* used by big city "dailies" have printing cylinders which carry 4 or 8 of these plates. Each time the cylinder turns, it will print 4 or 8 pages on one side of the paper and 4 or 8 on the other side. The continuous webs or rolls of paper are pressed against the printing cylinder by means of a second, or impression, cylinder. One press may contain several of these units. Each unit can produce about 50,000 impressions an hour. Smaller printing firms may use cylinder or *platen* presses.

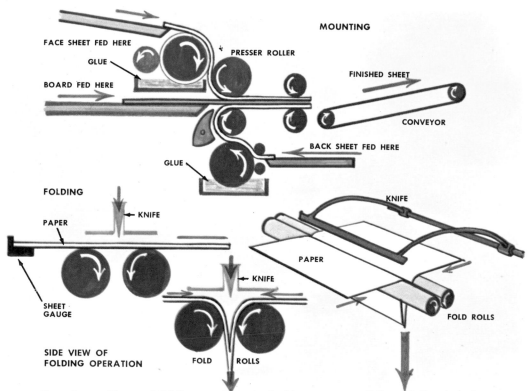

Mounting, cutting and folding are important side processes of the printing industry

PLANOGRAPHIC PRINTING

This method, one of the most recent, is based on the simple principle that grease and water will not mix. (Instead of being printed from a raised surface, both type and pictures are on a flat surface.)

Drawing or lettering was originally done on a thick porous stone with a crayon or ink mixed with tallow or wax. The surface of the stone was sponged with an acid, changing the surface not covered with wax into one which repelled grease and accepted water. The parts covered with wax accepted grease and repelled water. During printing, the stone was moistened with water, which soaked into those parts not drawn on. Printing ink, rolled over the surface, adhered only to the original drawing, which accepted ink.

Of course the heavy stone, still used in hand printing, is too awkward for commercial use. It has been replaced by a flexible, fine-textured *zinc* or *aluminum* plate. The image is photographed through a fine screen onto the plate. Since both text and pictures are printed from the same plate, the process is fast.

Commercially, planographic printing is called *offset lithography,* or *photo-offset.* In-stead of printing directly on the paper, the metal plate prints on a third roller, which transfers the print to the paper. The elastic, rubber roller is able to pick up fine dots and transfer them to rough paper, metal, wood, or canvas.

INTAGLIO PRINTING

In this process, both type and pictures are below the surface of the plate. Known before the time of Gutenberg, this method was called *engraving.* After the design or letters were cut into the steel or copper plate with a sharp V-shaped tool, the plate was covered with ink. Thus far, the process resembles block-printing. The entire surface wipes clean, however, so that the ink remained only in the lines. The plate, placed face down on a sheet of moist paper, was covered with felt and pressed with great pressure through a hand press. The ink was transferred to the paper by suction. The deeper the line, the darker the print.

Today this process is used for printing wedding invitations and certificates. The best known example is the printing of paper money and stamps by the Bureau of Engraving in Washington. The lines are severe, definite, and slightly raised.

Commercially, intaglio is known as *gravure printing—rotogravure* and *photogravure*. Pictures and words are reduced to small spots, which, instead of being raised above the surface as in relief printing, are small, square, microscopic wells below the surface. Although the cups are equal in size, they vary in depth. The deeper cups, which hold more ink, will transfer heavier deposits to the paper, thereby printing darker areas. Since the ink spreads over the paper, the dots overlap one another, giving a rich, velvety, slightly powdery quality. Big edition magazines, Sunday paper magazines and many high-quality art books are printed using the intaglio, or gravure printing, method. E. P. L.

SEE ALSO: COMMUNICATION, MACHINERY, PAPER, PHOTOGRAPHY

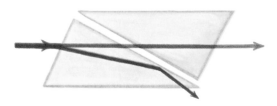

Polarization of light through a prism

Prism In geometry, a prism is a solid object the sides of which are equal *polygons* and the ends equal and parallel polygons. Some prisms are given special names according to the shapes of their bases. Some of the most common shapes are *triangular, quadrangular* and *rhombic.* These names also apply to some crystal structures which grow in the shape of prisms.

Probably the most common use for prisms is in the study of optics. One of the most interesting and simple applications of a triangular glass prism is to the study of the different wave-lengths of light. If the prism is placed in a narrow beam of sunlight, the light will be bent as it passes through the prism. Not all of the colors will be bent in the same amount, however, so that a strip of colors will fall on a screen. This strip of colors is called the SPECTRUM and this method of producing it was discovered by Newton. The violet end of the spectrum is

bent through a greater angle than the red end. The separation of the colors by this method is known as *dispersion*.

A rather specialized application of prisms in optics is the *polarization of light*. The prism employed in this process is called a *Nicol prism,* named after its inventor, W. Nicol. The prism is made of two pieces of calcite cut in a particular manner and cemented together with Canada balsam. Because the index of refraction of Canada balsam is between the indices of refraction for the two pieces of the prism, some of the light (extraordinary ray) passes through the prism and the rest of the light (ordinary ray) is reflected out the side. Hence, the light coming out the end is polarized. A. E. L.

SEE ALSO: LENS, MAN-MADE; LIGHT

Privet Privet is a shrub used in hedges. In summer it has small white flowers, and in the fall blue-black berries. Sometimes privet is clipped in odd shapes like arches and animal shapes. It is related to the lilac and the olive.

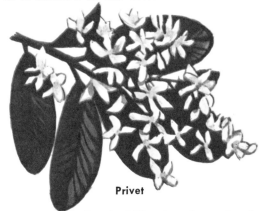

Privet

Probability Probability is a branch of MATHEMATICS which tries to determine which one of a number of events, all of which are the possible results of an act, is likely to occur, and how many times it is likely to occur.

Proboscis (pro-BOS-is) A proboscis is an elongation of the mouth, or an organ which protrudes in the area of the mouth. It may be the sucking organ of an insect or a grasping organ like the elephant's trunk.

Procyon (PROH-see-ahn) Procyon is a brilliant star which gets its name from the fact that it precedes the star *Sirius* in its nightly path across the heavens. Sirius is "the dog" and Procyon means "before the dog."

These two stars are called "dog stars" and are referred to in ancient literature. According to astrology, Procyon is the star that portends wealth, fame, and good luck.

Procyon, like the star SIRIUS, has a faint companion which is believed to be a white dwarf.   V. V. N.

Progesterone (pro-JES-ter-own) Certain organic chemicals called *hormones* are necessary for the body to carry on its functions. Progesterone is one of the hormones that regulates the reproductive processes of the female. It circulates in the blood stream.

Progesterone is produced by the *corpus luteum,* a tissue of the OVARY which develops after ovulation. Under the influence of progesterone, the lining of the uterus becomes highly developed and prepared to receive a fertilized egg. The continuous production of progesterone during pregnancy keeps the uterus in the proper condition for the development of the *fetus* or child. J. R. S.
SEE ALSO: ENDOCRINE GLANDS, HORMONE, MENSTRUATION, REPRODUCTIVE SYSTEM

Projectile Any particle or body which has horizontal motion and at the same time acts like a falling body can be classified as a projectile. A stone hurled in a horizontal direction is a projectile. Rifle bullets and torpedoes are the most commonly used examples of projectiles.

It may seem a bit odd that the horizontal motion has no effect on the vertical motion or vice versa, but nevertheless this is true if air resistance is neglected. If a projectile is fired horizontally, it will have a *velocity* in that direction equal to that given it initially. At the same time it is traveling horizontally, it will fall toward earth, due to *gravitational* forces exerted on it. While the

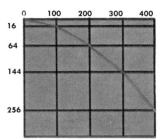

The path of a projectile can be shown on a graph to have a curve as above when the initial velocity is 100 feet per second. The fall is due to the regular action of gravity

horizontal motion is at *constant* velocity, the vertical motion is accelerated.

A simple method of showing the path of a projectile is to draw a series of equally spaced vertical lines on a piece of paper. The distance separating these lines represents the initial velocity of the bullet. The horizontal lines are drawn to represent the distance the projectile will fall in each second due to the action of gravity. These distances are 16, 64, 144, and 256 feet respectively for the first four seconds, figured from the formula $S = \frac{1}{2}gt^2$ where S is the distance, $g = 32$ ft./sec^2, and t is the time in seconds. A curve using the initial velocity as 100 ft./sec appears above. Other curves can be drawn using other initial velocities.

The earth's rotation also influences the path of a projectile. If a bullet is fired due north in the Northern Hemisphere, it travels east as·well as north due to the rotation of the earth. (The earth's surface does not travel as fast, however, the farther north one is from the equator.) Since the target would be farther north than the point at which the gun was fired, the bullet would fall to the right of the target. In the Southern Hemisphere the bullet would fall to the left since the target rotates faster than the gun if it is pointing north.   A. E. L.

Projection Projection in MAP-MAKING is the method of representing the surface of the earth, or some other celestial body, on a cylinder, a cone, or an *azimuth*. The best known is the *Mercator* projection in which the earth is presented as a rectangle, with all *parallels* and *meridians* represented by straight lines intersecting at right angles.

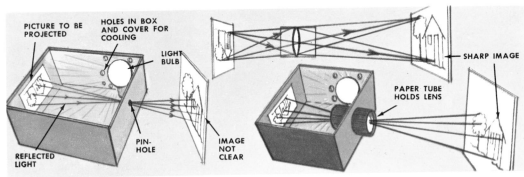

PICTURE TO BE PROJECTED

HOLES IN BOX AND COVER FOR COOLING

LIGHT BULB

SHARP IMAGE

PAPER TUBE HOLDS LENS

PIN-HOLE

IMAGE NOT CLEAR

REFLECTED LIGHT

A simple opaque projector; a convex lens fitted to a tube will make a sharper picture

Projector A projector is an optical device which sends out a beam of light. The projector contains a very bright source of light. This light can be gathered and directed by mirrors and lenses. The beam of light can be made to carry an image to be viewed on a screen.

A simple projector throws an image of any small picture onto a table or other surface. A box, with ventilation holes on the sides should be big enough to hold a light bulb and the picture to be projected. The light that bounces off the picture will have a path from the box and through the projection hole.

From all parts of the picture, bounced light gets out the hole to strike a screen. An image will show on the screen faintly but rather clearly if the hole is small, and bright but very fuzzy if the hole is large. The viewing screen cannot be very far from the box.

This type is called an *opaque projector*. No light passes through the picture being used. A convex lens fitted into a tube so as to slide and focus at the correct distance from the picture will cast a better image.

A *lantern-slide* type projector requires that light rays pass through a picture. A partly-transparent slide is placed between the light and the projector opening. The image depends on how much light is blocked or colored by the pattern.

How far an image can be projected depends on the brightness of the light source. As light spreads out and covers more screen it becomes more faint. As distance is increased or, for example, doubled (two times as far), the brightness at the screen is one-

fourth as much. If ten times as far, the brightness is only one hundredth. Projector bulbs are specially designed so that the filaments concentrate the source of light into a small area. A carbon ARC light is used in movie theatres.

For either opaque or transparent slide projecting, it is important to gather as much light as possible. The more light that bounces off or passes through a picture the brighter the screen image will be. Great amounts of light must pass through a slide film, and it is necessary that the light hitting the film is spread uniformly. White frosted glass is used and called a *diffuser*. Lenses called *condensers* are also used to direct intense beams of light on the film.

The arrangement of lenses that do the final projecting is most important. The bright light that leaves the slide must be brought to a sharp focus. The diagram on the next page uses points of color as they might appear on a cross-section of a slide. It shows they end up on a screen arranged in the same pattern but as a reversed or backward image. Anyone who has threaded a movie projector or slide projector knows that the film piece is fed into the machine upside down and backwards so that it comes out right side up on the screen.

A movie projector rapidly places one picture slide after another between a light

A lantern-slide projector

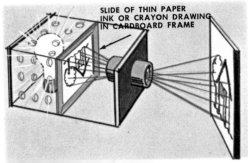

SLIDE OF THIN PAPER INK OR CRAYON DRAWING IN CARDBOARD FRAME

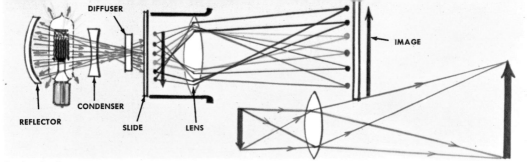

A simple lens system in a projector

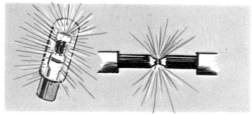

Projector light sources: bulb and carbon arc

source and a system of lenses. A shutter device flashes light just as the pictures come into position, or a special gear jerks the pictures along. A sound movie projector shows twenty-four pictures each second, but the eye sees each flash longer and blends the images together into a moving picture.

The index of refraction for any material varies with the wave-length of light passing through it. Thus, a lens forms an image at a different distance from the lens for each color. The lens in a projector is specially ground to minimize this effect.   F. R. W.

SEE ALSO: LENS, MAN-MADE; MOTION PICTURES; PHOTOGRAPHY

Promethium (proh-MEETH-ee-um) Promethium is an element in the rare-earth metal group. Only recently discovered in atomic research, it does not occur naturally. It is considered to be a man-made element. Promethium was named for the Greek god, Prometheus, who is supposed to have given fire to man.

The element was identified in the material obtained by bombardment of stable NEODYMIUM with slow neutrons in atomic piles, and among the fission products of uranium. Two main isotopes of promethium are a mass number 147, with half-life of 2.6 years, and 149 with a half-life of 52 hours.

The symbol for promethium is Pm. It has an atomic number of 61.   V. V. N.

SEE ALSO: ELEMENTS

Pronghorn see Antelope, Deer family
Prop roots see Banyan, Pandanus

Propagation (prah-puh-GAY-shun) New plants are made from some part of the old plant. A seed will grow into a plant. When a sweet potato is planted in soil it will grow into a plant. A tulip bulb will grow a beautiful flower. A branch of pussy willow when placed in a glass of water will grow new roots. All of these ways that new plants are made are called propagation.

Plants vary as to which part is best for propagating the species. Most annuals are grown from *seed*. In some plants there are many underground stems which are used for propagation instead of the plant's seed. Tulips, daffodils, and onions are *bulbs*. The white potato is a *tuber,* while the sweet potato is a *root*. Iris and quack grass are propagated by *rhizomes*. Crocus and gladiolus have underground stems for propagation called *corms*. The strawberry plant sends a stem along the top of the ground. This runner takes root at certain intervals and starts growing a new plant.

Man has found it more economical and sometimes necessary to use parts of the plant to produce new ones. Banana and seedless fruits must be started from the *root stock* of the mother plant. *Dahlia, man-root,* and *mangel* are produced by *root propagation*. New house plants of *geranium, coleus, ivy,* and *philodendron* can be produced by *cuttings*. A stem from the old plant can be placed in a jar of water until new roots are formed from the cut end of the stem. The LEAVES from *jade, gloxinia,* and *sansevieria* may be placed in moist sand. The end of the *petiole* of the leaf will root and a new plant eventually appears. When cross cuts are made on the veins under a *begonia* leaf and pressed into wet sand, new plants will appear at each cut. Many flowering shrubs can be propagated by cutting a branch off and placing it in a jar of water.

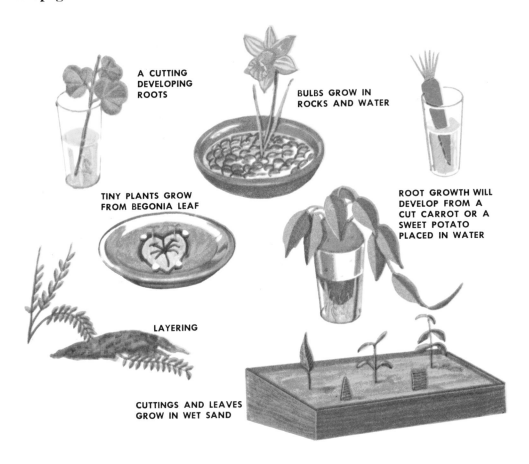

A CUTTING DEVELOPING ROOTS

BULBS GROW IN ROCKS AND WATER

TINY PLANTS GROW FROM BEGONIA LEAF

ROOT GROWTH WILL DEVELOP FROM A CUT CARROT OR A SWEET POTATO PLACED IN WATER

LAYERING

CUTTINGS AND LEAVES GROW IN WET SAND

Some home gardeners as well as nursery-men increase their shrub and woody vine supply by a method called *layering*. A branch of the existing plant is pulled over to ground level. At intervals along the branch, soil is piled over it. That part of the branch covered will root and send up a new shoot. When it is well established it can be cut from the original plant.

The propagating medium depends upon the species being produced. *Sand, mica* or *vermiculite,* and *sphagnum moss* are the most successful. Synthetic plant hormones are available. When these are added to the propagating medium they will speed up root growth. H. J. C.

Propane see Methane, Hydrocarbon

Propeller see Aircraft, Airplane

Prophase see Mitosis and meiosis

Proportion Proportion is a statement of equality between two ratios. A RATIO is the relation one quantity has to another. A proportion is written as

$a: b = c: d$ or $\dfrac{a}{b} = \dfrac{c}{d}$; a and d are the extremes, and c and d are the means.

Prostate gland see Reproductive systems

Protactinium (proh-tack-TINN-ee-um) Protactinium is a radioactive element whose symbol is Pa. Protactinium has an atomic number of 91 and a mass number of 231. It is found in nature in all uranium ores, and occurs in such ore to the extent of about one-fourth part per million parts of uranium.

An efficient method for separating this element from its ore is a *carrier technique; zirconium phosphate* is precipitated from strong acid solutions, and consequently *precipitates,* or carries down, the solid protactinium with the zirconium salt. Then the protactinium is separated by crystallizing the zirconium as an *oxychloride.* V. V. N.

SEE ALSO: ELEMENTS

CHAMELEON

WEASEL

ZEBRA

BITTERN

LEOPARD

FAWN

MONARCH BUTTERFLY

ICHNEUMON FLY

MASON WASP

IO MOTH

UNDERWING MOTH

ARCTIC FOX

BUFFALO TREEHOPPER

BUSH KATYDID

WALKING STICK

FLOUNDER

Protective coloration Animals have many ways of protecting themselves from their enemies. One way is by being able to fight. Another is by living in places where their enemies cannot get at them. A third way is called *protective coloration*. Animals that have protective coloration are hard to see when they are in the places where they usually live.

Some snakes and insects that live in grass are green. Tropical fish, which are so brightly colored that they are very showy in a tank, can hardly be

1375

seen when they are in their natural home among coral and water plants. Some tiny fish are so nearly transparent that they can be seen only when they move.

Even animals whose surroundings change color can sometimes change color to match. Some rabbits and weasels, for instance, shed their brown summer coats and grow white fur in winter. When an animal's body is in shadow, it looks darker than it really is, and many animals, as birds and fish, have undersides that are lighter than their bodies. Since their shadows are underneath them, their lighter bellies look the same color as the rest of them. This type of coloration is called *countershading.*

Another form of protective coloration consists of *patterning.* Stripes and spots make it difficult to see the animal's outline. This is the same principle that man uses in protective camouflage. The dappled back of a baby fawn blends into the leaf-shadows of the woods. Patterning and countershading are important types of protection called *concealing* or *cryptic coloration.*

Mimicry is a form of protective coloration that depends, not on making the animal invisible, but on making it look like something else. A harmless insect may have the same color pattern as one that stings. Shape as well as color may give this kind of protection. The insect known as a WALKING STICK looks like the twig on which it sits. Tree-hoppers are insects that look like thorns. Dead-leaf butterflies are blue and orange when flying, but when they fold their wings, they look like brown leaves.

Not all protective coloration makes the animal inconspicuous. Some animals, such as skunks, are left alone because they are seen and recognized. This is called *warning coloration.* The porcupine has a similar dark and light warning coloration.

Of course, animals cannot voluntarily take on protective coloration. It is one of the characteristics that enable them to survive and have young. Individuals that did not have either protective coloration or some other form of protection have not survived, and so natural selection has favored its development.

M. R. B.

SEE ALSO: BUTTERFLIES, CAMOUFLAGE, EVOLUTION, INSECTA, MIMICRY, MOTH, TROPICAL FISH

✳ **THINGS TO DO**

WHICH FOODS ARE RICH IN PROTEIN?

1   If a food containing protein is mixed with lime and copper sulfate, the mixture will be violet colored.

2   Make two solutions and keep them separate until you add a little of each to the food to be tested. Make solution 1 by adding as much copper sulfate as the small amount of water you are using can hold. Make solution 2 by dissolving lime powder in water.

3   Add equal parts of these two solutions to the food.

4   Is there protein in the following foods: hamburger, flour, butter, eggs, sugar, salt, cheese, and bread? Do some of these appear to have more protein than others?

Protein All living things are made up of cells. These cells are made up of protoplasm which is largely a mixture of proteins. The Greek word *proteios* from which protein is derived means "primary." These materials are of first or primary importance in living things.

Proteins are far more complex than most other substances. They are made up of smaller parts called *amino acids.* These giant molecules contain CARBON, HYDROGEN, OXYGEN, NITROGEN, and usually SULFUR. Albumin, a typical protein found in blood, has the formula of $C_{696}H_{1125}O_{200}N_{190}S_{18}$. Protein *molecules* are too large to pass through the walls of the intestine and blood vessels. They must be broken down into amino acids in digestion. The amino acids, which can be absorbed, are rebuilt into body protein in the cells.

Twenty-two amino acids are needed to build tissues. Fourteen of these can be made by the cells from FAT or SUGAR and nitrogen

Fossils remains of Pre-Cambrian worms

which has been freed by the breakdown of used proteins. The human body needs to obtain eight different amino acids from food, but not all protein food contains all eight. Therefore a varied diet is necessary to insure adequate protein nutrition. Muscle cells contain the greatest proportion of proteins.

All proteins are odorless and tasteless. Most are also colorless. They are very unstable compounds and undergo chemical change readily. Scientists often find it difficult to experiment with proteins because of their instability—the ease with which they break down.   J. K. L.

SEE ALSO: AMINO ACIDS, CARBOHYDRATES, NUTRITION, STARCHES, NUCLEOPROTEIN

Proterozoic Era (proh-ter-uh-ZOH-ick) The Proterozoic Era (*proto* means "earlier" and *zoic* means "life") occurred from 1700 million years ago to 500 million years ago. It lasted 1200 million years.

The Proterozoic Era was part, along with the ARCHEOZOIC ERA, of the *Pre-Cambrian* period. Pre-Cambrian rocks of these eras include *igneous, sedimentary,* and *metamorphic* rocks. Signs of past life are most often found in the sedimentary rocks. Even in these rocks very few distinct proterozoic fossils have been found. The lime deposits of blue-green ALGAE are the only known plant fossils. Animal fossils are even more rare and less distinct. They include the marine worms, jellyfish, sponges, and one-celled protozoans. These plants and animals are all among the simplest forms of life.

These plants and animals were all marine forms. Apparently no life existed on land. Because remains of very simple marine life occur in the rocks of this time, one can conclude that there probably was a good deal of such life in the oceans. The lack of fossils can be explained by the fact that most forms were very small and lacked hard parts such as shells, bones, etc., that could be preserved as fossils.

During this part of the Pre-Cambrian period intensive *volcanism* and *diastrophism* (uplifting) occurred. It was, however, interrupted by long periods of *erosion* and *deposition.* There was also another very important event. The first recorded *Ice Age* of the earth's history took place in eastern Canada. Geologists know this because it left *striated* boulders and other glacial deposits as evidence of its occurrence.

These mountain-building revolutions were not sudden, short periods of upheavals, but are known to have been many millions of years in length.   V. V. N.

SEE ALSO: GEOLOGIC TIME TABLE

Proton (PRO-tawn) The proton is one of the building blocks of all atomic nuclei. A proton is the nucleus of a hydrogen atom. The proton has a positive charge equal to the negative charge of an electron and a mass 1836 times the mass of an electron. The proton was first identified by Rutherford in 1919. Recent research has shown that the proton itself is surrounded by a "cloud" of MESONS.

The mass of a proton is 1.00759 atomic mass units (amu). The amu scale is based on assigning the lightest ISOTOPE of oxygen a mass of 16.00000.

High energy protons are produced in accelerators such as cyclotrons. When the nuclei of other atoms are bombarded by protons, new elements are formed. These elements are often radioactive. Very high energy protons have great penetrating power. A proton having an energy of 450 million electron volts can penetrate more than three feet of water. The proton gradually loses energy as it passes through the water. The average distance a proton travels before all its energy is lost is called the *range* of the proton.

Low energy protons in the form of hydrogen ions, H^+, are responsible for the acidic properties of substances such as hydrochloric acid (HCl), sulfuric acid (H_2SO_4), and acetic acid ($HC_2H_3O_2$).   J. H. D.

SEE ALSO: ATOM, NUCLEAR SCIENCE

Proton number see Nuclear science glossary

HOW MANY ANIMALS CAN YOU FIND IN A DROP OF WATER?

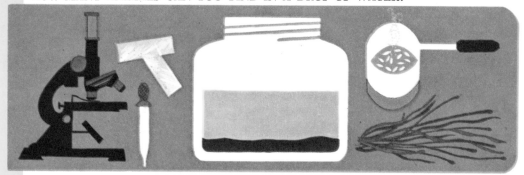

1 One-celled animals are found in most fresh water, streams, ponds, lakes, or classroom aquariums.

2 Take a large jar along with you when collecting. Fill the jar with an inch of mud from the bottom of the pond and then half full of pond water. Break off a handful of dried hay or grass growing along the bank. Add this to your culture.

3 Cook up about a dozen grains of rice. This will serve as additional food. Permit the jar to stand for one week undisturbed. Do not put it in direct sunlight.

4 Put a drop of this protozoa culture on a slide and observe under a microscope. It will be teeming with one-celled animals, as well as minute water insects, and flatworms.

Protoplasm Protoplasm is the general name for the material of which all plant and animal CELLS are made. It contains many large, specialized molecules (*macromolecules*).

Protozoa (proh-tuh-ZOH-uh) *Protozoa* means "first animal." Many scientists think that *Protozoa,* or animals like them, were the first animals to live on the earth. They are classed as the first, or simplest, group of lower animals because their bodies are made of a single cell. They are called *unicellular* animals. *Uni* means "one."

People are made up of many tiny cells which cannot be seen with the naked eye. For the same reason, most people have never seen protozoa. Most of them can be seen only under a microscope. If five of the largest were placed end to end, they would take up only one inch. It would take 25,000 of the smallest to measure one inch.

Even though each protozoan animal has only one cell, it takes in food, water, and oxygen. Protozoa build new materials for their cells and get rid of wastes. Like the larger animals with many cells, the protozoa are able to carry on all the activities that are necessary to stay alive.

All protozoa live in water. They may, however, live in microscopic bits of water. Those which live in the dry desert sand need only the thin film of water found between particles of sand. These small creatures have neither limbs nor muscles to travel great distances. Nevertheless, they are carried all over the world by wind, water, and other animals.

MOVEMENT OF PROTOZOA

According to the way they move from place to place, the protozoa have been divided into five large groups or classes. The *Flagellata,* or "whip-bearers," have one or more long flagella by which they swim. The flagella is a thin thread-like extension of the protoplasm, located at the front end of the body. As it is vibrated in a whip-like motion, the animal is towed behind.

The *ameboid* protozoa are called the *Sarcodina* after the Greek word *sarcos,* meaning "flesh." These animals put out *pseudopods,* or false feet, which are only temporary extensions of the protoplasm. Thus their bodies are continually changing shape. Since some members, like the *radiolarians,* are covered with shells, they must push the protoplasm through tiny holes in the shell.

The *Ciliata* are a group of agile protozoa which move by means of *cilia,* short hair-

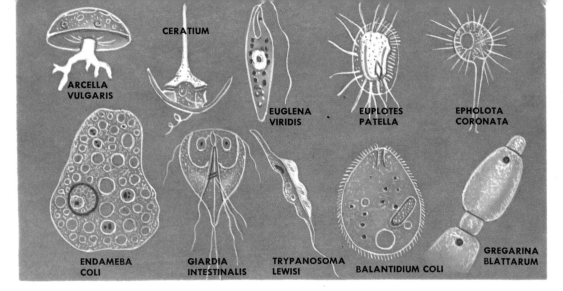

CERATIUM

ARCELLA
VULGARIS

EUGLENA
VIRIDIS

EUPLOTES
PATELLA

EPHOLOTA
CORONATA

ENDAMEBA
COLI

GIARDIA
INTESTINALIS

TRYPANOSOMA
LEWISI

BALANTIDIUM COLI

GREGARINA
BLATTARUM

Various protozoa with scientific names; top row are free-living, bottom are parasitic

like extensions of the protoplasm. By beating these rows of cilia, the animal is propelled much as a boat is rowed with oars.

Some members of the *Sporozoa* are enemies of man, since they cause such diseases as malaria and cattle fever. These protozoa have no particular type of locomotion because they are all parasitic. Instead, they rely upon water and animals to transport their spores, or offspring.

The *Suctoria,* or sucking protozoa, make up a special class. Although the young move by means of cilia, the adults attach themselves permanently to a solid surface. Since they have a long stalk and sucking *tentacles,* they resemble a tiny plant.

HOW THEY EAT

The method of obtaining food ranges from plant-like to animal-like habits. Some of the flagellates are able to carry on photosynthesis like a green plant, since their bodies contain chlorophyll. They manufacture and store starch from the food in water and soil. Other protozoa, like the large carnivorous animals, chase their prey. Some feed upon both plants and animals. BACTERIA, ALGAE, wood particles, and other small animals are common foods.

Some protozoa, like *Paramecium,* have permanent mouths or surfaces for ingesting food. The ameboid protozoa, however, take in food at any point on their bodies. The protoplasm simply flows around the piece of food. Suctorians have a unique method of sucking up the protoplasm of their prey by means of their long tentacles. Most parasites and many flagellates have another method. They absorb foods which have already been broken down into simpler substances.

THE PARTS OF THE BODY

Although each species is different in structure, all protozoa consist of a mass of living protoplasm which is surrounded by a thin membrane. For protection, there is often a thick, outer cuticle. Some have beautiful calcium or glassy shells.

Perhaps the most conspicuous parts of the cell are the *nucleus, food vacuole,* and *contractile vacuoles.* The nucleus is the controller of the cell, regulating all chemical processes. From two to many hundreds of nuclei may be present. Food vacuoles, present only after eating, are large droplets of water containing food. Instead of food vacuoles, protozoa which photosynthesize food have pigment bodies containing chlorophyll. For collecting excess fluid from the protoplasm, one or more contractile vacuoles are present.

SELF-PRESERVATION

To protect themselves, to rest, or to reproduce, many protozoa surround their bodies with a thick-walled sac, or cyst. This is practiced among most parasitic protozoa, especially as they move from host to host. When environmental conditions are unfavorable in deserts, ponds, and marshes, this covering becomes necessary for survival.

While reproduction is sometimes sexual, most protozoa produce new animals by *asexual* means. Some develop buds which break off, while others divide one or more times in order to produce two or more daughter cells.   E. P. L.

SEE ALSO: AMEBA; ANIMALS, CLASSIFICATION OF; CELLS; EUGLENA; EVOLUTION; MALARIA; PARAMECIUM; PARASITES; REPRODUCTION, ASEXUAL; STENTOR; VOLVOX

Shrub branches are pruned to increase bloom

Prune (cut back) When parts of a plant are cut off for the purpose of improving the plant, this process is called *pruning*. Pruning of the stem, branches, shoots, or roots benefits the plant by improving the shape or increasing the size of the flowers and fruits. Plants may be pruned by natural means, such as wind, ice, snow, shade, and overloads of fruit. The pruned plant is smaller after pruning, but because of the pruning it becomes stronger and larger. The branches should be cut close and clean, and large cuts should be covered with a protective paint or wax.

Most deciduous trees require severe pruning for many years. If a tree has two main branches that form a sort of Y, there is a tendency for the tree to split when it gets older. The smaller branch should be removed, leaving only one main stem. Dead and diseased stems should always be removed. In spring-blooming shrubs and trees, the pruning should take place immediately after flowering. In late blooming shrubs and trees, pruning should be done only in the winter or very early spring. Hedges are pruned or sheared to keep them compact. Annuals and perennials are pruned by removing all but the strongest stems, or by pinching back the tops. M. R. L.

Prune (fruit) see Plum

Pseudopodia Pseudopodia are temporary extensions of the body of a one-celled animal such as the ameba. They make possible a flowing type of movement or engulfing of food.
SEE: AMEBA, PROTOZOA

If this boy does not wish a certain girl to know that he likes her, excess blood may rush to his face causing him to blush when he sees her. This is a physical reaction to an emotion or thought

Psychology (sye-KAHL-uh-jee) Psychology is the scientific study of human and animal behavior. Like other sciences, it is concerned with research and application. Research finds out facts—in the case of psychology, facts about how people behave—and applied psychology uses these facts in schools, clinics, factories, and many other places.

As a science psychology is quite new. Of course people have always been interested in human behavior and have observed it and thought about it. Philosophy, theology, and literature have dealt with human behavior for centuries. Modern psychology differs from philosophy, theology, and literature because its method is scientific. Psychology proceeds by careful, objective observation, measurement, and experimentation.

Objective observation is illustrated by the studies made of the behavior of children in nursery schools. In such instances, various observers might watch the same child all morning and keep a record of everything the child did. When records by many different observers are brought together, the picture they present may be very different, and more accurate, than the observations of any one observer.

Certain kinds of behavior may be simulated with drugs. The rat at the top shows its normal pattern of movement. In the middle, it has had a depressant drug; at the bottom, a stimulant one

The man is afraid to argue with his boss, so he fights with his wife instead. He probably does not know the real reason for his anger. Psychology describes and tries to explain behavior of this kind

Measurement usually involves testing a great many people and establishing a scale on which they can be rated. *Intelligence tests* and *achievement tests* are examples of psychological measurements.

Experimentation includes trying something out in a controlled situation—where one factor may be changed while all others are kept the same. For instance, the same group of workers who do the same kind of work in the same factory are given coffee breaks in the morning and afternoon for one week. The next week the workers are not given coffee breaks. Such an experiment is designed to find out whether or not the men work better if they have short, frequent rests.

The knowledge gained in research is applied in many fields. Studies of how people learn most effectively are applied in education. Industry uses *aptitude tests* to place people in the kind of jobs they can do best. Studies of how people get along together in groups are used in business and industrial, as well as in educational and social, organizations. Clinical psychologists help people with problems.

A *psychologist* usually has a master's or a doctor's degree in psychology. A *psychiatrist* must have a degree from a medical school, as well as some training in psychology. A *psycholanalyst* must be trained in the method of psychoanalysis.

Since Wilhelm Wundt founded the first psychological laboratory in Germany in 1879, psychology has come to be regarded as one of the *behavioral* sciences, along with other sciences such as sociology, history, and political science. Each of these sciences has to find its own ways to observe, measure and experiment—procedures of investigation which are different from the methods of the physical sciences. In searching for methods to understand human behavior, psychologists have moved in different directions. These directions are represented by what are called "schools" of psychology. SIGMUND FREUD, for instance, presented a new direction for study when he observed that there is an *unconscious,* as well as *conscious,* activity of the mind. But whereas Freud felt behavior was greatly determined by the way man is allowed to express his creative and destructive instincts, J. B. Watson proposed that behavior is the result of physiological reaction to external stimuli. Other fields of psychology include educational psychology, opened by Froebel and Pestalozzi; social psychology, developed by William McDougall and Havelock Ellis; and there exist many others, such as child psychology, religious psychology, individual psychology, and even animal psychology.   D. A. B.

SEE ALSO: NERVOUS SYSTEM; PAVLOV, IVAN; REFLEX; SCIENTIFIC METHOD; STATISTICS; STIMULUS

Psyllium

Psyllium (SIL-ee-uhm) Psyllium seed is often used in medicine. It comes from a European species of plantain (*Plantago psyllium*). Most plantains are common weeds.

Ptarmigan see Grouse

Pterodactyl (ter-uh-DACK-tihl) The pterodactyl was a flying reptile that lived more than 60 million years ago. Although it could fly, it was not a bird. It had certain features similar to birds, but basically it was a reptile.

The pterodactyl belonged to a group of reptiles which lived during the MESOZOIC ERA when the great reptiles roamed the earth. The flying reptiles are referred to as *pterosaurs,* a word made from the Greek word *pteron* meaning "wing" and *sauros,* "lizard." These pterosaurs had forelimbs or arm-like parts adapted for flying or gliding instead of walking. Their bones were hollow as are the similar bones of birds today. They had no feathers, however. The wings were formed of a leathery membrane extending from a foreleg finger to the body, probably similar to that of the modern bat. The pterodactyl's hind legs were long and slender; its tail was generally short.

Pterodactyls ranged in size from those with one-foot wingspreads to the large *Pteranodon,* with a twenty-foot wingspread. It had a two-foot skull, no teeth, and a short tail. All forms are extinct today.   D. J. I.
SEE ALSO: BIRD, DINOSAUR, REPTILIA

Pteranodon, the largest of the pterodactyls
Chicago Natural History Museum

Ptolemy (TAHL-uh-mee) (127-151) Ptolemy (Claudius Ptolemaeus) was a noted Greek astronomer, geographer, and mathematician who lived in the second century A.D. He is best known for his system of astronomy, the *Ptolemaic System,* which declared the earth to be the center of the universe. His theory of the universe was believed by most people to be true until NICOLAUS COPERNICUS, a Polish monk, proved in the sixteenth century that the sun, and not the earth, is the center of the solar system.

Almost nothing is known about the life of Ptolemy. It is generally believed that he was born at Ptolemaius Hermii, a Grecian city in Egypt. The period of his life is estimated from the dates of his astronomical observations. It is believed that he made his observations and wrote in Alexandria.

The most important of Ptolemy's works was the *Almagest,* a thirteen-volume abstract of the astronomical science of the Alexandrian Greeks. In it Ptolemy explained his system of astronomy, giving Hipparchus credit as his chief authority. The system Ptolemy advanced was one in which the earth was a motionless globe. Around it revolved a spherical transparent shell in which were located forty-eight constellations and seven planets: the Moon, Mercury, Venus, the Sun, Mars, Jupiter, and Saturn. While making his observations, he discovered the irregular motion of the moon in orbit called *evection.*

Although Ptolemy is thought to have studied mathematics to make his astronomical observations more meaningful, his mathematical discoveries proved to be of greater value than those in astronomy. By explaining the mathematical theories of Hipparchus, he is considered by some to be the founder of *plane* and *spherical trigonometry.*

As a geographer, Ptolemy was almost entirely in error. He did, however, summarize all that the ancient world knew about the surface features of the earth. His main contribution to geography was an eight-volume *Guide to Geography,* the earliest effort to treat geography scientifically. He did not mention climate, natural resources, people,

or unique physical features of the countries with which he dealt. His map of the world and his twenty-six colored maps showed knowledge quite in advance of his time. The *Guide* greatly influenced the future study of geography. D. H. J.
SEE ALSO: ASTRONOMY, SOLAR SYSTEM

Ptomaine (TOH-mayn) Ptomaine is a word derived from the Greek word *ptoma* meaning "corpse." It is a term applied to substances (organic bases) which are formed by the action of bacteria on animal or plant matter, causing decay.

It is a compound containing nitrogen, produced by the putrefaction of proteins. Most ptomaines are harmless, but a few may be poisonous.

For a long time it was believed that the intestinal disturbance known as ptomaine poisoning was caused by eating food containing ptomaines. It has been established by medical authorities that this is not so, but that food poisoning is caused by specific bacterial poisons in spoiled food. W. J. K.

Puberty (PYOO-ber-tee) At about the age of twelve in girls and thirteen in boys, puberty or *adolescence* starts. The child is rapidly growing to be an adult. Among some people and in some religious groups, there are ceremonies to honor this new stage of human growth.

The word puberty is from the Latin *pubes,* meaning citizen. Today the word is narrowed to refer to the young person's beginning sexual and social maturity.

With the onset of puberty, bodily changes called *secondary sexual characteristics* gradually appear. In both boys and girls the sexual organs start maturing; sweat glands become more active; and hair commences to grow in the *axillary* regions (armpits) and *pubic* regions.

In boys the voluntary muscles develop more than in girls, and the shoulder bones broaden. The boy's voice deepens—often "cracking," and hair gradually grows on his chin and cheeks.

In girls starting puberty, the pelvic bones grow broader, the breasts start maturing,

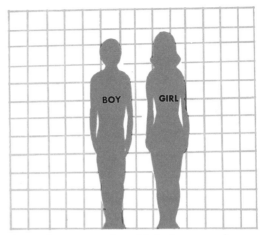

At twelve years, the girl is larger and more mature than the boy

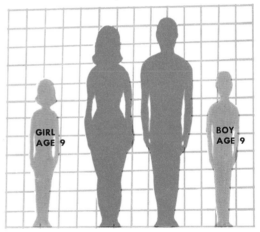

At fifteen the boy is usually larger and heavier than the girl. Adult body characteristics have begun to appear

and an even layer of fat tissue forms and rounds the outlines of the body. The teen-age girl's voice enriches to the feminine ranges from contralto to high soprano. The monthly cycle of MENSTRUATION also starts.

Accompanying these bodily changes are complex changes in the emotional sensitivities of adolescent boys and girls. Changes of mental outlook vary from those of a new excitement about the world and a heightened appreciation of human beings to spells of independence and severe criticism of that world. Adolescents are helped through the changes of puberty by the good example and guidance of parents and other strong adult leaders whom they can admire. D. A. B.
SEE ALSO: HORMONES, PITUITARY, REPRODUCTIVE SYSTEMS, SEX

Puff adder see Snakes

Puffin

Puffin   Puffin is a seabird of the AUK family. It has black-and-white plumage, a ducklike body, and short legs which make walking difficult. It is noted for its large, brightly-colored, triangular beak.

SEE: BIRD

Pulley   see Machines, simple

Pulse   The pulse is a rhythmic beat felt in any artery close to the skin. The contraction of the heart forces blood into the arteries, the arteries expand, and this expansion can be felt as beating or throbbing.

SEE: ARTERY, BLOOD, BLOOD PRESSURE, CIRCULATORY SYSTEM

Puma   see Cat family

Pumice   Pumice is hardened, frothy volcanic LAVA which has a high glass content. It is light enough to float on water. It is used in solid or powdered form as an ABRASIVE. It is a very porous rock.

SEE: ROCKS

Pumice is a light porous volcanic rock

Pump   A pump is a machine made to raise or move liquids or gases by suction or pressure.

Pumps serve many purposes. In rural areas, hand or electric-powered pumps lift water from a well. A pump removes water from washing machines. Pumps circulate water, gasoline, and oil within an automobile engine. Large electric pumps force water to houses in the city. Oil, gasoline, and natural gas are transported hundreds of miles through pipe lines by means of pumps. The animal heart is a very important pump.

One of the earliest known pumps was the Egyptian "chain of pots." This pump obtained water from the Nile river. Romans used pumps in connection with their skillfully-developed aqueduct and city water system.

Today, many types of pumps perform various jobs. Basically, pumps fall into three classifications: (1) *suction* or *reciprocating* pumps, including lift pumps, (2) *force* pumps, and (3) *centrifugal* pumps.

The suction pump is often found on farms. It consists of a piston which fits air-tight into a barrel or tube. On the piston, a valve opens upward. A handle is attached to a rod; and, in turn, the rod moves the piston up and down. At the bottom of the tube is another valve which also opens upward. When the handle moves the piston downward, the air in the tube is pushed out through the valve on the piston. When the piston is moved upward, gravity closes this valve and produces a partial VACUUM above the water in the bottom of the tube. The water is forced upward into the tube by the pressure of the air on the surface of the water in the well. After a few strokes of the handle, the tube is filled and water flows out the spout. Since it depends on air pressure, it can lift water only to a height equal to that pressure, about thirty-two feet.

A lift pump is a variety of the common suction pump. This type of pump is placed at the bottom of a well. It relies less upon the efficiency of its suction, but relies more on mechanically lifting water.

The force pump has no valve in the piston,

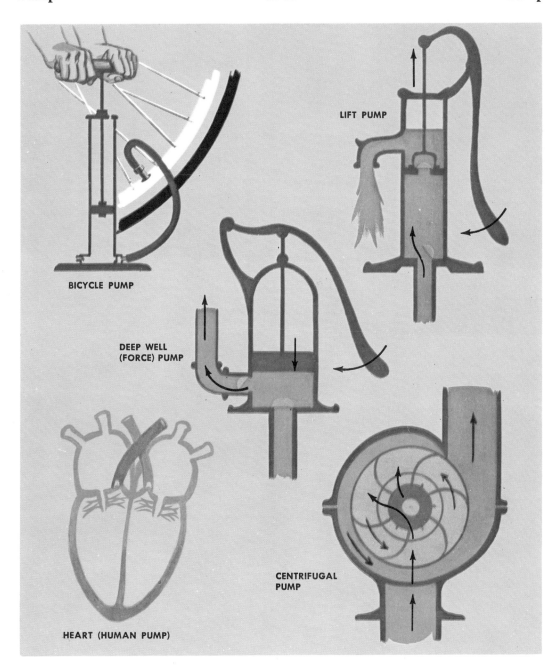

BICYCLE PUMP

LIFT PUMP

DEEP WELL
(FORCE) PUMP

HEART (HUMAN PUMP)

CENTRIFUGAL
PUMP

but rather has a valve at the spout or de-livery tube. This type of pump is used in deep wells and by fire engines. It works independently of air pressure. Force pumps are usually run by electric or gasoline en-gines.

A *mercury vapor* pump uses mercury as a piston. By removing mercury from a bulb or tube, a vacuum is created. Early light bulbs had air removed from them by this type of pump.

Centrifugal pumps are employed for re-moving a large quantity of water or other liquid, provided the lift is not great. Gen-erally, a centrifugal pump consists of a fan-shaped *impeller,* or blade. Inlets lead from the pump's center to its outer edge. An out-let is located on the edge of the pump. The impeller rotates rapidly, thus pumping the water by centrifugal force to the outlet. Washing machines use centrifugal pumps to pump out water. Modern water and sewage plants use this type of pump.   P. F. D.
SEE ALSO: WELL

Pumpkin and vine

Pumpkin The fruit of the annual pumpkin plant is large and fleshy. The leaves are broad and lobed. The climbing stem develops tendrils that curl around things.

Insects carry the pollen from the male flower to the female flower. The resulting edible berry-like fruit is often called a *pepo.*

Pumpkin seeds may be fried and salted for eating, and the field pumpkin is used for cattle feed. The pie pumpkin is usually made from *Cucurbita maxima,* a squash plant. Both pumpkin and squash are in the gourd family.   H. J. C.

Pupa see Metamorphosis

Pupil see Eye

Pure culture see Bacteriology

Purification Over the years, drinking water has been the most serious source of epidemic diseases. Many of the illnesses were traced directly to water that was not pure. Fortunately, the public water supplies today, particularly in the communities of this country, are well cared for. One rarely even gives thought to the safety of the water he uses.

Although purification is expensive, everyone should realize how important it is to protect and safeguard the water supplies. Whenever a community becomes careless about water, the threat of an epidemic of typhoid fever or other diseases may become serious.

Water supplies can be divided into two general groups: surface and underground. Surface-water supplies come from streams and lakes. Water from these sources is not considered safe unless it has been purified. Underground water supplies are obtained

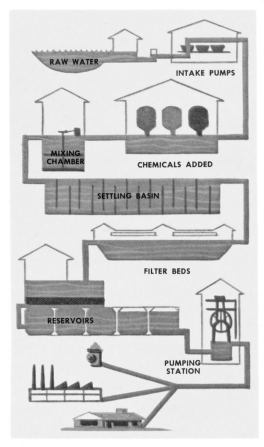

from springs and drilled wells. This water is usually safe provided it has not been contaminated with surface water or by drainage. This type of water supply should be tested periodically.

The water supplies of large communities are usually from lakes and streams, and therefore, it must go through a purification process. Two factors should be considered to make water fit for human consumption. First, the dissolved organic matter should be removed. Second, the bacteria must be destroyed. Almost all towns and cities use one or more of the following methods.

Settling: Water flows slowly into tanks, reservoirs, or basins. It is here that the organic matter sinks slowly to the bottom. Then the water is allowed to flow off on the opposite side of the settling basin from which it entered.

Chemicals: Particles of organic matter will settle more rapidly if certain chemicals such as alum are added to the settling tanks.

Filtration: Water is allowed to settle slowly through layers of sand, gravel, or charcoal. It loses much of its organic mat-

✳ THINGS TO DO

SETTING UP A FILTERING PLANT

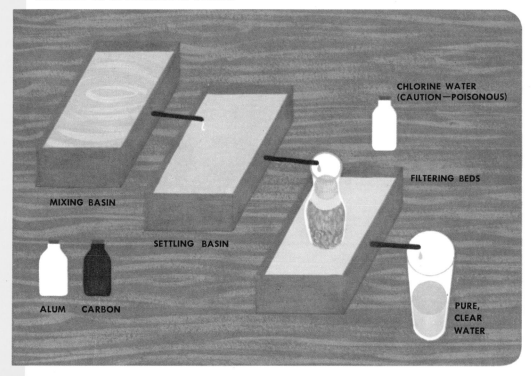

CHLORINE WATER
(CAUTION—POISONOUS)

FILTERING BEDS

MIXING BASIN

SETTLING BASIN

ALUM   CARBON

PURE,
CLEAR
WATER

1   Raw lake or river water must be treated before it is safe to drink. A model waterworks plant may be assembled by following the illustration.

2   Metal pans may be used for the mixing and settling basins. A glass chimney is suitable for the filtering bed. You will need to purchase alum which helps to clump the foreign particles and algae in the water to hasten the settling action. Carbon removes the fishy odors often found in water.

Put a piece of gauze over the lower opening of the chimney. Add a layer of small pebbles on the bottom, then a layer of coarse sand, and finally fine sand. In water plants, a small amount of chlorine (poisonous) is added to kill the bacteria.

3   The final product should be clean clear water safe for drinking but since your model is on such a small scale it probably will not do a very efficient job.

ter in this way and leaves as clear water.

Aeration: In many reservoirs, fountains force water up into the air. Here oxygen is dissolved in water and the flat taste is improved. Germs that are present are killed by the sunlight.

Chlorination: The gas chlorine is one of the most effective chemicals used to kill bacteria. It is used extensively in water purification. Many cities add this chemical to their water supply regularly, while others do so only when the bacteria count is higher than safety allows.

Bacteriological and chemical tests are run constantly so that people living in a large city can be sure that the water supply is healthful and safe.

Travelers and campers sometimes must use water they cannot be sure is safe for drinking. This water can be made safe by boiling it for a few minutes or by treating it with bleaching powder or chlorinated lime. Boiling water drives off the dissolved air. This results in the water having a flat taste. Air can be replaced by stirring, by shaking the container, or by a period of exposing it to the open air.   V. V. N.

SEE ALSO: ENGINEERING, WATER

Pussy willows with catkins

Purine (PYOOR-een) Purines are double-ring organic compounds which contain *nitrogen*. Purines are contained in NUCLEIC ACIDS, important building blocks of the body. Adenine and guanine are two of the purines contained in *ribonucleic acid* (RNA), a chemical active in heredity.

There are many known purines, but only twelve have been isolated from natural sources. The purine, *caffeine*, comes from the coffee bean and tea leaves, and thus is present in coffee and tea. Caffeine is used in the manufacture of cola drinks. Another purine, *theobromine*, is found in the leaves of the cacao. These purines give the stimulating effects peculiar to these drinks. *Uric acid* is also a purine.   J. R. S.

SEE ALSO: NUCLEOPROTEINS

Pus Pus is a semi-solid, yellowish discharge which appears at the site of an INFECTION. It is composed of dead *leucocytes, lymph, microorganisms*, and other debris.

Pussy willow The pussy willow is a shrub in the willow family (*Salicaceae*). When the early spring flower buds open, the young male flowers are furry and soft. They look like small gray kittens clinging to the branches. Later the flowers become long graceful catkins.

Leaves appear after the pussy willow flowers. They are smooth and long, bright green above and gray underneath. The catkins develop into larger clusters and are covered with yellow pollen and then form seeds or drop off the bush.

Pussy willows grow wild in low, wet spots, sometimes reaching twenty-five feet. They are planted to beautify a place and to attract songbirds.   P. G. B.

Putty Putty is a fine powdered CHALK (*calcium carbonate*) mixed to a thick dough with boiled linseed or other oil. It is used to hold glass in windows and to even out surfaces before painting them.

Pylorus see Digestive system

Pyramid see Geometry

Pyridoxine see Vitamin

Pyrimidines (pi-RIM-ih-dens) Pyrimidines are important in living material. Vitamins B_1 and B_2 contain them. Pyrimidines are organic ring compounds which contain nitrogen.

Pyrimidines have been found to be important in determining traits which are inherited. The *genes* which determine traits like eye color contain NUCLEIC ACIDS. *Uracil, thymine,* and *cytosine* are found in the

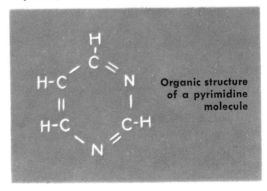

Organic structure of a pyrimidine molecule

nucleic acids which are present in the nuclei of living cells.

Some bacteria use pyrimidines to manufacture *folic* acid, a vitamin necessary for their existence. The pyrimidine ring is found in the sulfa drug, *sulfadiazine.* When bacteria are exposed to this drug, they will take it into their bodies. Since they cannot use pyrimidine in this form they die because normal metabolism is prevented.   J. R. S.

SEE ALSO: NUCLEOPROTEIN

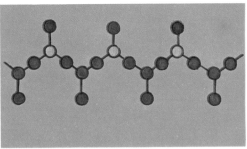

Pyroxenes are a group of minerals that are compounds of silica (SiO_2) and certain metals

Iron pyrite crystals are usually cubic

Pyrite (PYE-rite) Pyrite, or iron pyrites, as it is commonly called, is a mineral found throughout the world. Because of its glinting, brassy-yellowish appearance, it has many times been mistaken for gold, and is sometimes called "fool's gold."

The name pyrite is derived from the Greek word meaning "fire" because of the sparks which occur when it is struck with steel. Pyrite will also sustain fire, due to its sulfur content.

Pyrite is the commonest of the sulfide minerals. It is found associated with other sulfides, with oxides, and in quartz veins, in sedimentary and metamorphic rocks, in coal beds. It is also a replacement mineral found in fossils.

In some countries, where sulfur is not common, pyrite is used to obtain pure sulfur, but in the United States it is used commercially mainly for sulfuric acid. The formula for pyrite is FeS_2.   V. V. N.

Pyroxene (pye-RAHK-seen) A scientist selected the name pyroxene from the Greek, *pyr* meaning "fire" and *xenos,* "stranger;" thus the name

means "stranger to fire." This is not characteristic, however, for the various pyroxenes are typically minerals of the igneous or melted rock group.

Pyroxene belongs to a group of minerals which show a cleavage angle of 87 degrees to 93 degrees parallel to the fundamental prism. Chemically the pyroxenes are *metasilicates.*

Pyroxene crystals are generally short, stout, complex prisms. They are common in the more basic igneous rocks, and may be developed in the earth by pressure and moderate heat, as in *gneisses, schists,* and *marble.*   V. V. N.

Pythagoras (pih-THAGG-uh-russ) (582?-500?) Pythagoras was a Greek philosopher who was active about 530 B.C. Scarcely anything is known of Pythagoras' early life, but it is believed that he was born on the island of Samos.

He was important for having worked out a method of proving what is now known as the *Pythagorean theorem.* This theorem states that the square of the hypotenuse of a right-angled triangle is equal to the sum of the squares of the other two sides. D. H. J.

SEE ALSO: GEOMETRY

Python see Snakes

Pythagoras

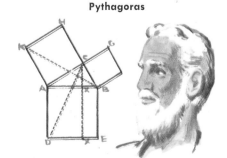

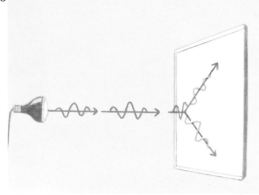

Quadruplets see Multiple births

Quail There are several types of quail known as mountain quail, valley quail, and Virginia partridge. Perhaps the most familiar name for quail is *bobwhite,* a name the quail has earned because of the sound of its song. This song is heard most often before rain. Many people say the quail forecasts rain and is singing, "more wet, more wet."

Quail are the size of plump robins. Their striped and mottled brown, black and white coloring is protective. They spend their lives in fields and farmlands searching for food of weed seeds and insects. They fly only on short flights and then only if suddenly frightened. About eighteen eggs are laid in ground nests. After twenty-four days, the fully-feathered babies hatch and immediately run about looking for food. Quail are sociable birds and always live together in groups called *coveys.* They sleep huddled in circles but always with heads pointed outward. Any unusual sound scatters them in all directions. Heavy snows and hunters are their enemies. Hunting this valuable game bird is restricted in most areas.   J. A. D.

Quantum theory (KWAHN-tuhm) In 1900 Max Planck, professor of theoretical physics in Berlin, found a mathematical formula that described the energy of a radiating substance. He found that the transfer of energy was not continuous, but instead included little packets, or bundles, called *quanta.* (The rainbow which appears to be a continuous band of color is really made up of little units, or bundles, of light of different energies.)

When a photon collides with an electron at the surface of a substance, the electron is excited into motion. This results in heat or electric current being produced, or a change in conductivity of the surface material, depending on the nature of the substance

When any piece of matter is heated, it starts to glow, gets red hot, and white hot at higher temperatures. This excitement of atoms, or molecules, of the matter is called *radiation.* When black materials are heated, the radiation depends solely upon the temperature. With colored materials, radiation is dependent upon more factors than temperature. Therefore, the radiation emitted by a black material at high temperatures is a suitable object for research because there is only the factor of temperature to consider. The radiation of a black body should be explainable in terms of the laws for radiation and heat. In the late 1800's Lord Raleigh and Sir James Jeans attempted to explain this hypothesis, but they failed.

When Planck attacked this problem, he turned from black-body radiation to radiating atoms. Experimental data on heat and light-radiating atoms led him to devise a mathematical formula to account for the behavior of such radiation energy. Surprisingly, his formula made it seem that atoms contain only *discrete* quantities, or quanta (*quantum* is the singular form) of energy, rather than their possessing continuous wave-like energy as classical physics had always assumed. The formula produced a puzzle such as one would face if a car can travel at 50 and at 52 miles per hour, but cannot go at 51 m.p.h.

In 1905, ALBERT EINSTEIN gave theoretical support for Planck's observations. Einstein's explanation was based on an experiment, the *photoelectric effect,* which showed that the energy of electrons emitted when light fell on a metallic surface depended, not

In this electroluminescent wall, an electric current frees electrons, which strike atoms of the phosphor which then emit photons (bundles of light energy)

upon how much light was present, but rather upon the frequency (or wave length) of the light. That is, the size of the radiation units called *photons* (quantum units) depended upon the rate of vibration of the atoms of the particular material; furthermore, the total energy emitted was related only to this rate, and thus could be expressed mathematically by merely three symbols, one of which was the "constant of proportionality." In honor of Max Planck, this constant was called *Planck's Constant*. The formula is: $E = Hf$; where E stands for the total energy of the emitted photon (in erg-seconds); f is the rate at which the radiant energy is vibrating, and H is Planck's Constant. (H is calculated to be 6.62×10^{-27}.)

In other words, Planck and Einstein stated that light (and other radiant energy) travels through space, in continuous waves, but is absorbed or emitted in energy packets, or quanta.

Shortly after the quantum theory was first announced, Niels Bohr, a Danish physicist, was able to apply it further to form a new theory about atomic structure. Bohr's original atomic model has been modified, but even the latest theories still agree with the idea of energy quanta.   J. R. S.
SEE ALSO: LIGHT, PHOTON, RADIATION

Quarantine Quarantine is the isolation of persons, animals, or plants which have been exposed to communicable diseases. The quarantine period lasts for a time equal to the incubation period of the disease.

Quarry (KWAWR-ee) A quarry is an opening in the earth caused by removal of stone. Such rocks as limestone, marble, sandstone, and granite are obtained by the procedure known as *quarrying*.

Quarrying is accomplished by the methods of *explosion, "plug and feather,"* and *channeling*. Explosion is done with dynamite or gunpowder to open or clear large areas. The resulting rubble is of primary use for roads or for smelting limestone rock.

The other methods are used chiefly for quarrying building stone. Plug and feather refers to a wedge with two half cylindrical pieces fitting on either side which are placed in a series of drilled holes in rock. Hammering the wedge spreads the "feathers" to apply pressure, causing a splitting of the formation.

Channeling involves a locomotive-like vehicle on a track with mechanical chisels to channel or cut the rock. This represents modern mechanized quarrying.   D. J. I.

Quarrying granite

Quartz Quartz is one of the most common minerals. It consists of *silicon dioxide,* or *silica*. It is found in many places and in many types of rock formations. Several varieties of quartz are used as gems. Others are building materials. Quartz is very hard.

There are many colors and many varieties of quartz. The color is due to other minerals and determines certain varieties. *Rock crystal* is pure, clear, transparent quartz. Purple quartz is called *amethyst*. These are crystalline varieties. *Agate* is an opaque type in which the color is distributed unevenly

J. Daniel Willems

ROCK CRYSTAL QUARTZ
IN NATURAL STATE

AMETHYST

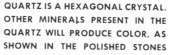
QUARTZ IS A HEXAGONAL CRYSTAL.
OTHER MINERALS PRESENT IN THE
QUARTZ WILL PRODUCE COLOR, AS
SHOWN IN THE POLISHED STONES

CITRINE

ROSE QUARTZ

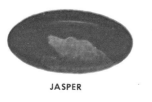
JASPER

CHALCEDONY

OPAL

FLINT

AGATE

CARNELIAN

through its mass. Sometimes the color runs through in curved bands. In *moss agate* specimens, the color is arranged so that it looks as if moss or other vegetable matter has been "frozen" in the quartz. Agate, *carnelian,* and *onyx* are usually considered as special types of quartz—*chalcedony.* Chalcedony is the *massive* form of quartz. Other varieties include bloodstone, flint, jasper, sand and gravel, sandstone, and quartzite.   C. L. K.

SEE ALSO: AGATE, AMETHYST, GEM, ONYX

Quartzite see Rocks

Quaternary see Cenozoic Era, Geologic time table

Queen see Ants, Bees

Queen Anne's lace see Wild flowers

Quicklime see Lime

Quicksand Quicksand is a bed of very fine, powdery, wet sand. It may look solid, but it is like a thick fluid. It will not support anything heavy. Men, animals, trains, or automobiles can be swallowed up if they move onto quicksand.

Under quicksand there is usually a layer of clay. The clay keeps the water from draining away from the sand. Quicksand is often found at the mouths of rivers where fine sand has been deposited on clay. It can also be found around lakes or ponds if a hollow pocket in a clay shore holds it and keeps it wet.

Quicksand is very treacherous. There are

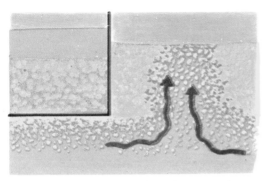

An underground spring that does not have enough outlets for the water may keep sand floating loosely. The upper left shows packed sand under still water, or water with outlets

Flowering quince

many tales of men sinking into quicksand. A man need not be swallowed up, however. If he remains calm and still and takes special care not to move his feet, he will stop sinking when he is in quicksand up to his armpits. His weight then will balance the weight of displaced sand.   C. L. K.
SEE ALSO: GEOLOGY

Quicksilver see Mercury (element)

Quill see Feather

Quince Flowering quinces are popular garden shrubs that are among the first to blossom in the spring. These shrubs belong to the rose family and come from eastern Asia. The five-petaled, showy flowers bloom before or with the unfolding of the leaves. They make fine specimen plants and are also used for hedges. They are easily raised in most soils and are propagated by cuttings or layering.

Japonica is a variety known as dwarf Japanese quince. It is a low, spreading plant that grows about three feet high and has red flowers.

Lagenaria is known as Japanese quince. It grows four to six feet tall and has spiny branches. Its flowers are scarlet or white, but some have pink flowers that turn red in the fall. It is the best flowering quince for hedges.

The hard, acid fruit called quince is related to the pear and apple. It is also a member of the rose family. The fruit is very tasty when it is cooked.   M. R. L.

Quinine (KWY-nyne) Quinine is a fever-reducing drug used in the treatment of MALARIA. It is a white, odorless, crystalline powder with a bitter taste. It comes from the bark of the *cinchona tree* originally found in South America. Because of the demand for quinine, the tree is now raised in the East Indies, Jamaica, Java, and other tropical countries. To prepare quinine, the bark is stripped from the trees and dried. It is then ground into a powder, from which the quinine is extracted.

Cinchona bark was used in early times by the Inca Indians of South America, who called it *quinaquina*. It was introduced in Europe in 1640, when it was used to cure the fever of the wife of the Peruvian Viceroy. She was Countess Cinchon, for whom the cinchona tree was named.

Before World War II, most quinine came from the Dutch East Indies. When the Dutch East Indies fell into Japanese hands, the supply of quinine for the Allied troops fighting in the tropics was cut off. It was necessary to develop synthetic drugs for the control of malaria, and *atabrine* became the best known.

Quinine is also used as a remedy for joint and muscle pain and for headaches, in the treatment of varicose veins, and as an appetite stimulant.   M. R. L.

Quintuplets see Multiple births

Quinine is obtained from the cinchona tree

Rabbit The rabbit family includes both hares and rabbits. They are small, furry, gnawing mammals with long ears and short tails. They can run fast, taking great leaps with their long, powerful hind legs.

Rabbits and hares are alike, except for size and nesting habits. Rabbits are much smaller than hares. European ones usually have their babies in an underground burrow which they have dug themselves, or which another animal has dug. Their babies are blind and helpless, and have no fur when they are born. American hares rarely dig burrows. They usually have their babies out in the open or in a shady spot under a clump of bushes. Baby hares are well-developed when they are born. They have warm coats of fur, their eyes are open, and they are soon able to care for themselves. *Jack rabbits, arctic hares,* and *varying* or *snowshoe hares* are all true hares. *Cottontails, pygmy rabbits,* and *swamp rabbits* are wild rabbits.

There are several groups of jack rabbits found on the plains of North America. They are big hares about twenty-eight inches long, weighing up to ten pounds. They have very long ears and very long hind legs. They are well-known for their speed. A mother jack rabbit may have as many as six litters each year, with two to four babies in each litter. When jack rabbits become too numerous and start to damage crops in their search for food, they are poisoned until their numbers are under control. Many rabbits

Courtesy Society For Visual Education, Inc.
Snowshoe rabbit, or varying hare, is a true hare. Its coat, or *pelage*, changes color as the seasons change

Courtesy Society For Visual Education, Inc.
Jack rabbit has especially long hind legs

Courtesy Society For Visual Education, Inc.
Cottontail rabbit, common through North America

J. W. Thompson
Pika, a short-eared member of the rabbit family

F. A. Blashfield

Domestic albino white rabbit

and hares also die from disease, such as rabbit fever (*tularemia*), which may also be fatal to man, and infectious *myxomatosis.*

Jack rabbits are active in the early morning and late afternoon. They spend the warm part of the day in a shady resting spot called a *form*. Each jack rabbit seems to have its own form.

The varying or snowshoe hare, found in the colder parts of northern North America, is white in winter and brown in summer. It sheds twice a year, growing a coat of brown in the spring and a coat of white in the fall. Its feet, which are long, broad, and heavily furred, serve as snowshoes in winter.

The arctic hare is a large white hare with short ears and legs and snowshoe feet. It feeds on mosses and grasses growing under the arctic snow.

Interesting members of the rabbit family are the *cony* or *pika,* living in colonies above the timberline in mountains in the Northern Hemisphere. They are small, brown animals weighing less than a pound. Their diet is grass and moss, which they store for winter.

The brown cottontail rabbit, common throughout North America, is easily identified by the white underside of its tail, seen as it runs away. It is a small rabbit, weighing about two or three pounds. Cottontails eat tender green plants, usually feeding in the early morning or late afternoon and spending the rest of the day under a bush or some other protective cover. The mother builds the grassy nest in a shallow hole in the ground, lining it with bits of its fur. Several litters of two to six babies may be born during the spring and summer.

Enemies of the cottontail include the fox, coyote, lynx, hawk, and owl, as well as man who hunts it for food.

Marsh or *swamp rabbits* are cottontails found in the swampy areas of southern United States. Their fur is a darker brown

and their tails are not as white. The Idaho pygmy rabbit, found on the prairies of California, Nevada, Oregon, and Idaho, looks like a small cottontail with similar habits.

There are also many varieties of domestic rabbits. Some are raised for their meat and fur, and some are raised as pets. D. J. A.
SEE ALSO: RODENTIA

Rabbit fever see Animal diseases, Rabbit

Rabies Rabies is a disease found among wild and domestic animals. It is sometimes called *hydrophobia,* which means "fear of water," because rabies causes paralysis of throat muscles, and the victim, although thirsty, cannot swallow.

In *dumb rabies* the infected animal is listless, dull-eyed and unable to swallow. The voice is hoarse, the mouth hangs open and the jaw drips saliva. There is no indication of unfriendliness, and many times the disease is not recognized until infection has passed on through a break in the skin of the animal's handler. *Furious rabies* is easier to recognize because the infected animal, in addition to hoarseness and slobbering, wanders off and becomes violent.

Rabies among wild animals, fox, bats, skunks, and squirrels, is referred to as *sylvatic rabies.* In domestic animals it is known as *urban* rabies. All pets should be given anti-rabies vaccinations for protection of the pet and the owner. Health departments make every effort to curb the disease by vaccinating stray animals, and issuing dog licenses. This dread disease can be transmitted to any unvaccinated pet by wild animals.

The rabies' *virus* lives in the salivary glands of the infected animal and can be passed on to humans through a bite. The VIRUS travels by nerve trunks to the central nervous system where it finally causes death to the nerve cells. The period between the entry of the rabies' virus into the body and the first signs of the disease may be from four to eight weeks.

For humans exposed to rabies, Pasteur anti-rabies VACCINE is administered for a period of 21 days for bites involving the head, and fourteen days for bites elsewhere on the body.   G. A. D.
SEE ALSO: ANIMAL DISEASES; PASTEUR, LOUIS

Courtesy Society For Visual Education, Inc.
North American raccoon

Raccoon The raccoon is a mischievous animal often called "little brother of the bear." Like the bear, raccoons have stocky bodies, pointed muzzles, and feet with naked soles. They are *plantigrades,* meaning that they walk on the entire sole of the foot. These flesh-eating animals have sharp, curved claws that cannot be drawn in. Although the body is covered with coarse, grayish hair, black patches often mark the eyes and black rings circle the tail.

Raccoons may be found throughout most of North and Central America. These curious little animals are nocturnal, usually sleeping during the day, and hunting at night. They eat fish, frogs, crayfish, and mussels which they catch in the shallow water along the edges of ponds and streams. They also eat fruit, berries, nuts, honey, corn and hunt birds, mice, reptiles, insects, and occasionally poultry. When water is available, they will carefully wash their food before eating.

Baby raccoons are born in late spring, either in a hollow tree, in a crevice among some rocks, or in a burrow in the ground.

Raccoons are hunted for their fur which is made into coats and coonskin caps in which the long bushy tail is used as a tassel. Raccoons are hunted at night with the help of dogs. Raccoons are courageous fighters. If captured young, these intelligent little animals are easily tamed and may be kept as pets.   D. J. A.

Race Race is a *subdivision* of a species. It is made up of animals or plants, usually of one locality, having a combination of physical characteristics, such as appearance or bodily structure, which distinguishes them from others of the species. These characteristics can be inherited.

SEE: EVOLUTION OF MAN, HUMAN BEING

Radar Radar is an electronic system that permits man to see objects at great distances regardless of darkness or bad weather. It is used to direct both air and sea traffic, and for detection and identification of unknown ships and aircraft.

Sound waves bouncing off hillsides or tunnel walls create an echo. Radar works in the same way by sending out short *pulses* of radio energy which bounce off objects in their path and return to the sender as a type of echo. The reflected impulses are shown on a screen, like that of a television set, as spots of light, or *blips.*

Most radar sets have six important parts: the *modulator,* which turns the transmitter on to send a pulse and off to receive an echo; the *transmitter,* which sends the very short, or *microwave,* pulses; the *antenna,* which focuses the pulses into a narrow beam and also receives the echoing signals; the *duplexer,* which, as a switching device, connects first the transmitter and then the receiver to the antenna; the *receiver,* which is a listening and amplifying device to strengthen weak echoes so that they will show on the radar screen; and the *indicator,* which displays the blips to the operator on its screen.

KINDS OF INDICATORS

While most radar sets work in the same way, there are several types of indicators, each designed for a particular job. The *Plan Position Indicator,* or PPI, is the most common type. It has a round screen with a compass scale around the outside. On this screen a beam of light, representing the beam of radar pulses being sent out of the antenna, rotates like the second hand of a clock. As this beam, or *trace,* sweeps around the screen, the blips appear as spots of light when it passes. The distance of the objects they represent is determined by their distance on the screen from the center, which is the station. The screen usually has rings showing distance from the center. Another type of indicator is the *Range Height Indicator,* or RHI, which measures the height of objects such as airplanes. The RHI has a trace that sweeps up and down and shows the range and height of an object in one given direction. It is used to assist pilots in

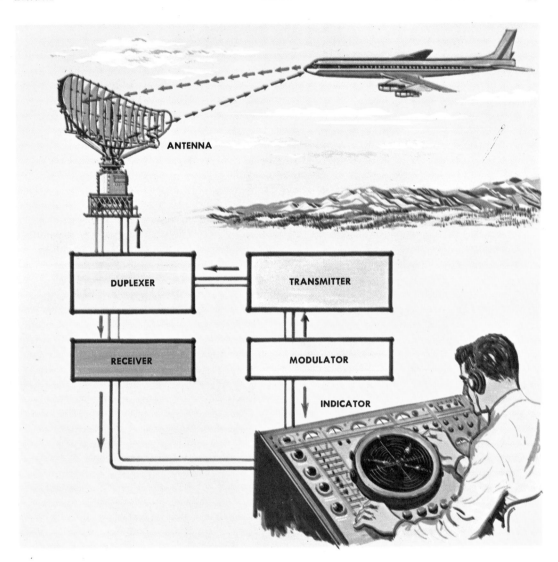

ANTENNA

DUPLEXER

TRANSMITTER

RECEIVER

MODULATOR

INDICATOR

instrument landings.

The A-scope and B-scope indicators give more details about the objects they detect, such as the number of aircraft in a formation.

SPECIAL USES OF RADAR

Police forces use *Doppler,* or *Continuous Wave,* radar to determine the speed of passing automobiles. This type of radar sends out continuous radio waves instead of pulses. The rate of vibrations, or frequency, of the returning echoes is different from the frequency of the transmitted signal, and this difference is measured to obtain the speed of the target.

The first radar that measured distance and direction was developed in 1934 by a U. S. Navy scientist, R. M. Page. Radar was used widely by the Allies and their enemies in World War II, and following the war was given many civilian applications. Today it is used in weather forecasting, in navigation, and in helping to prevent collisions between both ships and airplanes.   R. J. J.

SEE ALSO: INSTRUMENT LANDING SYSTEM

Radial symmetry see Animals, classification of

Radiant energy Radiant energy is ENERGY which travels in the form of electromagnetic waves. These waves are classified in order of decreasing wave length *as radiowaves, infrared waves, visible light, ultraviolet rays, X-rays,* and *gamma-rays.*

SEE: RADIATION

ALFRED B. NOBEL
1833–1896 •
Invented dynamite,
started Nobel Prizes

HIPPOCRATES
460–370? B.C
"Father of Medicine"

MARIE CURIE
• 1867–1934
Discovered radium
and polonium

ENRICO FERMI
• 1901–1954
Produced first atomic pile and first
controlled nuclear chain reaction

THOMAS ALVA EDISON
1847–1931 •
Invented light bulb,
phonograph and mimeograph

NICOLAUS COPERNICUS
• 1473–1543
First astronomer to say that Earth
goes around the sun

LUTHER BURBANK
• 1849–1926
Invented new
varieties of plants

EDWARD JENNER
1749–1823 •
Discovered smallpox vaccine

CHARLES DARWIN
1809–1882 •
Conceived the Theory of Evolution
through Natural Selection

WILLIAM HARVEY
• 1578–1657
Discovered the circulation
of the blood

GEORGE WASHINGTON CARVER
1864–1943 •
Experimented with
practical botany

SAMUEL F. B. MORSE
• 1791–1872
Invented telegraph and Morse code

LOUIS PASTEUR
• 1822–1895
Invented pasteurization

BENJAMIN FRANKLIN
• 1706–1790
Invented lightning rod

GALILEO GALILEI
1564–1642 •
Discovered law of pendulum motion

CAROLUS LINNAEUS
• 1707–1778
Classified the plant
and animal kingdoms

SIGMUND FREUD
• 1856–1939
Started psychoanalysis

GREGOR JOHANN MENDEL
1822–1884 •
Discovered principles of heredity

BARON ERNEST RUTHERFORD
1871–1937 •
Contributed to knowledge of
radioactivity and atomic structure

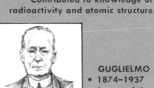

GUGLIELMO MARCONI
• 1874–1937
Invented the wireless telegraph

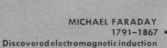

LOUIS AGASSIZ
• 1807–1873
Investigated glacial motion
and marine life

MICHAEL FARADAY
1791–1867 •
Discovered electromagnetic induction

SIR ISAAC NEWTON
• 1642–1727
Discovered laws of light,
gravity, motion and color

ALBERT EINSTEIN
1879–1955 •
Conceived the Theory of Relativity

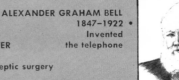

WILHELM KONRAD ROENTGEN
• 1845–1923
Discovered X-rays

ALEXANDER GRAHAM BELL
1847–1922 •
Invented
the telephone

JOSEPH LISTER
• 1827–1912
Started antiseptic surgery